Few operas have had more written about them than *Die Zauberflöte*, yet few are as often exposed to misguided comment – or to idiosyncratic productions. This book sets out to provide a straightforward account of Mozart's last opera, exposing the half-truths and legends that have proliferated since its first production in 1791. In chapter 1 a hitherto unsuspected source for the opening scenes is presented, and the complex relationship is revealed between the stories, essays and stage-works on which the plot is based. The second chapter studies the intellectual background, with special attention to Freemasonry. A detailed synopsis follows, then the history of the composition, based on documentary evidence and, in the case of the autograph score, the paper-types used. Chapter 5 examines the identity of the librettist and the qualities of his work, and chapter 6 is a detailed study (by Erik Smith) of Mozart's music and more generally of his late style. Chapter 7 covers the first performance, the cast, early reception, and then the rapid growth in the opera's fame; an outline history of productions concludes the chapter. Anthony Besch discusses the nature of the challenge to the director presented by *Die Zauberflöte* and suggests how the problems can be overcome. The volume contains illustrations, a bibliography and a discography.

Cambridge Opera Handbooks

W. A. Mozart
Die Zauberflöte

CAMBRIDGE OPERA HANDBOOKS

Published titles

Richard Wagner: *Parsifal* by Lucy Beckett
W. A. Mozart: *Don Giovanni* by Julian Rushton
C. W. von Gluck: *Orfeo* by Patricia Howard
Igor Stravinsky: *The Rake's Progress* by Paul Griffiths
Leoš Janáček: *Kát'a Kabanová* by John Tyrrell
Giuseppe Verdi: *Falstaff* by James A. Hepokoski
Benjamin Britten: *Peter Grimes* by Philip Brett
Giacomo Puccini: *Tosca* by Mosco Carner
Benjamin Britten: *The Turn of the Screw* by Patricia Howard
Richard Strauss: *Der Rosenkavalier* by Alan Jefferson
Claudio Monteverdi: *Orfeo* by John Whenham
Giacomo Puccini: *La bohème* by Arthur Groos and Roger Parker
Giuseppe Verdi: *Otello* by James A. Hepokoski
Benjamin Britten: *Death in Venice* by Donald Mitchell
W. A. Mozart: *Die Entführung aus dem Serail* by Thomas Bauman
W. A. Mozart: *Le nozze di Figaro* by Tim Carter
Hector Berlioz: *Les Troyens* by Ian Kemp
Claude Debussy: *Pelléas et Mélisande* by Roger Nichols and Richard
   Langham Smith
Alban Berg: *Wozzeck* by Douglas Jarman
Richard Strauss: *Arabella* by Kenneth Birkin
Richard Strauss: *Salome* by Derrick Puffett
Richard Strauss: *Elektra* by Derrick Puffett
Kurt Weill: *The Threepenny Opera* by Stephen Hinton
Alban Berg: *Lulu* by Douglas Jarman
W. A. Mozart: *La clemenza di Tito* by John Rice
Georges Bizet: *Carmen* by Susan McClary
W. A. Mozart: *Idomeneo* by Julian Rushton
Benjamin Britten: *Billy Budd* by Mervyn Cooke and Philip Reed

W.A. Mozart
Die Zauberflöte

PETER BRANSCOMBE
Professor of Austrian Studies, University of St Andrews

CAMBRIDGE
UNIVERSITY PRESS

Published by the Press Syndicate of the University of Cambridge
The Pitt Building, Trumpington Street, Cambridge CB2 1RP
40 West 20th Street, New York, NY 10011–4211, USA
10 Stamford Road, Oakleigh, Melbourne 3166, Australia

First published 1991
Reprinted 1993, 1996

Printed in Great Britain at the University Press, Cambridge

British Library cataloguing in publication data

Branscombe, Peter.
  W.A. Mozart, Die Zauberflöte / Peter Branscombe.
    p.   cm. – (Cambridge opera handbooks)
  Discography.
  Includes bibliographical references and index.
  ISBN 0-521-26491-X. – ISBN 0-521-31916-1 (pbk.)
  1. Mozart, Wolfgang Amadeus. 1756–1791. Zauberflöte. I. Title.
II. Title: Zauberflöte. III. Series.
ML410.M9B76 1991
782.1–dc20 90-40403   CIP MN

Library of Congress Cataloguing in publication data

Branscombe, Peter *1929–*
  W.A. Mozart – die Zauberflöte. – (Cambridge opera
  handbooks)
  1. Opera in German. Mozart, Wolfgang Amadeus, 1756–1791
  I. Title
  782.1

ISBN 0 521 26491 X hardback
ISBN 0 521 31916 1 paperback

WG

For Marina

Contents

List of illustrations	*page*	xi
General preface		xiii
Acknowledgments		xiv
Notes on the text		xv
	Introduction	1
1	The sources	4
2	The intellectual background: Freemasonry	35
3	Synopsis	45
4	The writing of *Die Zauberflöte*	67
5	The libretto	87
6	The music	
	by Erik Smith	111
7	Performance and reception	142
8	A director's approach	
	by Anthony Besch	178
9	Problems	205
	Conclusion	218
Notes		222
Select bibliography		235
Discography		239
Index		242

Illustrations

page

1 Act I, scene 17: 'Das klinget so herrlich, das klinget so schön!' – Papageno (with dulcimer rather than glockenspiel), Pamina and Monostatos. Engraving by F. John. Earliest surviving illustration of a production of the opera; Prague, 1792. (From the invitation to Professor Freiherr von Bretfeld's carnival ball, 1793; for 'breitfeld' see Mozart's letter of 15 January 1787.)   99

2 Act I, scene 14: opening bars of the duetto, no. 7, 'Bei Männern, welche Liebe fühlen', showing the absence of the clarinet and horn chords, and Mozart's rebarring.   123

3 Act I, scene 1: opening bars of the *Introduction* in Mozart's autograph score, showing the deleted clarini (trumpets) and timpani parts.   132

4 Act I, scene 1: p. 16ʳ of the *Introduction*, showing the last six bars of the cadenza for the Three Ladies.   133

5 Act I, scene 15: p. 7ᵛ of the finale, showing Mozart's rescoring of the accompaniment to the scene between Tamino and the Old Priest.   136

6 Watercolour by Philippe-Jacques de Loutherbourg (1740–1812): 'At the entrance to the temple'. This plate is one of eight surviving watercolours (*c.* 1787) that were probably commissioned by Cagliostro, inventor of the Egyptian Rite of Freemasonry. A woman neophyte, enjoined to silence by the guardian, approaches the curtained entrance to the temple; Mercury lies sleeping in the foreground.   181

7 Act I, scene 3: 'Hier meine Schönen, übergeb ich meine Vögel.' – Tamino, the Three Ladies and Papageno. Coloured engraving by Joseph and Peter Schaffer, published in the *Allgemeines Europäisches Journal*, Brünn, 1795.   185

8   Act II, scene 28: 'Hier sind die Schreckenspforten'. –
    Tamino, Pamina, the Two Men in Armour, and two
    Priests who, required neither by libretto nor score, may
    be assumed to have led in Pamina. (Coloured en-
    graving by Joseph and Peter Schaffer, published in the
    Allgemeines Europäisches Journal, Brünn, 1795.)   188
9   Act I, scene 15: 'Wie stark ist nicht dein Zauberton'. –
    Tamino enchants the animals and birds. Peter Rice's
    design for the Act I finale for Anthony Besch's produc-
    tion at the National Arts Centre, Ottawa, 1975.   193
10 Act I, scene 14: 'Bei Männern, welche Liebe fühlen'. –
    Valerie Masterson and Alan Opie as Pamina and
    Papageno in Anthony Besch's production (designs by
    John Stoddart) at the English National Opera, 1975.   200

The illustrations appear by kind permission of the following:
Plate 1, from an English private collection; Plates 2, 3, 4 and 5,
VEB Deutscher Verlag für Musik, Leipzig; Plate 6, Torre Abbey
Collection, the property of Torbay Borough Council; Plates 7 and 8,
Historisches Museum der Stadt Wien; Plate 9, the artist, Peter Rice;
Plate 10, the photographer, Andrew March.

General preface

This is a series of studies of individual operas, written for the serious opera-goer or record-collector as well as the student or scholar. Each volume has three main concerns. The first is historical: to describe the genesis of the work, its sources or its relation to literary prototypes, the collaboration between librettist and composer, and the first performance and subsequent stage history. This history is itself a record of changing attitudes towards the work, and an index of general changes of taste. The second is analytical and it is grounded in a very full synopsis which considers the opera as a structure of musical and dramatic effects. In most volumes there is also a musical analysis of a section of the score, showing how the music serves or makes the drama. The analysis, like the history, naturally raises questions of interpretation, and the third concern of each volume is to show how critical writing about an opera, like production and performance, can direct or distort appreciation of its structural elements. Some conflict of interpretation is an inevitable part of this account; editors of the handbooks reflect this – by citing classic statements, by commissioning new essays, by taking up their own critical position. A final section gives a select bibliography, a discography and guides to other sources.

Acknowledgments

It is a pleasure to express my gratitude to many friends and colleagues who have helped and encouraged me during the writing of this book. In particular I thank Anthony Besch, Roy Owen and Erik Smith for their contributions; Erik Smith has also read and commented on the entire manuscript. Peter Adamson, Leigh Bailey, Malcolm Humble, Susan Katzmann and Oswald Ruttner suggested source materials that I should otherwise have overlooked, and Hamish Scott, the late Martin Smith and Frederick Smyth offered valuable comments in areas in which their expertise corrected or confirmed my limited knowledge. Andrew Porter's constant encouragement over many years has been equalled only by the generosity of Alan Tyson, who has allowed me to benefit from his unpublished study of the paper-types and structure of Mozart's autograph score. Finally I thank the editors and advisers of the Cambridge University Press for their confidence and patience during the protracted gestation of this book, and Susan Ramsey for compiling the index.

Notes on the text

The principal source for all references to *Die Zauberflöte* is the full score published in the *Neue Mozart-Ausgabe* (*NMA*): II/5/19, Kassel etc., 1970, ed. Gernot Gruber and Alfred Orel. The edition of the libretto used is the facsimile of Schikaneder's original text of 1791, edited by M. M. Rabenlechner (Vienna, 1942).

References to the Mozart family correspondence are based on *Mozart. Briefe und Aufzeichnungen. Gesamtausgabe*, 7 vols., Kassel etc., 1962–75, ed. Wilhelm A. Bauer, Otto Erich Deutsch and Joseph Heinz Eibl. Letters are identified by date, and the passages quoted have been newly translated for this book.

Identification of scenes has been abbreviated; thus II, 17 = Act II, scene 17. The individual items in the score are numbered from 1 (*Introduction*) to 21 (finale), as in the *NMA* and most other editions; Mozart exceptionally numbered his autograph from 1 (overture) to 22.

Introduction

'Dined at Prince Schwarzenberg's ... after dinner charming music by Mozart. *Die Zauberflöte.*' Thus wrote Karl, Count Zinzendorf, in his diary on 19 February 1793;[1] there is a similar entry just over a year later. This music-loving aristocrat and prominent state official, whose comments after attending an early performance of the opera we shall find in chapter 7, is here unconsciously pointing to the extraordinary popularity that the music of Mozart's last opera achieved within a year or two of its première.

Of this success Mozart of course knew nothing, though his recognition of the opera's increasing hold on the public of the Freihaustheater auf der Wieden during the final weeks of his life gave him much pleasure. Perhaps the clearest indication of an opera's popularity at that time was to be measured by its appearance in the form of arrangements and adaptations. Apart from the piano scores and transcriptions that began to appear within weeks of the first night, there are in the case of *Die Zauberflöte* sets of variations and pot-pourris by Beethoven and Gelinek (several sets), Spohr and Sor; numbers from the opera make a saucy appearance in Lanner's waltz opus 196, *Die Mozartisten*, of 1842. The benign shadow of the opera lies heavily upon much of German-language literature and music in the next two centuries. Music from it appeared in arrangements for wind octet, flute quintet and quartet, string quartets, trios, duos (even for two cellos), guitar, and as German dances. In Victorian England, imagined to be unreceptive to *The Magic Flute*, there is evidence that many of the airs and duets ('The manly heart', for instance, as 'Bei Männern' was known) were familiar and well-loved items in the family circle and concert room. In Vienna, where the opera remained almost permanently in the repertory, a further sign of its hold on the public is to be found in the vocal quodlibets or pot-pourris prominent in innumerable plays with music in the popular theatres: no opera is as often quoted, from the early years of the nineteenth century on to

1

the death of that tradition that coincided with the passing in 1862 of its greatest master, Johann Nestroy (himself a Court Opera débutant as a very young Sarastro forty years before).

Die Zauberflöte has always been a controversial work: greatly loved and very frequently performed, yet also the object of heated scholarly debate and critical comment. The ordinary opera-goer does not find it difficult to come to terms with, though this has not prevented a large number of persons from feeling the need to interpret and explain what is at root a simple fairy-tale opera with a strong admixture of comic and more profound elements.

Two nineteenth-century comments suggested the nature of the problems it was held to present:

Here that which is eternal, valid for all times and all humanity (it is enough that I point to the dialogue of the *Spokesman* with *Tamino*!), is so irretrievably bound to the veritably trivial tendency of the play, intended by the poet simply to please a suburban Viennese public, that we need the intervention of an explanatory historical critique in order to be able to understand and endorse the whole work in its accidentally shaped uniqueness.

The second:

And yonder musician [i.e. Mozart], who used the greatest power which (in the art he knew) the Father of spirits ever yet breathed into the clay of this world; – who used it, I say, to follow and fit with perfect sound the words of the 'Zauberflöte' and of 'Don Giovanni' – foolishest and most monstrous of conceivable human words and subjects of thought – for the future 'amusement' of his race! – No such spectacle of unconscious (and in that unconsciousness all the more fearful) moral degradation of the highest faculty to the lowest purpose can be found in history.

The first writer is Richard Wagner; the essay is 'Das Publikum in Zeit und Raum' of 1878.[2] And the second writer is John Ruskin, in the Fifth Letter, 'Entertainment', of *Time and Tide* (25 February 1867).[3]

Belittlement of Schikaneder's libretto, like the numerous posthumous attempts to rob him of its authorship, have continued in the twentieth century, if on the whole to a less marked extent. This disparagement has done nothing to inhibit the enthusiasm for the opera of the general public, for whom the niceties of authenticity are of small concern.

In writing this book I have tried to maintain a balance between the needs of the ordinary opera-lover and the reader with a more specialized interest in Mozart's last work for the stage. I have also striven to thread my way through the thickets of the unusually prolific and luxuriant secondary literature, but above all to concentrate on the essentials, which must surely be to set out as directly as possible the ingredients, questioning traditional assumptions whilst as far as possible avoiding new speculation. This means that I have not attempted a detailed interpretation of the opera in Masonic terms, since the surviving evidence is incomplete, and to some extent contradictory.

The nine chapters (readers are advised against looking for any significance in the number of chapters or their sub-divisions) cover the most important sources for the opera, the intellectual background against which it was written, a synopsis, the genesis of the opera, essays on the libretto and the music, an outline history of the work in performance and reception, the interpretative and practical problems that face the director of a production, and brief consideration of some of the problems that recur in criticisms of the work.

1 The sources

The popular theatre and Mozart's links with it

More important than any one source of *Die Zauberflöte* is the whole tradition of the Viennese Popular Theatre, of which this opera is the supreme product – thanks to Mozart's musical and dramatic genius, prompted and aided by Emanuel Schikaneder. The tradition was already around eighty years old when *Die Zauberflöte* was written. The previous pattern of travelling companies of actors presenting a varied repertory of dramas, Singspiels and comedies was to continue until well after the establishment of a resident company at Vienna's Kärntnertor-Theater in 1710 or 1711. A notable ensemble was created under Joseph Anton Stranitzky, whose role of Hanswurst was descended from older comic types, native and foreign. His surviving repertory of *Haupt- und Staats-Aktionen* (plays about kings and queens, their advisers, and generals, with sudden changes of fortune, and liberally larded with the extemporized antics of comic servants) indicates that music, dance and spectacular scenic effects were within the capabilities of Stranitzky's company. Most of the plays were either parodies of, or satirical popular commentaries on, works performed at court or in the Jesuit theatre.

Stranitzky's successor in the mid-1720s, Gottfried Prehauser, built up the ensemble and repertory to a yet higher standard. His Hanswurst was admired for four decades, and he was supported by a strong team. During the 1750s, by when the rôle of music was extensive, Haydn wrote songs, and at least one complete Singspiel, for this company.

Well before the end of her reign, Maria Theresia had turned against this popular comic tradition; good taste and 'regular' (i.e. non-extemporized, Enlightenment) drama by the early 1760s were already excluding Hanswurst, or permitting him at most an anodyne rôle. But the tradition refused to die, and following the abandonment in 1776 of the restrictions limiting Vienna's theatres to two, both under court

4

control, troupes began to put on comedies on temporary stages and in adapted buildings. At the beginning of the 1780s, specially built suburban theatres began to open: in 1781 Karl Marinelli opened his Theater in der Leopoldstadt (a suburb to the north-east of the city); in 1787 Christian Rossbach opened his theatre in the Wieden suburb, to the south of the city, (the so-called 'Freihaus-Theater auf der Wieden'); and in 1788 Franz Scherzer built the Theater in der Josefstadt, to the north-west of the city centre; less permanent theatres existed in other suburbs. The Theater in der Josefstadt, and the Theater an der Wien, which in 1801 replaced the Theater auf der Wieden, still exist, much rebuilt.

The theatre in the Leopoldstadt was for some seventy-five years the principal home of popular comedy, with comic types like Kasperl and Staberl keeping alive the old Hanswurst tradition. From the late 1780s, after Joseph II abandoned his 'National-Singspiel' venture at the Court Theatre, Marinelli, seizing on the lack of light vernacular musical theatre, developed the musical side of his company, increasing the size and proficiency of the orchestra, and instituting a school for talented youngsters. Though the emphasis remained on dialect comedy, the musical repertory was adventurous (it included works by Schenk, Gassmann, Salieri, Dittersdorf, Paisiello, and had special success with German adaptations of two of Martín y Soler's operas); the farces often included music, with extensive ensembles.

When Schikaneder took over the direction of the Freihaus-Theater auf der Wieden in summer 1789 he brought with him from southern Germany the strengthening the company needed, especially in music. The most important new members, apart from himself, were Benedikt Schack and Franz Xaver Gerl, both composers as well as singers and actors. The three newcomers were responsible for the first production, the Singspiel ('comic opera') *Der dumme Gärtner aus dem Gebirge, oder Die zween Anton* ('The stupid gardener from the mountains, or the two Antons'), given on 12 July. Over the next six years it was followed by six sequels. The musical ambitions of Schikaneder, and the new direction he was taking with the magic opera, are both apparent in Paul Wranitzky's *Oberon, König der Elfen*, presumably commissioned, and certainly first staged, by Schikaneder (7 November 1789). *Der Stein der Weisen oder Die Zauberinsel* ('The philosophers' stone, or the magic island'), by Schikaneder, Schack and Gerl followed on 11 September 1790; it was clearly a forerunner of *Die Zauberflöte*, with its story from *Dschinnistan*, its magic element, and its pairs of lovers, one serious, one comic. The emphasis that

Schikaneder was placing on music is apparent in the appointment of Johann Baptist Henneberg as kapellmeister, in the vocal and orchestral concerts that began to be given in the theatre, and in the appearance of Dittersdorf in 1789 as composer of two new Singspiels, one of which he conducted. Schikaneder's principal achievement was to secure the services of Mozart as composer of *Die Zauberflöte*.

Mozart's links with the popular theatres of Vienna tend to go unremarked. At an unknown date, perhaps early in 1786, he sketched the scenario for the first four scenes of a comedy, *Der Salzburger Lump in Wien* ('The Salzburg dolt [rogue?] in Vienna'). And – perhaps early in 1787 – he wrote out some five pages of another comedy, intended to be in three acts, *Die Liebesprobe* ('The love-test'). The list of characters includes types familiar to any student of eighteenth-century Viennese comedy – Herr von Dumkopf ('Thick-head'), Leander, Wurstl (the familiar abbreviation of Hanswurst) and Kasperl. There is no suggestion in either fragment, however, that these were to be anything other than spoken comedies. In his own sphere, music, Mozart wrote the strophic 'Ein deutsches Kriegslied', 'Ich möchte wohl der Kaiser sein' ('A German war-song', 'I should like to be the Emperor'; K 539) for the benefit concert of the Leopoldstadt-Theater actor-singer Friedrich Baumann; the entry in Mozart's *Catalogue of all my works* ... carries the date 5 March 1788; it was performed two days later. The scoring – intended to have a patriotic ring at a time when hostilities had again broken out against Turkey – includes the 'Turkish' instruments of piccolo, cymbals and bass drum. On 17 September 1789 Mozart entered in his *Catalogue* the aria 'Schon lacht der holde Frühling' ('Sweet Spring is already laughing'; K 580) for his sister-in-law Josepha Hofer to sing in an intended but cancelled production in the Freihaus-Theater of Paisiello's *Der balbier von Seviglien* (as Mozart called it); and it seems likely that the lost German aria, 'Ohne Zwang, aus eignem Triebe' ('Without coercion, on my own impulse'; K 569), of January 1789, was also written for Josepha. On 8 March 1791 Mozart entered in his *Catalogue* the aria 'Per questo bello mano' ('For this lovely hand'; K 612) for two members of Schikaneder's company, 'Hr Görl und Pischelberger' – Franz Xaver Gerl, the first Sarastro, and Friedrich Pischelberger, the principal double-bass player of the theatre orchestra, and, given the difficulty of the piece, a talented performer. These works, like *Die Zauberflöte*, suggest that Mozart was confident of the competence and artistic skills of the performers, singers and orchestral players.

A further, apparently contemporaneous, link with Schikaneder's theatre is Mozart's last set of keyboard variations, on the song 'Ein Weib ist das herrlichste Ding auf der Welt' ('A woman is the most splendid thing in the world'; K 613). The tune, taken from the second of the *Anton* plays, *Die verdeckten Sachen* (26 September 1789), is light and attractive; the eight variations probably date from March 1791, some eighteen months after the première of the Singspiel, the time when Mozart is traditionally held to have been approached by Schikaneder with the invitation to compose his new magic opera. Whatever the precise chronology of *Die Zauberflöte*, it may be seen as emerging naturally from Mozart's increasing involvement with the popular theatre.

The story of Yvain
D.D.R. OWEN AND PETER BRANSCOMBE

The libretto of *Die Zauberflöte* was confected from a variety of sources; and though some have been plausibly identified, no satisfactory explanation has so far been offered for the origins of the opening scenes. Despite Papageno's Italianized name, we now have reason to suspect that he is of French ancestry, and that Tamino's opening adventures are derived at one remove from Chrétien de Troyes's Arthurian romance *Yvain*, or *Le Chevalier au Lion* (c. 1177). But how could this have come about?

The eighteenth century saw a great revival of interest in the poetry and legends of the Middle Ages, prompted partly by historical and antiquarian concerns, partly by the realization that here was a fund of good, well-told stories still capable of entertaining a wide public. In France much scholarly pioneering work was done by La Curne de Sainte-Palaye. Through his efforts and those of Etienne Barbazan and Le Grand d'Aussy, a host of texts was rescued from oblivion, sometimes to be excerpted or summarized in the *Bibliothèque universelle des romans* (1775–89) or otherwise given wide currency, even beyond the printed page: for instance, the thirteenth-century tale of *Aucassin et Nicolette*, was discovered and twice published in a modernized form by Sainte-Palaye in the 1750s, revamped by Le Grand d'Aussy in 1779, and in the same year presented as a comic opera, with Sedaine's libretto set to music by Grétry.

Much the same was happening in the German-speaking world. The Swiss J. J. Bodmer in mid-century produced a translation of Wolfram von Eschenbach's *Parzival* and the first edition of the *Nibelungenlied*;

his pupil C. H. Myller edited the same texts in the 1780s. The prolific C. M. Wieland drew liberally from medieval legend; his *Oberon* (1780), based on the Old French *Huon de Bordeaux*, was itself turned into an opera by C. L. Gieseke, presumably at Schikaneder's request, and it was presented, with Paul Wranitzky's music, in Vienna in 1789. It would not, then, be surprising to find a strand of medieval romance in the Mozart work.

Chrétien's *Yvain* had been translated into German by Hartmann von Aue in about 1200. Though Chrétien's work was known to Mozart's French contemporaries, it was Hartmann's version that first attracted critical attention when, in 1776, over a third of the text was published by K. J. Michaeler, to be followed in 1785 by a full edition by Myller, and in 1786–7 by another one, with modern translation, by Michaeler, custodian of the University Library. More significantly, Michaeler was a leading member of 'True Concord', the Masonic lodge which Mozart regularly attended, and was a co-editor of the *Journal für Freymaurer*, which furnished a further source for the libretto of *Die Zauberflöte*. It is hardly likely that Mozart would have been unaware of *Iwain, ein Heldengedicht vom Ritter Hartmann* ('..., an heroic poem by the knight, Hartmann'), as his edition was entitled.

We suggest that two episodes from *Iwain* are the main source of the opening scenes in the opera. The first tells of a knight's encounter in a forest with a strange human being. His account of his experience prompts Iwain, a prince, to undertake the same adventure shortly afterwards. The second occurs later in the romance and shows the hero, bereft of his senses, found unconscious in the countryside and rescued by three ladies, to be brought to a nearby castle, whose mistress needs his aid. We suggest that these two episodes were conflated by Schikaneder as a prelude to Tamino's main quest. In the following analysis we outline the events as presented in *Die Zauberflöte* and give opposite the parallels found in one or other of the episodes in *Iwain* (I, 1 or I, 2).

Die Zauberflöte	*Iwain*
In a desolate countryside, Tamino, carrying a bow, is pursued by a fierce serpent. Terrified, he falls unconscious. Nearby is a temple.	In a forest clearing a knight is terrified at the sight of fierce beasts. A chapel is in the vicinity. (I, 1) – He carries a bow. He lies unconscious [is asleep, having lost his wits]. (I, 2)

Three ladies come out of the temple, find the unconscious hero and release him from his peril without his being aware of it. They are the attendants of a high-born lady.

Three ladies from a nearby castle find the unconscious hero and cure his madness without his being aware of it. One is the mistress of the castle, the others are her attendants. (I, 2)

Moved by the hero's handsome appearance, they resolve to tell their mistress of his presence, thinking he may help her in her plight. They leave him lying there and return to the temple.

Recognizing the hero's nobility from his appearance, the lady who first saw him told her mistress he would be able to help her in her plight. They leave him lying there and return to the castle. (I, 2)

Tamino regains consciousness and wonders if he is dreaming.

Iwain regains consciousness and wonders if he has been dreaming. (I, 2)

He is confronted by an outlandish figure whose dress is made from the covering of the wild creatures over which he claims total authority. [This is Papageno, who is dressed in feathers.]

He is confronted by a monstrous figure whose dress is made from the hides of the wild creatures over which he claims total authority. [He is a herdsman, guarding fierce aurochs and bison.] (I, 1)

Tamino, who at one point doubts Papageno's humanity, asks him who he is, and receives the reply: 'A human being, like you!'

Iwain asks the herdsman, whose humanity he doubts, what kind of a creature he is. He replies: 'I'm a man, as you see!' (I, 1)

On being asked in turn who he is, Tamino replies in terms too affected for the simple but good-natured Papageno to understand: he is of princely stock. Papageno is unaware of the ways of the world, but gives him useful information regarding the supernatural inhabitant of the nearby dwelling.

When questioned by the herdsman, the traveller replies, in affected terms unintelligible to the simple rustic, that he is a knight in search of adventure. Though ignorant of such things, the herdsman gives him useful information regarding a nearby wonder. (I, 1)

Papageno boasts of his giant's might and the strength of his hands, accepting credit for having strangled the serpent.

The herdsman, a giant, boasts of the power of his hands to subdue his beasts. (I, 1)

In the company of the ladies, Tamino is received by their mistress and will help her to defeat her aggressor.

Iwain is conducted by one of the attendants to her mistress, whom he will champion against her aggressor. (I, 2)

Other details may or may not be significant. For example, having championed the threatened lady, Iwain chances upon a lion locked in combat with a venomous serpent. After some hesitation, he decides to help the lion, fearing only that the noble beast might turn on him once the serpent is slain. In fact the grateful lion becomes his faithful companion. In the opening number of the opera Mozart originally had Tamino as 'chosen victim of the grim lion' (see p. 48), before opting for the words printed in the libretto, 'chosen victim of the cunning serpent'; his initial indecision is curiously paralleled in Iwain's uncertainty as to which animal he should assist. Mozart keeps the lion in reserve for Sarastro's realm, having his inexperienced prince assailed by a creature more generally regarded as evil, and perceived as having sexual connotations.

Another curious coincidence is the occurrence both in the punishment inflicted by the Three Ladies on Papageno and in the information given to the knight by the herdsman of three particular elements: clear water, stone and gold. Papageno is told he must dine off the water and the stone, and has his mouth sealed with a golden padlock; Iwain is informed of the spring of clear water beside which stands a stone slab and where a golden cup hangs.

It appears, then, that Schikaneder devised a series of adventures to introduce his main plot by combining and rearranging romance material recently made available. His masterstroke was to turn a mysterious herdsman-figure into a birdman, for whom other prototypes have been found elsewhere (see pp. 98–101).

Terrasson's novel *Sethos*

It has long been recognized that the French novel *Sethos* exerted an influence on *Die Zauberflöte*, though commentators cannot agree whether it was the sole important source, or only of minor significance. *Sethos, histoire ou Vie tirée des monumens anecdotes de l'ancienne Egypte. Traduite d'un manuscrit grec ... Paris, 1731* is the legend on the title-page of the first of numerous editions; and it soon became accepted that Abbé Jean Terrasson is the anonymous author of this three-volume novel rather than the translator of a putative Greek original.

Readers of *Sethos* will soon perceive that details from the first four books (of ten) foreshadow incidents in *Die Zauberflöte*. A careful reading throws light on some problems presented by Schikaneder's libretto; it also gives the director of the opera valuable hints about solutions to problems of production and stage design, as well as background information about eighteenth-century views on the Egyptian Mysteries. The specialist will want to consult *Sethos* in the German translation used by the librettist of Mozart's opera, *Geschichte des egyptischen Königs Sethos ... Aus dem Französischen übersetzt von Matthias Claudius. Breslau ... 1777* (the second volume followed in 1778). The book continued to enjoy great popularity in France, where it was often reprinted; the earliest German translation, by C. G. Wend, was published in Hamburg as early as 1732–7.

The numerous similarities between Terrasson's novel and Schikaneder's libretto include a desolate and mountainous area where a fierce serpent holds sway (in *Sethos* it terrorizes the populace); in each case a young prince confronts the serpent. Sethos is successful, Tamino vanquished. In each work the prince comes to a splendid temple, to which he seeks admittance (in *Sethos* the site is identified as the Temple of Memphis); in each the aspirant must negotiate tests of fire and water before being received by the initiates as one of themselves. (The task of judgment imposed on Sethos immediately after his successful initiation points forward to the high priestly function that Tamino takes over in Goethe's sequel to *Die Zauberflöte*, and that Schikaneder himself posited in *Das Labyrinth*, though there Sarastro is persuaded to continue as high priest (the priests are also the country's judges in Terrasson's Egypt).

The linguistic parallels can be appreciated if Matthias Claudius's translation of Terrasson is set beside Schikaneder's text. In the novel, where the tests of fire and water are a stage in the neophyte's physical entry into the temple, the order of events familiar in the opera is not found. The relevant passage in the novel, literally translated, reads:

When Sethos was about to enter, his eyes were caught by an inscription with black letters written on a very white piece of marble which was set as a pediment on the moulding of the arch which formed the entrance to the path; he read these words: 'He who walks this way alone, and without looking behind him, will be purified by fire, water and air; and if he can overcome the dread of death, he will go out again, out of the bosom of the earth, and see the light again, and he will have the right to make his soul ready for the revelation of the secrets of the great Goddess Isis!'[1]

The words sung by the Two Men in Armour in the Act II finale of *Die Zauberflöte* are:

He who walks this path full of hardships will be made pure through fire, water, air and earth; if he can overcome the dread of death he will soar heavenwards from the earth. – He will then, illuminated, be in a position to dedicate himself wholly to the mysteries of Isis.[2]

An interesting omission in the opera libretto is of the warning against the aspirant's looking behind him. The parallel with the myth of Orpheus is more marked in the novel, where Orpheus is a recent initiate and present when Sethos is called upon to pass judgment on a Carthaginian prince accused of fratricide. In *Die Zauberflöte* the parallels with Orpheus are clear, but discreet – Tamino's quest is to rescue Pamina from what her mother claims to be infernal forces; the hero charms the animals and birds with his performance on the magic flute in I, 15 and II, 19. In the novel both Sethos and Orpheus pass through the trials of fire and water, and so does Tamino in the opera.

The other close, linguistic, parallel between the two books is the wording of Sarastro's hymn with chorus in II, 1 and the two hymns addressed to the trinity of Egyptian gods, and later specifically to Isis, in the novel. The first hymn, early in Book I, is introduced by Terrasson thus: '[In the middle of the sanctuary] large choirs sang with tones of mourning slow hymns taken from the old ritual and which were appropriate to the present crisis [the illness of Sethos' mother, Queen Nepthe (= Nephtys, sister of Isis?)].' The French text here contains as hymn four stanzas of six lines each, rhyming *aabccb*; stanza 1 is devoted to Osiris, stanzas 2 and 3 are devoted to Isis, and stanza 4 to Horus, child of Osiris and Isis, god of the sun, and by Terrasson also considered to be god of reason, or human wisdom. Claudius makes no attempt to do more than translate the text literally into heightened prose. The last stanza in particular contains several terms and concepts familiar from *Die Zauberflöte*:

Horus, god of discretion attained through wisdom, thou who succourest the innocent weak childhood of everything on its way to its journey, – preserve for a prince who, still a child, is thy blood, thine image, the assistance that to thee too, at his age, thy mother Isis granted.[3]

Sarastro's aria with chorus (originally not intended to be an aria, as the heading 'Chorus' in the libretto indicates) is a prayer for succour for Tamino and Pamina (she has no equivalent in Terrasson), but the more interesting difference is that Horus, the third god in the Egyptian trinity in Terrasson's novel, is at no point mentioned by Schikaneder. In view of the importance of the number three in the libretto, one might have expected that the young god Horus would find a place.

The other hymn occurs in the middle of Book III of *Sethos* and includes the words:

O Isis, great goddess of the Egyptians, give thy spirit to the new servant who has withstood so many dangers and tasks in order to appear before thee. Make him victorious also in the trials of his soul, and teach his heart thy laws, so that he may be worthy to be admitted to thy mysteries.[4]

There are other parallels between novel and libretto. For instance, the student of *Die Zauberflöte* who is alienated by Pamina's description (I, 14) of Sarastro's morning activity of hunting will find that the priests at Memphis in *Sethos* indulged in various not obviously priestly activities (incidentally, Prince-Archbishop Colloredo, Mozart's unloved employer, was a keen huntsman). There are no clear distinctions between the sacred and the profane activities of the ancient Egyptian priests in Terrasson's novel — in addition to their religious duties they act as judges, warriors and counsellors of kings. Initiates, in fact, needed to be all-rounders. The terrors of the tests were enough to scare away all but the bravest, yet such was the respect in which the people held the initiates, owing to their great virtues and incorruptible sense of justice ('Tugenden ... und ... Gerechtigkeit'), that there were always candidates for admission. Initiates were respected even by the kings

who regarded them not only as men intrepid in battle, but also as the most enlightened ministers they could have, and often, too, as mediators between themselves and the priests, whose authority they at times could not help fearing; finally, nothing is more pleasant for a private individual than to have all the rights of priesthood without its obligations and burdens ...

A related area of misunderstanding concerns the presence of women in the temple. The priests' music in the opera — the choral contributions to Sarastro's 'O Isis und Osiris schenket' (no. 10) and to the quintet 'Wie? Wie? Wie?' (no. 12), and the chorus 'O Isis und Osiris, welche Wonne' (no. 18) — is for tenor and bass voices only; however, the chorus parts in both finales include soprano and alto lines — for musical reasons, but also because it is clear from Terrasson's description of life in the temple, including specifically mixed choral singing, that women played an important part in its activities: there were priestesses (as the wives of the priests were honorifically termed; it is clear from the injunctions placed on Sethos at the time of his tests that he may salute the priestesses (cf. Tamino's gestures to Pamina in II, 18), but must not speak to them); and the reader has earlier learned that the officers of the second order (temple guards, workmen, acolytes and servants, including failed aspirants for initiation) could marry and have families. The subordinate rôle of women in Sarastro's temple may well owe something to Masonic practice in the lodges of Mozart's day, from which women were entirely excluded (see pp. 23 and 40).

The frequent stage-direction 'thunder' in the first scene of Tamino's and Papageno's initiatory trials (II, 2–6) finds an interesting equivalent in the descriptions of ceremonies at the Temple of Memphis in the third book of *Sethos*. There we learn that what the people and the aspirants take to be thunder is in fact the rumble and clang, augmented by the resonance of the underground chambers and passages, of the great gates of the temple being closed. Again, in the middle of Book III we learn that the drawbridge mechanism, by means of which the aspirant is conveyed into the temple itself from the canal he has just swum, makes a noise of thunder. This is a signal to the priests in the sanctuary that the aspirant is at hand, though the common people who happen to be present take the noise for a sign that a god is about to unveil a mystery.

One of the strongest contrasts in the opera, that between night and day, darkness and light, is also a feature of the novel. Amedes, Sethos' tutor and guardian, determines to let the prince visit the interior of his father's as-yet vacant burial pyramid. 'As it was a matter of traversing dark and deep places, Amedes was convinced that this was an excellent test against the panic dread which overcomes most people in darkness, and against the fear of ghosts, with which, according to popular rumour, uninhabited buildings were then, as now, filled' (penultimate paragraph of Book II). The parallels with the scenes set in darkness in *Die Zauberflöte* (II, 2–6 and 7–12, followed by the promise of dawn at the opening of the second finale) are clear.

The emphasis placed on personal qualities in *Die Zauberflöte* is also a feature of *Sethos*. The last lines of the second book contain a warning to Sethos to observe discretion in respect of the knowledge he has already gained from Amedes: '... keep secret ('seyn Sie verschwiegen') the little I have told you in order to prepare yourself for greater matters'.[5] When Sethos determines not to turn back at the gates that lead to the tests of fire and water, Amedes warns him 'for the last time to combine presence of mind ('Klugheit') with courage ('Muth')'. Just previously the general point had been made that the inscription above the entrance leading to the tests was sufficient to persuade most aspirants who had had the courage to progress thus far to go back while there was still time – only those with extreme curiosity and boldness ('Kühnheit') even reached that place.

Having passed the warning text the aspirant is given an initiate to guide him before he proceeds to 'a very strict examination on all the other virtues' (apart, that is, from courage). The opera can convey no sense of the distance that the aspirant must wander in the vaults – more than a league, we read in the novel – before he arrives at 'a small door, all of metal, that was closed; and two paces further, three men armed with helmets, on top of each of which was an Anubis head [Anubis: god and guardian of the dead, usually represented by a jackal].' One of these men addressed the candidate thus:

We are not here to stop you on your way; pursue it, if the gods have given you courage. But if you are unfortunate enough to retrace your steps, we shall stop and hold you here. Now you may turn back; one moment later, and you will never leave this place except you at once follow the route forward without turning your head or taking a backward step.

The comparable passages in *Die Zauberflöte* is the Spokesman's advice to Tamino early in II, 3:

Prince, there is still time to turn back – one step further, and it is too late.

For Papageno the message is made clear in II, 23, when the Spokesman informs him:

Strictly, you deserve to wander for ever in the dark clefts of the earth; – but the merciful gods release you from that punishment

(as in the novel Orpheus is granted remission after failing the final test at the entrance to the temple).

Terrasson's description of the tests of fire and water is not exactly comparable to those through which Mozart's Tamino and Pamina must pass, but provides valuable suggestions for a stage-designer and director who wish to benefit from a fictional example familiar in the late eighteenth century. The aspirant who is not daunted by the admonitions finds himself drawing near a recently lighted fire. The path ended here, leading into a vaulted chamber more than one hundred feet long and broad. When one entered there were on the right and left side two pyres, or rather, two upright piles of various logs, very close to each other, around which, vine-like, were twisted branches of Arabian balsam, Egyptian thorns, and tamarinds, three very supple, odiferous and readily combustible kinds of wood. The smoke escaped through long tubes placed there for that purpose. But the flames, which easily licked up to the roof and then fell back in waves, gave the whole space that they encompassed the appearance of a glowing furnace. Further, Sethos found on the floor between the two pyres a metal grille eight feet wide and thirty feet long, reddened by the fire. This grille was formed of lozenge-shaped segments which scarcely left space between them for a human foot. Realizing that he could only proceed by this way, he did so with as much speed as care. Historians ignorant of the basic facts or wishing to exaggerate the miraculous element say that such a person passed through the flames, instead of saying that he passed between two hedges of flames; and that he walked on red-hot iron, instead of saying that he walked between segments of red-hot iron.

Having passed this test, Sethos finds himself facing a wide canal, which flows through the subterranean chamber. Just before it reaches the chamber it has descended a waterfall, the noise of which he has confused with the fire. Beyond the canal he can just make out a flight of steps in an arcade, ascending into darkness. The canal to left and right is blocked by barriers, and iron balustrades extend from the far bank of the canal towards the steps. Relighting his torch, he binds his clothes to his head and swims the canal, holding the torch in one hand. He dresses himself and ascends the steps to the platform from which the aspirant is transported by wheel mechanism through a quarter circle until the great gates of ivory swing open and, from the complete darkness which had followed the extinction of his lamp, he finds himself in the blazing light of day (or in an equally brilliant lamplight). This is the last trial. Strikingly similar is the final stage-direction in II, 28 of the opera: 'At once a door opens; one sees an entrance to a brightly lit temple.' To his amazement Sethos finds that he has ascended from beneath the same statues of Osiris, Isis and Horus in front of which he and the people had prayed for the recovery of his mother. 'He was received by the priests, who stood in two rows at the rear of the sanctuary. The high priest embracing him first praised him for his courage and congratulated him on the happy outcome of his trials.' While Sethos is prostrating himself before the altar, the high priest speaks the words: 'O Isis, great goddess of the Egyptians ...' (see p. 13). These words, echoed in chorus by the priests, recall phrases in Sarastro's aria with chorus, no. 10 ('O Isis ... gieb deinen Geist dem neuen Diener, der so viel Gefahren ...'), just as a later phrase — that Sethos will remain 'in diesen heiligen Oertern' ('in these sacred precincts') — may remind us of the opening words of each verse of Sarastro's second aria (no. 14), the last line of which ('Verdienet nicht ein Mensch zu seyn') echoes a phrase of Sethos ('... sind es nicht werth Menschen zu seyn').

The reader will probably have been struck as much by the differences as the similarities between *Sethos* and *Die Zauberflöte*. Schikaneder has run together the quite separate sets of tests that Sethos undergoes as a candidate for initiation (the trials of courage: fire, water and gaining entry to the sanctuary; and the three stages of purification: fasting, or purification of the body, purification of the soul, and 'Manifestation', or revelation). Thus the test of silence, part of the purification of the soul in *Sethos*, is imposed on the aspirant in *Die Zauberflöte* along with the testing of his courage; and the trials of fire and water (which perhaps represent progression to the Second Grade in Masonic terms) are the final stage that we witness in the process of initiation for Tamino and Pamina, rather than the early stage they represent for Terrasson's hero.

A few further details in *Sethos* claim attention. The emphasis on the figure three hardly needs emphasizing in the opera – three chords, Three Ladies, Three Boys, three temples and threefold appearances of several of the characters. Three plays an even more important part in the novel, with three stages to each kind of initiation, three questions to Sethos, each posed three times, and to be answered after nine days, three Men in Armour at the gates of metal, three dominant gods (Osiris, Isis and Horus). The entrance by which Sethos and Amedes enter the pyramid measures three feet square; but these examples could be multiplied – doubtless threefold.

The reader of *Sethos* will gain useful hints about the duties of the priests that we may find puzzling in *Die Zauberflöte*. Common to both is the appointment of a priest or initiate to instruct and accompany a candidate for admission; at other times, a candidate may be kept under observation, and his discourse overheard, by unseen priests who are summoned to the scene by the sound of the closing of the metal doors; in this way, and also by investigation of the candidate's past life, information is made available to the senior priests and judges that assists their judgment, and increases the awe in which they are held by the candidate by reason of their knowledge of him. The priests adopt a deliberately casual attitude towards an aspirant – 'they seemed ready and willing, merely obliging him to inscribe his name and his desire, and at once appointed an initiate to instruct him about the tests he had to undergo'.[6]

We read later of the solemn vows the initiate has to take that he will never betray any of the secrets to which he has access. However, not only the initiates but the young priests and the officers of the second order were advised never to affect that air of reserve which merely excites in others a vain curiosity, and which in part betrays the very secret one wishes to keep. Thus they accustomed themselves to affect a certain affability which prevented most people from suspecting that they knew so large a number of things about which they did not speak. Something of this studied casualness and feigned ignorance attaches to the priests who accompany Tamino and Papageno during their tests, particularly to the Second Priest, who jokes with the bird-catcher in II, 3, finding its musical expression in the otherwise puzzlingly jaunty, even flippant duet 'Bewahret euch vor Weibertücken', no. 11.

A final detail: in a lengthy section in the middle of Book II, Terrasson describes the music room in the temple, and the instruments available, many of them precious antiques. 'One learned that ... the wind instruments were discovered first. One even saw here in first place the flute with numerous reeds of varying length, which was in use before Osiris invented the simple flute which was by itself capable of producing all the notes of the earlier instrument.' In other words, the primitive panpipe of Papageno is specifically identified as the predecessor of the perfected flute presented to Tamino.

Thamos, König in Egypten

In the context of *Die Zauberflöte*, one of Mozart's earlier compositions demands consideration. This is his score of incidental music (the only incidental music he wrote) to Baron Tobias Philipp von Gebler's five-act heroic drama *Thamos, König in Egypten*, K 345/336a. Gebler's play, published at Prague and Dresden in 1773 both separately and as the final work in the third and last volume of his *Theatralische Werke*, has interesting thematic and musical links with *Die Zauberflöte*. *Thamos* is set in the Temple of the Sun at Heliopolis. The high priest, Sethos − he is also, unrecognized, the deposed king, Menes − watches over the education and the lives of his daughter, Tharsis (who does not know his real identity), and of Prince Thamos, the son of the king who overthrew him. Thamos' false friend, Pheron, plans to marry Tharsis and become king; he is aided by Mirza, first sun-maiden. Sethos reveals himself as the rightful king, unites the young lovers, and the conspirators receive their deserts.

It is not difficult to detect resemblances with *Die Zauberflöte* –
notably in the pairings Sethos and Sarastro, Thamos and Tamino,
Tharsis and Pamina, Pheron and Monostatos, Mirza and the Queen
of Night – even if the differences are almost as striking.

Mozart's score for *Thamos* consists of five orchestral numbers –
four entr'actes and a postlude – and three choruses. Until recently
it has been accepted that the two big choral numbers, and probably
the entr'actes, were written in 1773, the choruses being thoroughly
revised in the late 1770s, when the closing chorus with bass solo was
added. Wolfgang Plath and Alan Tyson have concluded that the
autograph of the final version of the orchestral numbers was written
in 1776–7 and that of the choral numbers in 1779–80 (that is,
separated by the lengthy journey to Mannheim and Paris that Mozart
undertook with his mother).

It would be easy to underestimate the importance of *Thamos* in
the prehistory of *Die Zauberflöte* were it not for the clear indication
in Mozart's letter to his father of 15 February 1783 how highly he
valued the music, regretting that the limited success of the play
deprived him of the chance to see his score more widely performed
(however, by around 1785 it was being given with Plümicke's play
Lanassa). Those who have claimed that the revised version of the
Thamos music was commissioned by Schikaneder for performance
during his Salzburg season of 1780–1 are almost certainly wrong:
Gebler's play does not appear in the repertory list which E. K. Blümml
has reconstructed from contemporary records. It is much more likely
that Mozart revised his score for the company of Johannes Böhm,
who played in Salzburg in 1779 (and, in light of the findings of Plath
and Tyson, unlikely that the task was carried out for Karl Wahr, who
is known to have given the play in Salzburg in 1775–6).

The dignity and beauty of Mozart's *Thamos* score are indisputable;
the two choruses to Gebler's words in their later form, and the final
choral number with its opening bass solo for the high priest, are
worthy predecessors to the priests' music in *Die Zauberflöte*. The three
choruses are the most extensive choral settings that Mozart undertook in German. With their rapid changes of dynamics, tempo and
mood, their solo and duet passages, and their rich orchestration these
movements would have taxed the resources of a court opera company
in the 1770s, let alone the travelling troupe for which they were
written. An incidental detail is worth mentioning: the falling rhythmic
figure at bars 24–5 and 168–9 of the opening chorus of *Thamos* (to
the words 'schon wird von Ägypten dir neues) Opfer gebracht' – 'new

sacrifice is brought to thee from Egypt') occurs in almost identical form in the last apostrophe of the Three Ladies and Monostatos in the Act II finale of *Die Zauberflöte* (bars 805–6; the words are 'sei unsrer Rache] Opfer gebracht' – 'may a sacrifice to our vengeance be brought'). Further, verbal phrases from *Thamos* would not be out of place in the opera: the first words of Gebler that Mozart had to set are 'Schon weichet dir, Sonne, des Lichtes Feindin, die Nacht!' ('Already, o Sun, light's foe, night, yields to thee!'); the phrase 'Sanfter Flöten Zauberklang' ('soft flutes' magic sound') is also imaginable in *Die Zauberflöte*. The strongest pre-echo occurs in one of the purely instrumental numbers. The stirring C-minor Allegro (no. 2) that closes the first act opens with a Maestoso threefold knocking figure which one hesitates to link with Freemasonary, less because Mozart was still some way from seeking admission to the order than because these chords are immediately followed by one of several explanatory notes written into the autograph by Leopold Mozart that indicates that treachery is afoot: 'The first act concludes with the decision taken by Pheron and Mirza to set Pheron on the throne.'

Ignaz von Born's essay

The most outspokenly Masonic source of *Die Zauberflöte*, and the product of a man close to Mozart, is the long essay 'Ueber die Mysterien der Aegyptier' which appeared in the first number of the *Journal für Freymaurer* in 1784. This treatise 'On the Mysteries of the Egyptians' was signed 'I.v.B.M.v.S.', that is, 'Ignaz von Born, Meister vom Stuhl' (Master)'. For further information on Born, see pp. 40–1. The periodical, 'published by the Brethren of the Lodge "Zur wahren Eintracht" in the Orient of Vienna', was initiated by Born and edited by the poet Alois Blumauer; for the three liveliest years of Freemasonry in Austria it provided a very important vehicle for Masonic opinion.

Born's essay, 116 pages long, relies heavily on his extensive reading of classical authors, to whom he frequently refers in footnotes. The most often cited authors are Diodorus Siculus (the *World History*), Herodotus (the *History*), Plutarch (*De Iside et Osiride*) and Apuleius (the *Metamorphoses*). 'Ueber die Mysterien der Aegyptier' is a rather dry, scholarly piece of work. There are, though, verbal pre-echoes of *Die Zauberflöte* and interesting details of aspects of Egyptian civilization. To take first an example from the field of religion, the words 'bey dem tiefen Stillschweigen der Eingeweihten' ('while the initiates maintain a profound silence', p. 86) remind us of the stage-direction in II, 21 of Schikaneder's libretto: 'Eine Stille herrscht bei allen Priestern' ('Silence reigns among all the priests'; Pamina comments 'Welch eine fürchterliche Stille!', 'What a dreadful silence!').

The essay is divided into three sections, preceded by a short but weighty introduction. The first section is a survey of the circumstances of the Egyptian people in the earliest times, including the history of Osiris, his deeds, murder and deification. The second concerns the constitution, duties and knowledge of the Egyptian priests. And the third compares the ceremonies and customs of the Egyptian mysteries with those of Freemasonry.

The introduction (*Einleitung*) mentions the Temple of Truth (Tempel der Wahrheit) in which the lost records of 'one of the most enlightened and oldest nations' were stored. Citing Diodorus Siculus, Born lists some of the gods and kings of the ancient Egyptians, including Osiris ('Osiris was a mortal. We call the sun, this unchanging symbol of the godhead, by his name.'). And he continues – now citing Plutarch, and thus placing the emphasis firmly on the twin deities invoked in *Die Zauberflöte*:

Knowledge of nature is the final purpose of our application. This procreatrix, nourisher and preserver of all creatures we honour under the image of Isis. – Only that man lifts her veil unpunished who knows her whole might and strength.

That Schikaneder had a copy of Born's essay before him, or was at least recalling details of its phraseology, is suggested by the verbal echoes – 'Verschwiegenheit' ('discretion'), the phrase 'rein und lauter' ('clean and pure') on p. 23, and 'Heiligthum' ('sanctuary') and 'Fremdling' ('stranger') on the following page. Born then sets out his aim in the essay; it is 'to satisfy my curiosity which commands me to instruct myself in everything that may have a relevance to our honourable Order, – and to the closeness of its relationship to the Mysteries of olden times.' And he concludes this opening section by mentioning his studies of the ceremonies, religious practices and duties of the Egyptian priests and initiates, 'and finally I compared the customs and ceremonies of the Egyptian Mysteries with those of Masonry'.

It is difficult to sift the sources in such a way that no doubt is left as to the origins of specific details in the libretto of the opera – there is, for instance, no reason to suspect that Schikaneder had read Diodorus or Plutarch. But the occurrence of both these authors as major sources for *Sethos* and Born's essay certainly does not entitle us to accept that the one, but not the other, was familiar to Schikaneder. For instance, in Part I of the essay the contrast between bare, mountainous country, and the richly fertile land by the Nile is a feature of Terrasson's account as well as Born's; in *Die Zauberflöte* that contrast is striking in the two outdoor settings in Act I – the rocky, mountainous terrain of the Queen, with a scattering of trees, and the 'pleasant and charming valley' (as the Second Lady describes it) in which Sarastro's temple is situated.

In the second section of 'Ueber die Mysterien der Aegyptier' Born discusses the hidden meanings of hieroglyphic writing:

The profane man saw, for example, Osiris and Isis in the image or sign of the sun and moon. According to mystical meaning ... the sun was the highest unique godhead, the primeval source of all good, and the moon the image of the omnipotence of the creator, and the sign of the sun often betokened the spirit and the fiery particles, and the sign of the moon, on the other hand, the waters and the little parts of the earth to which, as the effective causes of the whole creative process, according to their teaching, the air owes its existence.

The moon, the heavenly body we associate with the Queen of Night, has here no evil connotations. This section of the essay closes with a summary of the qualities of the priests: 'In short, gentleness, tolerance, submissiveness and obedience towards their rulers, and exact adherence to the laws, marked out the Egyptian priests as much as did their knowledge and their way of life.'

The third and longest section concerns the qualities of the ancient Egyptian priesthood and those of the Masons; it is the one of greatest interest to us. Everything that occurred in the Mysteries had a threefold purpose,

a moral, an historical and a mystical meaning. Wholly impenetrable, however, is – owing to the profound silence of the initiates and the older writers about everything that was carried out in the innermost part of the temple – the mystical meaning. Hardly ever will even the most far- and clear-sighted Brother of our Fellowship be able to unravel it; for that our so-called illuminated Brothers cannot herein come to our assistance, is beyond all doubt ... In their anxious search they wander from the prepared path on which they were led when they were admitted to the Order; bury themselves in labyrinths, wander from the twilight into the night, and their cry that they see light where the deepest darkness reigns, that they are quenching their thirst for truth at the source of life, leads many a good Brother from the straight path, leads him to the pool of nonsense, from which he thinks he is drinking wisdom, and diminishes the little band of the elect which, under the guidance of reason, this special light that the greatest architect has given man to guide him, slowly but surely approaches the desired goal.

Two pages later come revealing comments about the practice of the Viennese Masons: 'We, too, make it clear to the initiate, as soon as he has seen the light, that we are not ordained to be a secret and hidden society, but that we, when tyranny and vice gained the upper hand, secretly banded together in order to oppose that stream the more surely.' In Born's essay, as in *Sethos*, a king's son must yield precedence to the son of an initiate; we note from II, 1 that Tamino, at the age of twenty, is past the minimum age for initiation, which is eighteen (Sethos was sixteen). Born is firmer than Terrasson in excluding women from the Mysteries, as from the throne. The sub-ordinate rôle of women is emphasized – 'the Egyptian priests believed women to be incapable of the higher knowledge which was the priests' task, and doubted their discretion'. The most a woman could hope for was to be permitted to feed the animals that were sacred to the Egyptians – a condescension that she owed to the respect in which Isis was held. Women, we read further, were also excluded from the secrets of Masons, lest they disturb the Brothers in their work by their charms.

Born goes on to quote from the *Metamorphoses* of Apuleius, singling out the passage from Book XI (= Chapter XVIII in Robert Graves's translation in Penguin Classics, *The Golden Ass*, Harmonds-worth, 1950, p. 241) in which the ass describes the apparition of Isis and the events of the day of his initiation. He develops the parallels between the experiences described by Apuleius and those of the new Mason: the aspirant is informed when he is to appear in the temple, he is admitted not by one priest but 'in a general assembly' held in the evening, there are similarities in the signs used, the linen clothing of the aspirant; and in each the aspirant is led by the right hand into the temple so

that in darkened chambers he may be faced with the terror of death and brought back, passing through all the elements, to his previous position, and so that he might see bright light at midnight. This was noticed, and no one will fail to recognize the similarity between the initiation of the Egyptian priest and that of the Mason.

Further, Born enquires: 'Are not the various initiations into the secrets of Isis, or nature, of Serapis, or inner knowledge of nature, and of Osiris, or full recognition of the highest godhead, approximately the same as the various degrees in Masonry?' We might be aware of more parallels, he says, had there been traitors among the Egyptian priesthood 'as in part the self-interested authors of some Masonic writings have become traitors to our Order.' (It is difficult to identify contemporary betrayers of Masonic secrets, but the defection and subsequent vehement antagonism of Leopold Alois Hoffmann and others lay in the near future.) The quality of discretion ('Verschwiegenheit') is emphasized (citing Plutarch, *De Iside et Osiride*) by the pressing of Solomon's seal to the tongue of the new Mason.

Plutarch is also the source for the story of the saving of the life of the young prince Horus from the serpent with which his evil uncle's mistress intended to kill him; his servants saved Horus by killing the serpent, and in commemoration of this a rope was thrown into the middle of the temple during the Mysteries and was symbolically chopped into pieces. It is surely permissible to see here the origin of the first scene of *Die Zauberflöte*. Excluded from the libretto, on the other hand, are a series of references from the third section of Born's essay to more or less familiar Masonic topics – the grades of Apprentice (Lehrling), Journeyman (Gesell) and Master (Meister), the spirit-level, set-square, plumbline, circle and drawing-board as symbols of the mathematical sciences, and the trowel as specific symbol of architecture (the art traditionally believed to have been invented by Osiris), with the hammer held to have its origin in the shape of the Egyptian plough.

Present in Born's essay, on the other hand, are references to metallurgy (he was himself a metallurgist), which he links with Osiris, and to the Nile. Each year an Egyptian was sent blindfold on a pilgrimage to the temple of Isis at Sais, and he always arrived safely; the Egyptian equivalent of the 'travels of our Brothers the Journeymen' were 'the travels of Osiris, who to the accompaniment of music and a train of nine girls or Muses passed through Egypt, in order to draw to him the rude inhabitants through the magic of music, song and dance, and to make them more sociable.' Common to the Egyptian priesthood and to Masons were their code of conduct and their resilience in the face of oppression ('our Masonic zeal, too, is perhaps more fanned than suppressed by persecution and prohibition').

Though there is no mention in *Die Zauberflöte* of the sphinx, nor any surviving picture of an early production that includes a representation of the sphinx (as in the epoch-making sets designed for Berlin in 1816 by Karl Friedrich Schinkel), the description of the qualities of the sphinx in Born's essay leaves an important mark on the opera.

The sphinx, says Born, combines the beauty of the female form with the strength of the lion to produce wisdom. 'Are not wisdom, beauty and strength ('Weisheit, Schönheit und Stärke') also the properties that the Mason must have in his mind's eye when designing the building he is creating?' These three qualities are praised in the closing chorus, in which 'strength ... crowns beauty and wisdom with an eternal crown as their reward'. Three was a holy number for the Egyptians, as it is for Masons; metal was represented by a triangle, as were the sacred bird, the ibis, and the elements of fire and water. These last, equilateral triangles resting on their base and on their point, are represented by Masons on their key and trowel in homage to Hermes Trismegistus (= Thoth the Very Great). The sun was worshipped as 'the symbol of the unchanging eternal godhead'.

Born's peroration takes the form of three questions: 'Is truth, wisdom and the promotion of the happiness of the entire human race not the actual ultimate purpose of our Fellowship? ... Is it not our duty to oppose vice, ignorance and foolishness, and to spread enlightenment? ... And can there possibly be a more exalted and noble ultimate purpose than to broaden our knowledge through mutual instruction, through shewing everyone who joins our circle the straight way to perfection on the path of virtue, to lead him back fraternally if he strays, to encourage ourselves each day to perform virtuous deeds, to practise all that is good, and to prevent all evil?' These precepts are recalled in the second act of *Die Zauberflöte*, notably in the opening words of the Spokesman in II, 6, and in Sarastro's aria in II, 12. The whole essay ends with the solemn exhortation, soon to be frustrated by events in Vienna: 'May superstition and fanaticism never desecrate our lodges!'

Dschinnistan

In 1786 there was published at Winterthur the first volume of a collection of fairy-tales destined to have far-reaching influence. This was *Dschinnistan oder auserlesene Feen- und Geister-Märchen, theils neu erfunden, theils neu übersezt und umgearbeitet* ('Dschinnistan or selected tales of fairies and spirits, partly newly invented, partly newly translated and revised'). The first volume contained five tales; the second, published in 1787, contained seven; and the third, which appeared in 1789 and included a foreword signed 'Weimar den 18. Merz 1789. Wieland', thus ending the already transparent anonymity, also contained seven tales. Wieland's foreword indicated that the issue of a fourth volume would depend on public encouragement; despite the popularity of the collection, no further instalment appeared. A cheaper edition without the attractive copperplate engravings was announced in the Jena *Allgemeine Literatur-Zeitung* in May 1793; and the individual stories were beginning to appear separately in Vienna in 1791, brought out by Mathias Ludwig, the publisher of Schikaneder's theatre almanac for 1791.

The vogue of *Dschinnistan* lasted many years – Ferdinand Raimund based his first play, *Der Barometermacher auf der Zauberinsel* (1823), on 'Die Prinzessin mit der langen Nase', the fourth tale of the final volume. Wieland is rightly given the credit for the enterprise, but the foreword indicates that his collaborator (and son-in-law) J. A. Liebeskind was responsible for about a third of the stories, including the one most often mentioned in a Mozartian connection, 'Lulu oder die Zauberflöte', the last story of the whole collection.

Mozart and Schikaneder derived motifs and incidents from so many sources, and the debt to 'Lulu' is so limited, that Liebeskind's story has been given more credit than it deserves; though it is indeed the primary source for the magic opera by Joachim Perinet and Wenzel Müller, *Der Fagottist oder Die Zauberzither* – familiarly known as *Kaspar der Fagottist* (see below, pp. 29–31).

The principal stories from *Dschinnistan* to which the libretto of *Die Zauberflöte* is indebted are as follows: 'Adis und Dahy' (volume I, story 2) contains a character named Torgut, 'a very ugly black slave' who spies on the heroine, suspecting that her mockery of him is connected with her love for someone else; he reports his suspicions to his master, the Brahmin, and – with the heroine (in this respect Pamina is more kindly treated) – is punished instead of rewarded. 'Neangir und seine Brüder' (volume I, story 3) contains the detail – also familiar from other sources – of the hero falling in love with the heroine's portrait, and determining to set off at once and rescue her, before he has ever set eyes on her. 'He became quite beside himself at the sight, and his heart, which had never experienced what love is, was put into the pleasantest apprehension by a thousand unknown stirrings' (the similarity of situation is backed by one of vocabulary; words like 'Bildnis', 'Herz', 'Liebe', 'Regung', 'Entzücken' and 'Feuer' are common to aria and *Märchen*).

'Der Stein der Weisen' (volume I, story 4) is rich in Egyptian atmosphere: Misfragmutosiris, an adept 'of the true and secret school of the great Hermes', narrates how he entered the great pyramid at Memphis and won the secret papyrus roll from the sleeping (or dead)

Hermes Trismegistus, making his way through tests of flood, fire and wind, in the depths of the pyramids (the resemblance to *Sethos* is clear). The motifs in an illustrative vignette include a genie on a lotus-leaf, holding a flaming torch, with his finger to his lips, and an open-jawed serpent facing the king.

'Die klugen Knaben' (volume III, story 3) tells of a tyrant who is finally overthrown by a goatherd who loves the woman whom the king covets as mistress (Alide, steadfast in the face of every threat, resembles in this respect the heroines of *Die Entführung aus dem Serail* and *Kaspar der Fagottist*). The happy outcome is due to the courage and determination of the goatherd and his beloved, but also to the wise advice of the three boys who give the story its title (the title-engraving shows each of the boys seated at the foot of a palm-tree – the leaves of the palms, we read, are golden, like those in the opening scene of Act II of *Die Zauberflöte* – with the hero approaching respectfully). The boys' parting injunction to the young man is like the advice their counterparts give to Tamino in I, 15: 'Sey standhaft, erdulde gelassen, alles was dir dabey begegnen wird, und hüte dich einen Laut von dir hören zu lassen!' ('Be steadfast, suffer patiently all that will befall you, and take care not to let a sound escape you' – an instruction reduced by Schikaneder to 'Sey standhaft, duldsam und verschwiegen!' – 'Be steadfast, resolute and discreet!'). The boys' arrival at the end of the tale as little *dei ex machina*, descending on a white, shining cloud to prevent a tragic outcome, is echoed in the opera by the descent of the Three Boys to prevent first Pamina, then Papageno, from committing suicide.

Finally, 'Lulu oder die Zauberflöte' (volume III, story 7) is the principal source of Perinet's libretto for Müller's *Kaspar der Fagottist*, to which it keeps very close; it also exerted an influence (often exaggerated) on Schikaneder's libretto for Mozart's opera. The relationship between these three works will be analysed in the last section of this chapter.

Wranitzky's *Oberon*

The influence of Paul Wranitzky's *Oberon, König der Elfen* ('Oberon, king of the elves'), first performed in the Freihaus-Theater auf der Wieden on 7 November 1789, has been much debated. In the first edition of his *Mozart's Operas* (London, 1913), E. J. Dent claimed that the Priests' march that opens Mozart's Act II was derived from Wranitzky: a claim not repeated in the second edition (London, 1947).

The modern student, more aware than Dent could have been of other theatre music of the 1780s, may well be more readily reminded of Wranitzky's debt to the Mozart of *Die Entführung* in particular than of any possible musical influence of *Oberon* on *Die Zauberflöte*. Wranitzky's score is colourful, and melodically attractive, but hardly memorable, and it surely left no mark on the score of *Die Zauberflöte*.

More to the point are studies of the influence of the text of *Oberon* on Schikaneder's libretto, though it has long been recognized that Gieseke, the named author of Wranitzky's libretto, deserves little credit for what is largely a plagiarism. The north German actress Friederike Sophie Seyler published the libretto of her 'romantic Singspiel' in five acts, *Hüon und Amande* (to give it the original title that was only replaced by the familiar one after the initial success of Wranitzky's opera) at Flensburg in 1789, just before her death. Gieseke's *Oberon, König der Elfen* is hardly more than a mild revision of Seyler's book. When Komorzynski revealed Gieseke's lack of originality he fatally weakened the principal argument for Gieseke's having had a significant hand in the text of *Die Zauberflöte*.

Certainly there are linguistic echoes of the text of *Oberon* in *Die Zauberflöte*; more important, there are dramatic situations common to the two works – the trials of two pairs of lovers before they are finally united, the use of a magic instrument (Hüon's horn, Tamino's flute). But the popularity of Wieland's verse epic *Oberon* (1780) was such that one need not look to Seyler or Gieseke for touches that have their origin in the epic itself. Mozart owned a copy of the Wieland poem, and Schikaneder was so conscious of his indebtedness to Wieland (though not specifically for *Oberon*) that he remembered him in his will of 17 December 1803. Schikaneder was possibly acknowledging Wieland as the progenitor of the Wranitzky opera which Schikaneder had presumably commissioned and which certainly gave him a box-office success. However, it is for his edition of oriental tales that Schikaneder expressed his gratitude to the German poet, the source of *Der Stein der Weisen*, Schikaneder's first magic opera, and in part of *Die Zauberflöte*: 'I bequeath to the famous poet Herr Wieland in Weimar, as author of *Tschinnistan*, 300 Gulden' – which sum, in the event of Wieland's predeceasing him, was to be paid to 'Herr Schiller, our German Schaekspair, who wrote *Kabale und Liebe*, for which bequest however Herr Schiller is requested to write a theatrical work and send it to every theatre in Germany', the proceeds to be made over by Schiller to encourage young dramatists. Schikaneder died, poor and insane, a few months before Wieland.

The most famous production of *Oberon* was at Frankfurt on 15 October 1790 for the coronation of Leopold II as Holy Roman Emperor, but it was given widely and often in Germany, and F. L. Schröder (vol. II, p. 115) comments, after the long-awaited first performance of *Die Zauberflöte* in Hamburg on 19 November 1793, that Mozart's opera was only slowly establishing itself as superior to *Oberon*, and even to Hensler's and Müller's *Das Sonnenfest der Brahminen*, at his theatre.

Komorzynski's claims that atmosphere, situations and precise textual phrases in *Oberon* and *Das Sonnenfest* recur in *Die Zauberflöte* are exaggerated. Hensler's work performed in the Theater in der Leopoldstadt on 9 September 1790, given ninety-one times in fifteen years, and also published by at least three German houses, certainly conveys a humanitarian message like that of *Die Zauberflöte* (Hensler was a Freemason, and it fell to him to deliver the Masonic Oration in memory of Mozart). In respect of atmosphere and story-line *Das Sonnenfest*, set on an Indian island, recalls rather *Les Pêcheurs de perles* than *Die Zauberflöte*. In any case, the phrases in the Gieseke and Hensler texts that may remind the reader of Schikaneder's libretto are typical of the limited vocabulary and restricted choice of rhymes available to the contemporary librettist; it is not surprising that such formulations were 'in the air'.

Kaspar der Fagottist

A persistent claim advanced by commentators inimical to Schikaneder is that far-reaching changes he is held to have made to the libretto of *Die Zauberflöte* at an advanced stage of composition were due to the success of a play with music on the same subject, staged by his rival director Marinelli in the Theater in der Leopoldstadt just under four months before the première of Mozart's opera. *Der Fagottist, oder Die Zauberzither* ('The bassoonist, or The magic zither'), a Singspiel in three acts by Joachim Perinet, with music by Wenzel Müller, was first given by Marinelli on 8 June 1791, and it enjoyed great popularity – 129 performances in that theatre, and numerous productions elsewhere, as well as a sequel.

The relationship between fairy-story and Singspiel will be clear from the following tabulation:

J.A. Liebeskind: 'Lulu oder die Zauberflöte'

Prince Lulu is led by a white gazelle to the castle of the fairy Perifirime. Because of his modesty, courage, wisdom and innocence he is entrusted with the task of recovering the fairy's magic tinder-box from the evil magician who stole it. [The tone, and elements of the vocabulary, of Perifirime's words are echoed in the Queen of Night's opening recitative to Tamino.] His reward for success will be 'the best of my possessions'. Perifirime gives Lulu a magic flute ('It has the power to win the love of all who hear it, and to incite or still all passions that its player wishes'; cf. the words of the Three Ladies in no. 5 of the opera). She also gives him a ring which, if turned on his finger, will make him appear young or old, and which, if thrown from him, will summon help. She takes him in her cloud-chariot most of the way to the castle of the magician, Dilsenghuin, and warns Lulu of Dilsenghuin's suspicious nature – he holds a girl against her will and is trying to win her love.

Lulu gains admittance, disguised as a minstrel, through his offer to use his flute to win the girl's love for Dilsenghuin. Lulu reveals himself to the girl, Sidi, frustrates the magician's plan to marry her, seizes the tinder-box and throws the ring from him. The fairy appears, punishes Dilsenghuin and his accomplices, and takes Lulu, Sidi and her companions back to her castle, where the two kings – the fathers of the young lovers – are waiting to celebrate their marriage.

J. Perinet: *Kaspar der Fagottist*

Act I. Prince Armidoro and his servant Kaspar have become separated from their companions during the pursuit of a deer with a golden collar. When the prince hits it with a javelin, Perifirime, 'the gleaming fairy', appears and enjoins the pure young prince to recover her magic tinder-box from the magician, Bosphoro, who also holds a young woman against her will. Armidoro accepts the task and is given talismans – a magic zither, a ring that will change his appearance when twisted on his finger, and the advice to cry 'Pizichi' if danger threatens. Perifirime provides a hot-air balloon (a topical allusion to Blanchard's attempts to make balloon-flights in Vienna) to transport them to Bosphoro's palace.

They arrive, and Bosphoro's fat harem-keeper, Zumio, is so impressed by the prince's singing and zither-playing that he admits him, convinced that his music will win Sidi's heart for Bosphoro. Meanwhile, Pizichi – a little genie – appears and gives Kaspar a magic bassoon, with which he softens Zumio.

Act II. Armidoro charms Sidi with his singing, and with loving glances; and Kaspar woos Sidi's companion, Palmire. Kaspar's basson-playing soon has everyone

dancing, though complications
arise when Sidi, having fallen in
love with Armidoro, loses the
power to oppose Bosphoro's will.
The latter, suspicious of the
visitors, determines to have them
drowned in a boating 'accident'.
Perifirime comes to their rescue,
and it is Zumio who gets a
soaking.

Act III. Bosphoro and Zumio now
plot to poison Armidoro and
Kaspar, and steal their magic
instruments. With the help of
Pizichi, and of additional talismans, both dangers are averted;
the *Tafelmusik* provided at dinner
by the prince and his servant puts
everyone else to sleep. Armidoro
then takes the tinder-box from
around Bosphoro's neck, throws
down the magic ring – and
Perifirime appears and punishes
the villains. The scene changes to
the fairy's palace, where the
prince's hunting companions greet
their lost master. The work ends
with preparations for a double
wedding, and with praise for
Pizichi.

As can readily be seen, Perinet's principal contributions were to
build up the comic element (Dilsenghuin alone is portrayed as being
semi-comic) and to introduce additional material so as to extend the
story into a three-act Singspiel. The prince's companion is the
timorous, greedy, grumbling Kaspar, complete with magic bassoon
and satirical local (i.e. Viennese) allusions. The opposition is so
unconvincingly drawn that Armidoro and Kaspar, equipped as they
are with all manner of talismans, have an easy task. Such are the
contents of the work that has for generations been held to have led
Schikaneder and Mozart to alter the story-line of *Die Zauberflöte*.
So superficial and inconsistent is it that, despite its amusing comic
scenes and Wenzel Müller's tuneful, lively score, we can readily
understand Mozart's dismissive comment to his wife after he had
attended the fourth performance of *Kaspar der Fagottist* on 11 June

1791: '... then, to cheer myself up, I went to the new opera the *Fagottist* in the Kasperl Theatre, which everyone is talking about – but there's absolutely nothing to it.'

No one who is familiar with Perinet's play could accuse Mozart of belittling a feared rival of his own forthcoming opera. Of its kind, *Der Fagottist* is a good and successful example – plenty of opportunities for Johann La Roche, the star attraction of Marinelli's theatre, to delight his fans, and for the designers and machinists to show their skills with transformation scenes and other *coups de théâtre*: Kaspar's bassoon spouts red wine (I, 3); Armidoro, Kaspar and their young ladies are rescued by tritons when the storm sinks their boat in the finale to Act II.

Some parallels and differences between 'Lulu', *Kaspar der Fagottist* and *Die Zauberflöte* invite comment. Perinet follows Liebeskind in making a mystery of the identity of the girl held captive by the evil magician; both do so clumsily. Schikaneder has the Queen reveal from the start that her own daughter is the captive – a more effective touch, showing that the appeal to Tamino is personal, and primarily erotic. I suggest that the so-called break in the story-line of Schikaneder's libretto, whereby our initial impressions of good queen and evil magician are corrected, was designed to supply a dramatic interest and tension which in the source was unsatisfactorily provided by the retarded revelation of the heroine's identity. The scope for psychological character-depiction is greater in Schikaneder's book. Whereas in 'Lulu' and *Kaspar der Fagottist* our expectation that the good fairy and intrepid hero will be victorious is made the more certain by the comic gullibility of the villain and his henchmen, Sarastro and the Queen of Night are complex and credible antagonists. The replacement of the gilded tinder-box (press its spring, and spirits appear to do one's bidding) by the sevenfold circle of the sun is an example of the restraint and high purpose of Schikaneder and Mozart: in *Die Zauberflöte* the powers of this emblem are not ennumerated, and thus trivialized. The magic ring that can disguise its wearer, and summon help instantly, has no place in the ethos of the opera, which concerns human virtue put to the test and ultimately triumphant.

One related detail that seems to be unsatisfactorily handled in all three versions of the story is the hero's motive for undertaking his mission. In the tale from *Dschinnistan* it is to reclaim the tinder-box; Lulu is only told of the girl held against her will when Perifirime is taking him towards the magician's castle. And when Lulu tells Sidi that he has been sent to free her, it is not true. Further, her identity as the queen's daughter is not disclosed until near the end. Perinet has Perifirime reveal that both a maiden and a tinder-box are at stake, but as clumsily handled retarding elements: mutual recognition comes only at the close. Schikaneder holds back until II, 8 the revelation that the Queen is keener to get back the circle of the sun than her daughter. Tamino's mission is chivalric rather than materialistic. Yet, instead of thinking solely of the girl he has come to rescue, he is deeply impressed by the beauty of the temples to which he has been led and muses (at first subconsciously) on the ambiguity that a place where wisdom, industry and the arts dwell should be inhabited by a kidnapper. That this ambiguity is only apparent is demonstrated by the fact that Tamino's newly awakened desire for the attainment of love and virtue has Pamina as its object, the personification of both qualities.

It remains to discuss half a dozen small similarities between *Kaspar der Fagottist* and *Die Zauberflöte*. Armidoro's aria 'Der Lenz belebet die Natur' ('Spring reawakens nature'), in which he accompanies himself on his magic instrument, is also accompanied by the chirruping and rhythmic swaying of birds; in Tamino's flute aria 'Wie stark ist nicht dein Zauberton' ('How powerful is thy magic sound') in the Act I finale 'The birds whistle in accompaniment'. Zumio's threat to Sidi and Palmire, 'Wart – ich will euch Mores lehren', is close to Monostatos' cry to the fleeing Pamina and Papageno, 'Wart, man wird euch Mores weisen' ('Wait – I will/someone will teach you manners'). Kaspar, like Papageno, misses a summons by claiming that he must be allowed to finish his meal first. In III, 14 Kaspar and Palmire are threatened by Zumio and the slaves; Kaspar plays his bassoon and enchants Zumio and the slaves so that he and Palmire can slip away, as in *Die Zauberflöte* (I, 17) when Papageno's glockenspiel captivates Monostatos and the slaves. Both works also contain illuminated writing, and food and drink that appear by magic.

It is tempting to argue in favour of direct influence of Perinet on Schikaneder; however, touches like these are commonplace in the Viennese popular theatre. One could as easily argue that Schikaneder and Mozart were parodying Perinet's clumsily delayed dénouement in details like the clarity and immediacy with which (I, 3–6) Pamina is identified as the Queen's daughter, or the dignity of bearing and avoidance of triviality of Tamino in contrast to Armidoro. One could also argue that in outline and in tone the plot of *Kaspar der Fagottist* more closely resembles *Die Entführung aus dem Serail* than *Die Zauberflöte*. Given the uncertainty about when *Der Fagottist* was written (its inconsequentialities suggest it was tossed off rapidly), and about the stage Schikaneder and Mozart had reached by the second week of June 1791, the wisest course is to assume that Perinet's work did not materially influence that of Schikaneder and Mozart.

2 The intellectual background: Freemasonry

Vienna in the reigns of Joseph II and Leopold II

Ten years separate the libretti of Mozart's two full-length German operas. Not the least interesting point of contact between them is their attitude towards punishment. In *Die Entführung aus dem Serail* the bloodthirsty Osmin threatens Belmonte and Pedrillo with all manner of tortures, and Konstanze's second aria shows her preparedness to endure the torments she can expect if she continues to oppose the Bassa's desires. If in the end the tribulations of the lovers are replaced by jubilation when the Eastern despot proves to be more generous than Belmonte's father had been, the happy outcome owes more to the spirit of the Enlightenment, and to operatic *bienséance*, than to psychological realism. Certainly it would be misguided to look for a comment on contemporary reality in such a context.

Largely owing to the vigorous campaign of Joseph von Sonnenfels, which in its crucial final stage was supported by Joseph II himself, torture had been abolished in 1776, and after 1781 the death penalty was maintained only for high treason. All the same, cruel and public punishments were frequently meted out under Joseph II. The morality of *Die Entführung* reflects a pre-Josephist outlook. *Die Zauberflöte* is a late flowering of the spirit of the Enlightenment; Sarastro promulgates the message that humane values must prevail, that love should triumph over vengeance. In the finale to Act I, Monostatos is sentenced to seventy-seven strokes with the bastinado for threatening Pamina's virginity. That this punishment was commuted is made clear by Monostatos' monologue in II, 7 (though the point is generally misunderstood, even when the lines in question are not cut), and the ineffectiveness of the threat is demonstrated by his further attempt on Pamina in II, 7 and 10, this time augmented by blackmail; Sarastro's reaction is to dismiss (banish?) him: 'Geh!'[1] The toleration of Monostatos in Sarastro's temple, and the physical punishment to which he is sentenced, point to an inconsistency that is more likely to strike a modern spectator or reader than it would have done Mozart's contemporaries.

The paradoxes of life in Vienna during the reigns of Joseph II and Leopold II were unusually strong. On the one hand, Joseph's desire for change encouraged hopes of freedom of all kinds; on the other, the forces of reaction had begun to halt, indeed to reverse his enlightened policies by the middle of his sole reign. Well before the death of Maria Theresia in 1780 Joseph as her oldest son and co-regent had begun to introduce large-scale reforms in religious affairs and court ceremony, and to the military, judicial and educational systems, the economy and the constitution. But opposition from the landed aristocracy and the Church, the provincialism typical of most areas of the empire, crises in Hungary and Belgium, as well as the external threats posed by Prussia and Turkey, dissipated his energies so that he managed to see few of his plans through to their successful real-ization. The contradictory nature of the decade of Joseph's sole rule is nowhere more clearly seen than in the field of censorship. In 1781 strict control over publications was relaxed. In that year, Gottfried van Swieten – well known for his connections with Haydn and Mozart – was appointed President of the Commission for Education and Censorship in addition to his post as Keeper of the Imperial Library. His influence with the emperor was strong enough to with-stand the opposition of Cardinal-Archbishop Migazzi to the flood of anti-clerical pamphlets and regularly published critiques of the sermons preached in Vienna's churches; and the emperor often showed himself remarkably tolerant of criticisms directed at himself and his policies.

The rise to prominence of the businessman and publisher Wucherer in 1785 may be seen as marking the turning-point in the history of the freedom of the press and of the publishing and bookselling trade in the Josephist era. Wucherer was enterprising enough to specialize in subversive literature, whilst attempting to ingratiate himself with Joseph by presenting him with special copies of unimpeachable publications. In 1786 he was attacked by Johann Rautenstrauch, writer and Freemason, for piracy, profiteering and unpatriotic bearing. Wucherer not only exchanged blows with Rautenstrauch, he also became 'diocesan', or chief representative in Austria, of the German Union, a secret society with leanings towards Illuminism, and which aimed to secure a monopoly in the book trade. It is hardly surprising that Count Pergen, the newly created Minister for Police, and his deputy, Court Councillor Beer, ultimately persuaded Joseph to banish Wucherer – though early in Leopold's reign Wucherer exploited the anti-Josephist backlash and set up business again in Austria, until Pergen was able to bring about his second expulsion. It has not been established whether Wucherer owed his success to Masonic support, or that of the Hungarian aristocracy opposed to Joseph; but his case showed how difficult it had become for the emperor to sustain a liberal outlook. The increase in cheap newspapers and the ever-increasing flood of critical pamphlets led directly both to the promotion of the police department to full ministerial status, and to the Patent of January 1790 which formalized the strict reintroduction of censorship – so that the democratizing tendencies of Joseph's first years as sole monarch were finally countermanded. An early sign of this reaction was the emperor's Patent of December 1785 which severely curtailed the activities of the Freemasons.

Freemasonry in Vienna

Masonry had been introduced to Vienna in 1742, when the lodge 'Aux Trois Canons' was constituted under the auspices of a lodge in Breslau. Although Franz Stephan von Lothringen, from 1745 Emperor Francis I, was admitted a Freemason in 1731, there is no evidence that he took any practical part in the rise of the craft in Austria, though it was probably he who prevented the publication in Habsburg lands of the papal bull condemning Freemasonry in 1751, and he may also have provided the Masons with a meeting-place. Certainly the distrust and disapproval of Maria Theresia is well known, and it was 1770 before the first comparatively long-lived Viennese lodge was inaugurated, 'Zur Hoffnung' ('Hope'), which from 1775 was known as 'Zur gekrönten Hoffnung' ('Crowned Hope'). The number of lodges, and their size, grew rapidly. 'Zu den drei Adlern' ('The Three Eagles') was founded in 1770; it gave birth to the lodge 'Zum Palmbaum' ('The Palm-Tree') in 1776; the two were united in 1781. 1771 saw the foundation of 'Zum heiligen Joseph' ('St Joseph'), constituted under the Grand Lodge of Berlin, which was dissolved in 1785, as was the other lodge under foreign patronage, 'Zur Beständigkeit' ('Constancy'), which was formed in 1779 under the aegis of 'Zu den drei Schlüsseln' ('The Three Keys') of Regensburg, to which Schikaneder briefly belonged. The most influential of all the Viennese lodges, 'Zur wahren Eintracht' ('True Concord'), was formed in 1781. The last two of Vienna's St John lodges, 'Zu den drei

Feuern') ('The Three Fires') and 'Zur Wohltätigkeit' ('Beneficence')
were founded in 1783.

The situation was complicated by the foundation in 1784 of
the National Grand Lodge of Austria and by the existence of further
lodges that observed other rites: from 1772 until 1778 'Zu den drei
Schwertern' ('The Three Swords') was Rosicrucian (also Rosicrucian
was 'Zur Liebe und Wahrheit' – 'Love and Truth', 1790); and
from 1784 'Zu den sieben Himmeln' ('The Seven Heavens') observed
the rites of the Asiatic Brethren. It was to control the dissipation
of Masonic activity that some of the leading Masons favoured
regularization. Joseph II was not himself opposed to Masonry,
and he was kept closely in touch with affairs by Johann Baptist,
Prince Dietrichstein, Provincial Grand Master, and Leopold, Count
Kol(l)owrat-Krakowsky, Deputy Master of 'Eintracht' and Supreme
Chancellor. It became clear, however, that the price for official
recognition and protection of the Masons would be high; Kolowrat
reported to 'Eintracht' in August 1785 that the emperor would require
lodges to register with the police, to reduce their number, and to
supply full lists of members. This was merely an informal preliminary
formulation of the imperial edict promulgated on 11 December 1785,
in which Joseph recognized the Order, but also ended its brief period
of intellectual and artistic splendour.

The tone of the 'Masonic Patent' (terms like 'trickery' and
'extortion' occur) makes it clear that the emperor was disturbed both
by the spread of Masonry to the smallest towns and to aristocrats'
country seats, and by the excesses and favouritism that unsupervised
secret societies could nourish. He allowed the Masons to continue their
activities because of the good they did, but he also announced his
intention 'to take them under the protection and guardianship of the
state'. He made four specific provisions: only one lodge in the capital
of each province, which must announce to the police details of
forthcoming meetings; two, or even three, lodges to be permitted in
Vienna, but none in smaller towns, in rural areas, and in castles; the
chairman of each lodge to provide the governor of the province with
a list of members for transmission to the central administration, such
lists to be updated each quarter, and any change in the mastership
to be reported; finally, this restructuring of the lodges would exempt
them from further inquiries, and permit 'this Brotherhood, which
consists of so many honest men who are known to me, truly to shew
itself useful to its fellow-men and to learning', whereas irregularly
constituted lodges and gatherings were to be abolished. The provincial

governors added the inducement that anyone reporting an offence would be rewarded with one third of the fine imposed, would be exempt from punishment, and his identity would be kept secret. The decree, published in the official *Wiener Zeitung* on 17 December, took effect from 1 January 1786.

The Masons wasted no time in effecting the reorganization demanded, though it caused grief and considerable ill feeling. The Grand Master of the Grand Lodge, Prince Dietrichstein, seconded by Ignaz von Born, the Grand Secretary, supervised the task, though not without adding to the sense of betrayal and alarm already felt. Of the eight existing lodges, 'St Joseph' and 'Constancy' elected to close completely (though 'St Joseph' reopened in 1790). The remaining six lodges reformed as two: 'True Concord', 'The Three Eagles' and 'The Palm-Tree' reconstituted themselves under Born's leadership as the united lodge 'Zur Wahrheit' ('Truth'), which opened on 6 January 1786; the other three – 'Crowned Hope', 'Beneficence' and 'The Three Fires' – formed the united lodge 'Zur neugekrönten Hoffnung' ('New-Crowned Hope') under Tobias, Baron Gebler. Since the maximum size of a lodge was to be 180 members (a figure not strictly adhered to), a large number of Masons, perhaps more than 600, were excluded, or would have to wait for vacancies.

Comparatively few records survive of Masonic activity during the following years. Many of the leading figures – including Dietrichstein and Born – ceased to be active Masons within months of the imperial edict. The high summer of Austrian Masonry was over, but it remained an important force in cultural and intellectual life until it was driven to suspend all its activities in December 1793 under Francis II.

The limited quantity of documentary evidence, far from acting as a warning to scholars, has encouraged speculation, some of it wild, about the activities of the Viennese Masons, and Mozart in particular, during the years leading up to the composition and performance of *Die Zauberflöte*. Fortunately, additional evidence has been brought to light in recent years. Else Radant's discovery of a list of members of the lodge 'Zur [neu-]gekrönten Hoffnung' for 1790[2] fills an important gap; and Philippe Autexier has recently unearthed a number of documents about Vienna's Freemasons and suggested a revaluation of more familiar material.[3]

The lodge 'Zur wahren Eintracht' and Ignaz von Born

Two of Vienna's lodges deserve to be singled out: 'Zur gekrönten Hoffnung', distinguished by the number of leading aristocrats and persons from the world of the arts among its members, and 'Zur wahren Eintracht'. The latter was founded on 12 March 1781 by a small group of Brethren from 'Hoffnung', adherents of the Zinnendorf observance. Under its first Master, Ignaz Fischer, the new lodge grew in size, but it attained notability only in the autumn of 1781, when the famous African prince, Angelo Soliman, himself only recently entered as Master, proposed that Born should be incorporated. Born was passed to the Second Degree on 19 November and raised to the Third Degree two days later; on 9 March 1782 he was elected Master of the lodge by a large majority.

Ignaz von Born (1742–91) was one of the outstanding men of his era. His reputation as a scientist, civil servant, enlightened thinker and man of letters would have kept his name alive even if he had not been Vienna's foremost Mason, a member of the Bavarian Order of the Illuminati – and frequently mentioned in the context of *Die Zauberflöte*. As a young man he was for some months a novice in a Jesuit seminary, before studying first law and then mineralogy in Prague. In 1776 he was summoned to Vienna to take charge of the imperial natural history collection, and in 1779 he was appointed Court Councillor in the Department of the Mint and Mines. His highly anti-clerical views inform a brilliant satirical attack on monasticism (the *Monachologia*, published in Latin in 1783, then in German editions and translated into several foreign languages, including English. The German translation gave the author's name as Ignaz Lojola Kuttenpeitscher: 'Cowl whipper'.) This brought him notoriety which did him little harm before the tide turned against liberalism in the second half of the decade; but it is unlikely that the authors of *Die Zauberflöte* intended to honour him directly in the figure of Sarastro at a time when Masonry and the spirit of the Enlightenment were already under threat. Furthermore, Born's total withdrawal from the Craft in August 1786, within a few months of his accepting office as Grand Master of the newly formed lodge 'Zur Wahrheit', certainly damaged the cause. In addition, the anti-feminist line of Born's essay 'On the Mysteries of the Egyptians', though it accords with Sarastro's early pronouncements, is alien to the new spirit of sexual equality that informs the Act II finale ('a woman who is not afraid of night and death / is worthy, and will be initiated').[4]

But this is to anticipate. In 1784 we find 'de Born' as one of the subscribers to Mozart's Lenten concert-series and at about the same time, the first volume of the *Journal für Freymaurer* was published, its first item being Born's paper on the Egyptian Mysteries with which he had inaugurated the lodge's new research programme. The *Journal*, though intended only for Masons, was printed in a run of 1,000 copies. A more specifically scientific journal published by the lodge under Born's editorship was the *Physikalische Arbeiten der einträchtigen Freunde in Wien* ('Physical works of the Friends of Concord in Vienna'). Born's supreme achievement as a scientist was his perfection of a new amalgamation method for the extraction of precious metals. He was given a knighthood for this, and at the celebration on 24 April 1785 a grand concert was held at the 'Crowned Hope' lodge, at which Mozart's cantata *Die Maurerfreude* was first performed. Born was also honoured by foreign academies.

Vienna's intellectual élite was strongly represented in the 'Eintracht' – the poets Blumauer, Alxinger, Ratschky, Retzer and Leon, the dramatist Major-General Ayrenhoff, the leader of the Austrian Enlightenment, Joseph von Sonnenfels, a number of prominent surgeons, philosophers, lawyers and academics, the famous traveller Georg Forster, the publisher Artaria, Haydn, and several of Austria's most powerful aristocrats.

Mozart as Mason

On 5 December 1784 the secretary of the lodge 'Zur Wohltätigkeit' circulated to the Viennese sister lodges the name of 'Kapellmeister Mozart' as a candidate for initiation. On 14 December, at 6.30 o'clock, the attendance register for the lodge records that 'Wenzel Summer, Chaplain at Erdberg, and Mozart, Kapellmeister' were duly initiated. The Master of 'Wohltätigkeit', Otto, Baron von Gemmingen-Hornberg, was an old acquaintance of Mozart's from Mannheim in 1779, and the author of the drama *Semiramis* which Mozart planned to set to music as a melodrama. The lodge was a small one, and it used the same premises as 'Zur wahren Eintracht' at the house 'Zum roten Krebsen' ('The Red Crayfish') on the Kienmarkt. It was as a 'Visiting Brother' that Mozart next appears in the Masonic records, attending a meeting of 'Eintracht' on Christmas Eve. At the same lodge, on 7 January 1785, at the request of 'Wohltätigkeit', 'Brother Wolfgang Mozard' was passed to the Fellow Craft Degree. We do not know when he became a Master – records of attendance for most of the lodges survive only fitfully – but he must have been raised before attending the Master Lodge at 'Eintracht' on 22 April (on which occasion the signature of his father, then only a journeyman, was crossed out as ineligible).

Haydn should have been initiated at 'Eintracht' on 28 January, and Mozart was present for the ceremony. However, Haydn did not receive the notification in time, and when he was admitted, on 11 February, Mozart was unable to attend – not only had his father arrived that day, it was also the first of his six Friday concerts at the 'Mehlgrube' casino.

Though there are good grounds for agreeing with Einstein's judgment that Mozart's adagios for winds including basset-horns, K 410 and 411 (484d and a), which probably date from 1782–3, are Masonic in mood, and perhaps also in purpose, the earliest undisputed work for the Craft is the song 'Gesellenreise' ('Fellow Craft's Journey'), K 468, written on 26 March 1785 in readiness – it is assumed – for his father's forthcoming passing to the Second Degree. On 20 April he completed *Die Maurerfreude* (K 471) in honour of the special celebration of Born's ennoblement, to be held at the 'Gekrönten Hoffnung' on 24 April. Apart from Mozart's cantata, sung by Valentin Adamberger (who had created the rôle of Belmonte in *Die Entführung* three years earlier), music by Paul Wranitzky was also performed on this occasion. The cantata was published in full score in August, for the benefit of the poor, in a handsome edition for which all responsible were Masons, and whose illustrated title-page positively proclaims its Masonic nature. Mozart's next, and most widely known, Masonic composition, the 'Masonic Funeral Music' (*Maurerische Trauermusik*) was written in July. It was given on 17 November 1785 at the Lodge of Sorrows for two prominent Masons, and parts for double bassoon and two further basset-horns were added for a later performance.

Four days before Mozart took part in an especially grand Masonic concert at the 'Crowned Hope' on 15 December, the imperial edict was published which led to the reorganization of the Craft. From this time forward, little evidence survives of lodge meetings and Masonic activities. Certainly Mozart does not seem to have written music for any Masonic occasion between the three-part choruses with organ, 'Zerfliesset heut, geliebte Brüder' ('Dissolve this day, beloved brothers') and 'Ihr unsre neuen Leiter' ('O ye, our new leaders'), K 483 and 484, which he wrote for the opening and closing ceremonies of the first meeting of the newly formed lodge 'Zur neugekrönten

Hoffnung' on 14 January 1786, and summer 1791 (with the possible exception of two further and lost choruses, which may, however, have been written in 1785).

Mozart maintained contact with his Masonic friends and colleagues during the intervening years, but it is only over the last months of his life that he again composed Masonic works. The 'Little German Cantata' *Die ihr des unermesslichen Weltalls Schöpfer ehrt* ('Ye who honour the creator of the boundless universe'; K 619) of July 1791 is not strictly a Masonic work, though the man who commissioned it and wrote the words, Franz Ziegenhagen, was a Brother in Regensburg. One could argue that *Die Zauberflöte*, too, is not a Masonic work since it was written for performance in a public theatre. There is, however, no doubt about the last work Mozart was to complete, and to direct, *Eine kleine Freymaurer-Kantate* ('A little Masonic Cantata'; K 623) is what he entitles it in the *Catalogue* on 15 November 1791, and despite its name it is considerably the longest of his Masonic works. Mozart fell ill two days after he conducted the first performance of the cantata on 18 November at the ceremony of inauguration of the new temple of 'Zur neugekrönten Hoffnung'; he died seventeen days later. The cantata was published by subscription 'in order to assist his distressed widow and orphans'; it appeared in November 1792. At the end of April the dramatist Karl Friedrich Hensler delivered a Masonic Oration in memory of Mozart at a Lodge of Sorrows held by the 'New-Crowned Hope'.

Schikaneder and Freemasonry

Documentary evidence for lodge membership and attendance at meetings of 'Zur Wahrheit' and 'Zur neugekrönten Hoffnung' becomes erratic and scarce after the reorganization of Vienna's lodges at the end of 1785. This makes it difficult to state firmly that a particular individual was a Freemason at a particular time. Emanuel Schikaneder is a case in point. It is known that he petitioned to be admitted to membership of the lodge 'Zu den drei Schlüsseln' ('The Three Keys') at Regensburg on 4 July 1788, and the tone of the letter makes it plain that he was not already a member of the Craft. That his application was successful is clear from an excerpt from the lodge's minutes for 4 May 1789, requesting him to absent himself from meetings at the forthcoming Festival of St John and for the following six months, owing to unpleasant rumours about his private life as well as his self-aggrandizement.[5]

Although Schikaneder wrote a letter of apology, in which he looked forward to being welcomed back at meetings in due course, he moved to Vienna within a matter of weeks, to take over the direction of the Freihaus-Theater auf der Wieden (he was performing there by mid-July), so his appeal to the Regensburg lodge will have been at best inconclusive. There is no evidence that he was ever a member of one of the Viennese lodges; certainly his name does not appear (as Mozart's does) among those of the 212 members of 'Zur gekrönten Hofnung' (*sic*; the 'neu' had by then been dropped from the title) in 1790.[6]

The claim that he was the author of the text of Mozart's *Eine kleine Freimaurer-Kantate* (K 623) cannot be sustained if he was not a member of 'Gekrönte Hoffnung', since the first edition, published early in 1792, indicates that 'its words are the work of a member of the same'. A variant of the text was published in another edition in 1792 in honour of Emperor Franz II, with text by 'G...e'. This may well have been Gieseke (he appears as 'Giesege Karl Ludwig actor First Grade', i.e. Entered Apprentice, in the 1790 list of members of the lodge). This is not to claim that Gieseke necessarily wrote the original words of the cantata; Franz Petran, the poet of *Die Maurerfreude* and in 1790 still a member of the lodge, is another obvious candidate. Given the persistent claim that Gieseke was the author of the libretto of *Die Zauberflöte* it would be a posthumous compensation if his name could convincingly be linked with that of Mozart as author of the *Kleine Freimaurer-Kantate*.

As for the authorship of the libretto of *Die Zauberflöte*, the fact that Schikaneder probably did not belong to a Viennese lodge is of little importance. His experiences at lodge meetings in Regensburg during the months of his membership would have provided him with a knowledge of the workings of the Craft sufficient to enable him with Mozart's help and advice to fashion the libretto of the opera. Certainly a copy of the solitary 'private' Masonic source of the opera, Born's essay in the first volume of the *Journal für Freymaurer*, would not have been hard to come by in the Vienna of 1790–1, and even if Mozart did not have one of his own, copies would have been available in the lodge library.

3 *Synopsis*

Characters

Sarastro	Bass
Tamino	Tenor
Spokesman ('der Sprecher')	Bass
First Priest ('Old Priest')	Bass
Second Priest	Tenor
Third Priest	Speaking rôle
The Queen of Night	Soprano
Pamina, her Daughter	Soprano
First Lady	Soprano
Second Lady	Soprano
Third Lady	Soprano
First Boy	Soprano
Second Boy	Soprano
Third Boy	Soprano
An Old Woman (Papagena)	Soprano
Papageno	Bass
Monostatos, a Moor	Tenor
First Man in Armour	Tenor
Second Man in Armour	Bass
First Slave	Speaking rôle
Second Slave	Speaking rôle
Third Slave	Speaking rôle
Priests, Slaves, Attendants	

Orchestra

2 flutes (piccolo), 2 oboes, 2 clarinets (basset-horns), 2 bassoons; 2 horns, 2 trumpets, 3 trombones; timpani; *istromento d'acciajo* (glockenspiel); strings

Act I

	Key	pan-pipe	piccolo	flute	oboe	clarinet	basset-horn	bassoon	horn	trumpet	trombone	timpani	'istromento d'acciajo'	violins I and II	viola	violoncello	double bass
Overture	E♭			2	2	2		2	2	2	3	2		✓	✓	✓	✓
1 Introduction	C minor → major			2	2	2		2	2	2	3	2		✓	✓	✓	✓
2 Aria (Papageno)	G	✓		2	2			2	2					✓	✓	✓	✓
3 Aria (Tamino)	E♭					2		2	2					✓	✓	✓	✓
4 Recitativo ed aria (Queen)	B♭				2			2	2					✓	✓	✓	✓
5 Quintetto	B♭				2	2		2	2					✓	✓	✓	✓
6 Terzetto	G			1	2			2	2					✓	✓	✓	✓
7 Duetto (Pamina, Papageno)	E♭					2		2	2					✓	div	✓	✓
8 Finale	C	✓		2	2	2 →	2	2	2	2	3	2	✓	✓	div	✓	✓

Act II

	Key	pan-pipe	piccolo	flute	oboe	clarinet	basset-horn	bassoon	horn	trumpet	trombone	timpani	'istromento d'acciajo'	violins I and II	viola	violoncello	double bass
9 Marcia	F			1			2	2	2		3			✓	✓	✓	✓
10 Aria con coro (Sarastro)	F						2	2			3				div	✓	
11 Duetto	C			2	2	2		2	2	2	3	2		✓	div	✓	✓
12 Quintetto	G			2	2			2	2	2	3	2		✓	div	✓	✓

		pan-pipe	piccolo	flute	oboe	clarinet	basset-horn	bassoon	horn	trumpet	trombone	timpani	'istromento d'acciajo'	violins I and II	viola	violoncello	double bass
13 Aria (Monostatos)	C		1	1		2		2						✓	✓	✓	✓
14 Aria (Queen)	D minor			2	2			2	2	2		2		✓	✓	✓	✓
15 Aria (Sarastro)	E			2				2	2					✓	✓	✓	✓
16 Terzetto	A			2				2						✓	✓	✓	✓
17 Aria (Pamina)	G minor			1	1			1	2					✓	✓	✓	✓
18 Coro (Priests)	D			2	2			2	2	2	3			✓	div	✓	✓
19 Terzetto (Pamina, Tamino, Sarastro)	B♭				2			2						✓	✓	✓	✓
20 Aria (Papageno)	F			1	2			2	2				✓	✓	✓	✓	✓
21 Finale	E♭	✓		2	2	2		2	2	2	3	2	✓	✓	div	✓	✓
9^A Threefold chord	B♭			2	2		2	2	2	2	3						
11^A Duetto (Tamino, Papageno)	B♭			2	2	2		2	2					✓	✓	✓	✓

Figure 1.   Table of instrumentation

Act I

OVERTURE (Adagio – Allegro – Adagio – Allegro, E flat.) Solemn tutti chords – which according to the individual student's interpretation may be taken as being three or five in number – give way to a calm, mysterious twelve-bar-long passage before the tempo changes and a fugato is introduced as the main Allegro theme. The flute and oboe dominate the quieter second subject, below which the fugato maintains an urgent presence. The development section is delayed by wind chords (Adagio, B flat), three times three, which in Act II will take on a specific function as marking key stages in the initiation of Tamino. Thereafter the Allegro follows its brilliant course, with high spirits running hand in hand with masterly contrapuntal ingenuity, bold dynamic contrasts and a powerful coda.

First set

The theatre is a rocky region, with trees here and there; on both sides there are practicable mountains (i.e. that can open up), near a round temple.

Scene 1 No. 1 INTRODUCTION (Allegro, C minor): 'Zu Hilfe! Zu Hilfe! sonst bin ich verloren.' Tamino, wearing a splendid Japanese[1] hunting-costume, enters right; he descends from a rock; he has a bow, but no arrows; a serpent pursues him (Mozart at first wrote in his score the text: 'dem grimmigen Löwen zum Opfer erkoren', that is 'chosen victim of the fierce lion'). Tamino cries for help from the gods as the serpent draws nearer. As he faints, the temple door opens, and three veiled Ladies emerge, armed with javelins, with which they kill the serpent, chopping it into three. Their brief song of triumph gives way to gentler music as they admire the handsome stranger and voice the hope that he may be able to restore their Queen's former calm. Each of the Ladies is keen to stand guard over the youth while the others report to the Queen. After a short Allegretto section in G major, $\frac{6}{8}$ time, in which each considers unselfishly withdrawing, leaving the others on guard, they decide in a closing Allegro in C major that, however much each would love to have the youth for herself, they will all leave together – once they have bidden him a tender farewell in three-part harmony.

Dialogue: Tamino regains consciousness, muses about his deliverance and his whereabouts, but is interrupted by the sound of a distant panpipe, and then (according to a stage-direction in the libretto that

Mozart did not obey) speaks during the ritornello of the approaching Papageno's entrance-song. Tamino comments that he can see a man coming this way, and then conceals himself behind a tree.

Scene 2 No. 2 ARIA (Andante, G major): 'Der Vogelfänger bin ich ja.' Papageno enters; he has on his back a large bird-cage protruding far above his head, and in both hands he has a panpipe which he plays before and during his song. That he wears a costume of feathers is made clear in the ensuing dialogue and by the illustration included at this point in the first edition of the libretto. His strophic song cheerfully depicts the joys of being a skilful bird-catcher, as well as his wish that he could catch girls, too, and become better acquainted with the one he liked the best, and make her his wife. (The third strophe, containing Papageno's most intimate wish, is not included in either the original libretto or the autograph score, but it does occur in early vocal scores (e.g. that of Simrock, Bonn, 1793); it could be that the words initially entered by Mozart at the start of the second strophe, following the refrain, and then heavily over-written, were 'Wenn alle Mädchen ...', the first words of the third stanza; they would not have fitted the music, lacking as they do the four-line refrain that opens the first two stanzas.)

Dialogue: Papageno and Tamino get into conversation, each puzzled by the presence and identity of the other. Papageno's rôle of clown is soon clear, and he instructs the Prince about his life as well as the little he knows about his origins (he was brought up by a funny old man; he never knew his mother, who was said to have been a servant of the 'Star-flaming Queen'). When Papageno learns that Tamino is heir to an empire, he sees the chance for indulging in some business speculation with his birds – for he is bird-catcher to the Queen and her Ladies, who each day give him food and drink in exchange for his catch. Tamino gradually realizes that this must be the Queen about whom his father has often told him, though he has no idea how he has got to her realm. His thoughts are constantly interrupted by Papageno's chatter and boastfulness which, when it has led him to claim that he killed the monstrous serpent with his bare hands, provokes a further interruption:

Scene 3 The Three Ladies return, punish Papageno for his claim that it was he who killed the serpent when they had done so – he is given water, not wine, a stone rather than fancy bread, and in place of sweet figs a golden padlock is placed before his mouth – and they hand Tamino a miniature portrait of the Queen's daughter, telling him that if he is not indifferent to her features, then fortune, honour and fame await him. While the Ladies continue to banter with Papageno, the Prince becomes totally absorbed with the portrait.

Scene 4 No. 3 ARIA (Larghetto, E flat): 'Dies Bildnis ist bezaubernd schön.' For the words of Tamino's 'Portrait' aria Schikaneder has provided a very tolerable sonnet (rhyming *aabbccddeedffd*) in iambic tetrameters, though Mozart obscures the fact in his setting, which alters the structure by its use of repetitions and its own compelling musical logic. (For a detailed analysis of this aria, see pp. 114, 121, 124–5.) For once, the cliché of falling in love with a picture carries total conviction as the young man gradually comes to recognize the new emotion that fills his heart, and names it. His ardour increases at the thought that, if he could find her, if once she were standing there before him, he would – and he pauses for a moment before self-questioning gives way to the passionate and exultantly repeated conviction that he would embrace her and make her his for ever.

Scene 5 Dialogue: He is about to exit after his aria when the Ladies return to inform Tamino that the Queen, who has overheard him soliloquizing about the beautiful girl of the portrait, intends to entrust him with the task of rescuing Pamina – for such is her name. She has been kidnapped by 'a powerful, evil demon' and is held not far away in the tyrant's stronghold. Tamino swears to rescue her; immediately – and here the libretto's instruction is not followed by the composer – a shattering chord heralds the advent of the Queen. The mountains part, and the theatre is transformed.

Second set

A splendid chamber. The Queen is seated upon a throne which is decorated with transparent stars.

Scene 6 No. 4 RECITATIVE AND ARIA (Allegro maestoso, B flat; Aria: [Andante], G minor – Allegro moderato, B flat): 'O zittre nicht, mein lieber Sohn.' After ten imposing bars of orchestral introduction the Queen bids the young man not to tremble; she flatters him, calling him innocent, wise and good, and telling him that it is in his power to bring comfort to her deeply troubled maternal heart. The slow introduction to the aria ('Zum Leiden bin ich auserkoren'), $\frac{3}{4}$, expresses the Queen's grief at the abduction of her daughter; the tone of pathos is briefly replaced by anger as she mentions the villain responsible, but as she relives the scene for Tamino's benefit it is her own powerlessness that is emphasized. In the concluding Allegro moderato section ('Du, du, du wirst sie zu befreien gehen') the Queen moves to confident exhortation of the young man, promising him in fiery coloratura (it conveys the harder, more ruthless side to her character which will later predominate) that her daughter will be his for ever if he succeeds in rescuing her. The Queen and her Ladies disappear, and the set takes on its previous appearance.

Scene 7 Dialogue: Left alone, Tamino begs the gods to succour him and strengthen him for his task. He is about to leave when Papageno bars his way.

No. 5 QUINTET (Allegro, B flat – Andante, B flat): 'Hm! Hm! Hm!' Papageno can only hum and gesture to Tamino that he wants to be released from the padlock. Tamino regrets that he is powerless to help.

Scene 8 The Ladies return (F major), free Papageno's mouth and warn him against lying in the future. All five join in singing the first of the moral aphorisms of the opera ('If all liars had their lips padlocked, love and brotherly ties would replace hatred, slander and black gall'). The First Lady thereupon gives Tamino a golden flute (cf. II, 28, where Pamina describes it, not necessarily in total contradiction, as having been carved from oak-wood) which will protect and succour him in his quest – a magic flute that can beneficently transform the emotions of its hearers. After all five have praised the flute, Papageno tries to slip away, but the Ladies tell him that he has been designated as the Prince's companion for the journey to Sarastro's citadel; Sarastro is here identified as the 'demon'. Papageno is only talked out of a cowardly refusal by the gift of what the libretto calls 'eine Maschine wie ein hölzernes Gelächter' ('a machine like wooden laughter') and the score 'ein stählnes Gelächter' (literally 'steel laughter').[2] Once he has been assured that he will be able to play it, Papageno abandons his objections to accompanying Tamino. Their departure is delayed by the realization that they do not know the way. The tempo changes to Andante for an aethereal passage in which, to the accompaniment of clarinets and bassoon with pizzicato violins, the Ladies tell the Prince and Papageno, *sotto voce*, that they will be led by three wise Boys. (The music may be thought to imply the presence of the Boys; they do not in fact appear until I, 15, when they advise Tamino, as Papageno has made clear in the previous scene. This takes care of the objection that the essentially good Boys would not, or would no longer, be at the disposal of the scheming Queen.) Farewells are repeated, and everyone leaves the stage.

Third set

Scene 9 Dialogue: The scene changes to a splendid Egyptian room, into which two slaves carry cushions and a fine Turkish table; they are busy spreading out carpets when a third slave enters, laughing at the news that Pamina has escaped from their bullying overseer, the Moor Monostatos. The Third Slave relates that Pamina saved herself from the Moor's unwelcome attentions by calling on the name of Sarastro, which halted him long enough for her to be able to hasten to the canal and escape to the palm plantation in a gondola.

Scene 10 Their rejoicing is short-lived, for Monostatos is heard shouting for fetters; Pamina, recaptured, is led in.

Scene 11 No. 6 TRIO (Allegro molto, G major): 'Du feines Täubchen, nur herein!' Monostatos is implacable in his threats; Pamina pities her mother. The slaves fetter her and are then dismissed so that Monostatos can have his way with her, she having sunk in a faint on to a sofa.

Scene 12 At that moment, Papageno enters, having first peeped inquiringly through the window. He sees Pamina first, but when he and Monostatos come face to face, each is comically scared of the other, begs for mercy and runs off. So much happens in this splendid trio that one notes with surprise and admiration that it plays for little more than a hundred seconds.

Scene 13 Dialogue: Pamina calls for her mother as she wakes from her brief nightmare, and then laments her wretched plight.

Scene 14 Papageno recovers his composure quickly and re-enters, opining that since there are black birds in the world, why not black men, too? He introduces himself as an emissary of the Star-flaming Queen, and tells Pamina about the handsome Prince who has fallen in love with her picture (which he uses to check her identity). We learn that the promised guides did not materialize, and that Papageno has been sent ahead by the Prince to announce his arrival. She warns him of the danger if Sarastro should catch him – it is nearly noon, and at that hour he normally returns from hunting. They are about to leave when Pamina suddenly has second thoughts – what if this should be a trick? But she regrets her unworthy suspicions, recognizing in Papageno one with a feeling heart. When she learns that he has no girl-friend, let alone a wife, she is confident that heaven will soon provide him with a female companion.

No. 7 DUET (Andantino, E flat): 'Bei Männern, welche Liebe fühlen.' This is a duet about the comforting power of love, rather than a love duet. Love raises man and woman towards the level of the gods (or rather, since Mozart replaced Schikaneder's 'die Götter' by 'die Gottheit', towards divinity). The wind sextet (pairs of clarinets, bassoons and horns) is used sparingly in this radiant number (the problems which it presents are discussed on pp. 128 and 208–9).

Fourth set

Scene 15 The scene changes to a grove with, at the back of the stage, a beautiful temple with the words 'Temple of Wisdom'; a line of columns leads to two other temples, the one on the right being designated 'Temple of Reason', and that on the left 'Temple of Nature'. Three Boys, each holding a silver palm-frond, lead Tamino in.

No. 8 FINALE (Larghetto, C major, passing through several keys and tempi to Presto, C major): 'Zum Ziele führt dich diese Bahn.' To music which exquisitely balances dotted rhythms and legato chords the Boys warn the Prince to be steadfast, tolerant and discreet, but they are not allowed to tell him whether he will be able to rescue Pamina. Left alone, he muses in a fascinatingly innovatory blend of accompanied recitative and brief arioso passages on the nature of his quest and task. It is at once clear to him that he is in a place where wisdom, industry and the arts dwell, and that he will not find here the cowardly villain the Queen's words had led him to expect. He strides boldly up to the Temple of Reason, determined to rescue Pamina, but a voice bids him stand back. The same thing happens at the Temple of Nature.[3] He knocks at the central door, that of the Temple of Wisdom, and is met by an old Priest (traditionally but probably wrongly identified as 'der Sprecher', the Orator, or Spokesman; see pp. 148–9), who questions him in measured tones as to his motives, noting at once the young man's vengefulness towards Sarastro, which is at odds with his protestation that love and virtue are his goal. The Priest assures the impetuous youth – who is about to leave when he is told that Sarastro does indeed hold sway in the Temple of Wisdom – that the latter could justify his action in abducting Pamina, and that in due course the confusion sown in Tamino's mind by a woman's wiles will give way to full understanding, once the hand of friendship – and here the dialogue broadens into four bars of particularly solemn arioso (Andante) – leads him into the lasting ties of their inner sanctum. Left alone to wonder when seemingly eternal night will give way to light, he is told by a four-part offstage male chorus, softly supported by three trombones and strings, that it will happen soon, or never. When he asks the voices if Pamina is still alive, he learns that she is. In joy and gratitude he takes out his flute, plays it for the first time, and in a C-major solo (Andante: 'Wie stark ist nicht dein Zauberton') praises the power of its magic tones, with which, Orpheus-like, he charms the beasts and birds that come forth to listen. He breaks off disconsolately when he realizes that Pamina is not there, though when the last five notes of his G-major flute scale are taken up off-stage by Papageno's piping the same five notes, he thinks perhaps Pamina will be with him. In a brief G-major Presto passage (Mozart originally wrote 'etwas geschwinder', that is, 'somewhat faster' (than the previous Andante)) the Prince expresses his excitement, before rushing off to find her.

Scene 16 (Andante, G major): 'Schnelle Füsse, rascher Mut.' Papageno and Pamina, the latter now free of her fetters, enter without having seen Tamino. They fear capture unless they find Tamino swiftly, and they call and pipe in vain for him.

Scene 17 Then Monostatos hurries in (Allegro), mockingly taking up their last words ('Nur geschwinde' – 'just be quick') – a clever touch by Mozart for which the libretto gives no hint. Monostatos summons slaves to bind the fugitives, but in the nick of time Papageno thinks of his glockenspiel (as he now calls it). He plays, and Monostatos and the slaves, bewitched by the simple charm of the music, march off, singing (many editions of the libretto and the score contain the inauthentic stage-direction 'exeunt dancing'). The moment they have the stage to themselves – immediately before the whole bar pause – Papageno and Pamina burst out laughing (Mozart wrote the word 'lacht' in the glockenspiel staves that they are about to take over for their duet). They then sing ten lines (of the fourteen that Schikaneder included in the libretto) of improving doggerel about the benefits of magic bells and the joys of harmony and friendship (Schubert's 'Heidenröslein' hardly seems to lie twenty-four years ahead). As they complete their moral ditty, trumpets and drums ring out (Allegro maestoso, C major), and a tiny off-stage choral greeting heralds the entry of Sarastro. The fugitives just have time to regret their plight (Papageno wishes he were a mouse or a snail, able to hide himself away), and Pamina radiantly to assert the necessity of telling the truth.[4]

Scene 18 Upon this a procession arrives, preceding Sarastro, who drives in on a triumphal chariot drawn by six lions. He is praised as a wise and good leader (Larghetto, F major). Pamina kneels to tell him that, though she had tried to flee, it was Monostatos' demand for love that drove her to do so. Sarastro bids her stand, tells her that he knows that she is in love with someone else, will not force his own love upon her – but will not give her liberty. When she starts to plead filial duty he warns her of her mother's baleful influence and says that women require a man's guiding hand. This scene rivals the earlier one between the Old Priest and Tamino in its inspired freedom of expressive musical language, which covers every gradation between recitative and the most lyrical arioso, and surpasses it in range and subtlety of orchestral coloration – the basset-horns make their first, hesitant, appearance in the score at the opening of the Larghetto, soon to combine with oboes in yearning accompaniment to Sarastro's words about knowing the state of Pamina's heart (with poignant chromatic flute taking over). **Scene 19** (Allegro, F major): Monostatos drags in Tamino, but the latter and Pamina have eyes only for each other, and fall into each other's arms. Their breathless ' 'Tis he!' – ' 'Tis she!', delightedly taken up by later parodists, is in fact a wonderfully direct and economical passage (just one bar of singing in thirds before their voices join for one note!). But Monostatos separates them angrily and looks to Sarastro for reward for his vigilance; the 'reward' Sarastro apportions is a rather startling seventy-seven lashes on the feet (and he is immediately led away to receive them – though his soliloquy in II, 7 suggests unequivocally that the sentence was commuted). Nevertheless the chorus praise Sarastro for his divine wisdom and discernment. He bids the priests cover the heads of the two strangers and lead them into the temple of examination. A brief and stirring chorus (Presto, C major) praises the qualities of virtue and righteousness, which make a heaven of earth, and mortals like gods.

Act II

Fifth set

Scene 1 A palm grove; the trees are all like silver, the leaves of gold. Eighteen leafy seats, and on each a pyramid and a large, black horn, chased in gold. The largest pyramid and the largest trees are in the middle. Sarastro and other Priests enter in stately procession, each with a palm-frond in his hand. A march with wind instruments accompanies the procession.

No. 9 PRIESTS' MARCH (F major): this solemn march, both parts of which are marked to be repeated, lacks a tempo indication (Mozart headed it merely 'Marcia'). It is scored for flute, pairs of basset-horns, bassoons and horns, three trombones and (despite the indication in the libretto that it was for wind instruments alone) strings. Like much of the priestly music it features both legato ties and dotted rhythmic figuration.

Dialogue: Sarastro informs the assembled priests of Osiris and Isis that this is one of the most important assemblies of their time. Tamino, a king's son, and twenty years of age, seeks admission to the brotherhood (he actually expresses it more obliquely – 'he paces up and down at the north gate of our temple and sighs with virtuous heart for an object which we must all struggle arduously and industriously to attain'). Sarastro tells them, in answer to their questions, that Tamino is virtuous, discreet, beneficent; and for the first time since the overture the thrice-repeated wind chords (now with basset-horns in place of the clarinets of the overture) mark the Priests' agreement that Tamino is a worthy candidate; following his example they raise their horns to their lips. Sarastro further indicates that Tamino's initiation will help destroy the prejudice against 'our difficult art', and that Pamina is intended by the gods for Tamino. This, he tells the assembly, is the reason why he tore her away from her haughty mother. Tamino will help secure their firm foundation against the deception and superstition with which the Queen seeks to ensnare the people. Second sounding of the threefold chord. The Spokesman is concerned that Tamino's royal blood may equip him ill for the trials that await him; but Sarastro has confidence in his humanity. If he were to perish during his trials, he would experience the joys of the gods earlier than they would. For the third time the horn-blasts signify assent. The Spokesman and another priest are appointed to supervise the instruction of Tamino and Papageno; they leave at once, and the remainder of the priests gather round Sarastro, holding their palm-fronds.

No. 10 ARIA WITH CHORUS (Adagio, F major): 'O Isis und Osiris, schenket.' Sarastro apostrophizes the sister and brother deities and invokes their protection over 'the new pair' (by which, as the context makes clear, he means Tamino and Papageno, not Tamino and Pamina) during their trials. Schikaneder intended this number to be a plain 'chorus', as the libretto informs us; instead, it is a hymn-like bass aria, with four-part men's voices echoing in varied form the last line of both verses. The instrumentation is as unexpected as it is atmospheric: pairs of basset-horns and bassoons, three trombones, divided violas and cellos.

Sixth set

Scene 2 (Night; distant thunder.) A shallow courtyard in the temple, with remnants of broken columns and pyramids, and some thorn-bushes. On both sides practicable doors, tall and in ancient Egyptian style, which imply side-buildings. Tamino and Papageno are led in by the Spokesman and the other Priest; the sacks covering their heads are removed, and the Priests depart.

Dialogue: As the thunder grows louder, so Papageno becomes more frightened, despite Tamino's admonishment that he should be a man ('I wish I were a girl!' retorts Papageno).

Scene 3 The two Priests return, with torches. Tamino fearlessly answers the Spokesman's questions: he seeks friendship and love, and is prepared to risk his life to gain them; in token of his agreement to undergo every trial, he shakes the Spokesman's hand. The Second Priest finds in Papageno a child of nature, requiring only sleep, food and drink, and — if possible — a pretty wife. But he is not prepared to risk his life by undergoing the trials, and declares he will stay single. When told he may see the girl Sarastro has in store for him, like him in colour and dress, young and beautiful, and called Papagena, but that he may not speak to her until the appointed hour, he offers the Priest his hand in token of his agreement. The first test is of silence; they will see their women, but must not speak to them.

No. 11 DUET (Andante (an earlier marking, Allegretto, was replaced), C major): 'Bewahret euch vor Weibertücken.' The Priests warn Tamino and Papageno against feminine wiles: the first duty of the brotherhood. Many a wise man has succumbed to that temptation. The last line of the duet ('Tod und Verzweiflung war sein Lohn' — 'Death and despair was his reward'), set to a memorable and surprisingly jaunty melody accompanied by bassoons, trombones and strings, and then echoed *piano* by full orchestra, was quoted by Mozart in the letter to his wife which can be dated to 11 June 1791. For a suggested interpretation of this number, see pp. 17–18, 129.

(No. 11ᴬ DUET (Andante — Allegro, B flat): 'Pamina, wo bist du?' For a discussion of the origins of this seldom-heard and perhaps inauthentic number, see pp. 207–9. Tamino and Papageno search in vain for Pamina and Papagena, separation from whom is the greatest hardship. Much of the Allegro section is a solo for the Prince, who sings that to see Pamina, and to ask if she loves him, will prepare him for entering on the path towards a new life; the number ends with the two men making repeated calls for silence.)

Scene 4 Dialogue: Left alone by the Priests, Papageno has hardly time to call for lights, and Tamino to interpose that they must patiently accept what the gods will.

Scene 5 No. 12 QUINTET (Allegro, G major): 'Wie? wie? wie? Ihr an diesem Schreckensort?' Suddenly the Three Ladies appear from a trapdoor to warn Tamino and Papageno that they are doomed, and that the Queen is close at hand, having penetrated the temple. Tamino is steadfast, but Papageno keeps chattering to the Ladies, without ever quite addressing them directly. All five conclude that a man is of firm resolve and thinks before he speaks. The Ladies are about to leave, their mission unaccomplished, when from off-stage the chorus of Priests briefly interpose that the holy precinct has been desecrated, and send the Ladies to hell. They sink with a threefold shriek, echoed by Papageno. Immediately the threefold chord (its fourth appearance) heralds the renewed approach of the two Priests.

Scene 6 Dialogue: The Spokesman praises Tamino's steadfastness, but warns that further dangerous tests lie before him; he re-covers his head and leads him away. The Second Priest elicits the response from Papageno that he is lying in a faint, and leaves it to his powers of reason to work out why he must be exposed to so many frights and tribulations if the gods really do have a Papagena for him. He, too, is led off, blindfolded and complaining.

   Seventh set

Scene 7 The scene changes to a pleasant garden, with a horseshoe pattern of trees. In the middle is a bower of flowers and roses, in which Pamina lies asleep. The moon shines on her face. In the foreground is a grassy bank.

Monologue: Monostatos enters, sits down, and comments wrily that Pamina is the tender but insignificant plant because of his interest in which he was to have been bastinadoed. He says he owes it merely to the fact that this is a special day (see II, 1) that he can still walk with his skin intact. Desire rises within him again, and he will risk stealing a kiss.

No. 13 ARIA (Allegro (replacing an earlier marking of Allegretto), C major): 'Alles fühlt der Liebe Freuden.' The instruction 'The whole number to be sung and played *piano*, as if the music were coming from a great distance' occurs, contrary to widespread belief, in the earliest editions of the libretto; Mozart marks the number 'sempre pianissimo' (though he includes two *mfp* chords in each of the two stanzas). The use of a piccolo (usually in unison with the first violins) gives a 'Turkish' flavour; the scoring otherwise includes flute, pairs of clarinets and bassoons, and strings. Monostatos asks why, because he is black, he is supposed to avoid falling in love. In the second strophe he asks the moon to forgive him for falling for a white girl, and to close its eyes if it objects to the sight of his kissing her. He steps stealthily towards the sleeping Pamina.

Scene 8 Dialogue: The Queen, accompanied by thunder, appears from the middle trapdoor right in front of Pamina. Monostatos lurks to watch and listen as Pamina throws herself into her mother's arms, and the Queen sternly inquires what has happened to Tamino. When she learns that he has dedicated himself to the initiates, she tells her daughter that she is lost to her for ever. Pamina would flee to her mother's protection, but she has lost all her power since her husband died: he bequeathed the all-powerful sevenfold circle of the sun to the initiates, to whose guidance he commended his wife and daughter. Sarastro now wears the emblem on his breast. Pamina's only hope of being united with Tamino is to persuade him to flee by way of the vaults before daybreak; she cuts no ice with her mother by pointing out that her father was close to the wise men of the temple, and that Sarastro is no less virtuous. In her frenzy the Queen chides Pamiņa for loving her arch-enemy's ally and hands her a dagger, made sharp for killing Sarastro. She is to carry out the task, and then return the circle of the sun to her mother.

No. 14 ARIA (Allegro assai, D minor): 'Der Hölle Rache kocht in meinem Herzen.' The Queen reveals herself in her true colours in this furious and dazzling outburst, which begins and ends with the words spat out as if in accompanied recitative. The vengeance of hell boils within her, death and despair (and here she takes up the 'Tod und Verzweiflung' from the end of the priests' duet, No. 11) flame about her. Pamina will be disowned if she does not kill Sarastro; this is the Queen's oath of vengeance. She sinks out of sight.

Scene 9 Dialogue: Pamina, with the dagger in her hand, rejects the command to kill, even as she stands deep in thought.

Scene 10 Monostatos comes out quickly, stealthily and cheerfully from his hiding-place, exulting in the information he has overheard. Pamina, not yet aware of his presence, wonders what she is to do;

Monostatos, seizing the dagger, says that she must entrust herself to him: a word to Sarastro, and her mother will perish, drowned in the underground waters that cleanse the initiates. Her only way to save her mother is to love him. She refuses, and he raises the dagger to kill her.

Scene 11 Sarastro appears, dismisses Monostatos – despite the latter's protestations that he was only avenging the threat against Sarastro (the generally spoken line, 'ich bin unschuldig!' – 'I am innocent!' is an inauthentic accretion). As he departs, Monostatos mutters that, having failed with the daughter, he will join the mother.

Scene 12 Pamina pleads for her mother; Sarastro reveals that he knows everything. Provided that Tamino is steadfast, Pamina, too, will be happy, and her mother will return in shame to her own citadel. **No. 15 ARIA** (Larghetto (replacing an earlier marking of Andantino sostenuto), E major): 'In diesen heil'gen Hallen.' Sarastro tells Pamina that vengeance is unknown in these sacred halls; if a man falls, he is led back to duty by love and friendship: forgiveness is the duty of anyone calling himself a man. Like Sarastro's earlier aria, this is also in two strophes, this time in straight *dal segno* form (the verbal and musical motif of walking is more appropriate in the first stanza). The instrumentation consists of pairs of flutes, bassoons and horns in addition to strings.

Eighth set

Scene 13 The scene changes to a hall in which the flying-machine of the Three Boys can operate. (The description of the flying-machine is given in detail in a stage-direction here, though the reference to its opening door presumably only becomes appropriate for the appearance of Papagena in II, 29.) There are two grassy banks in the foreground.

Dialogue: Tamino and Papageno, their heads uncovered, are led in by the Priests. The Spokesman tells Tamino that he and Papageno are to wait in silence until the dread trumpet (that is, the threefold chord) is heard; then they are to move towards its sound. The Second Priest warns Papageno of the dire consequences of breaking the rule of silence. The Priests leave.

Scene 14 Papageno soon begins to talk, ignoring Tamino's shushings and gestures, arguing that he can talk to himself or to Tamino, since they are both men. He complains that they have not even been provided with a glass of water.

Scene 15 An ugly old woman comes up through a trapdoor, offering Papageno a big goblet on a tray. He drinks, hoping in vain that it will prove to be more interesting than water, and then gets into conversation with the Old Woman, who sits down beside him. She tells him she is eighteen years and two minutes old, and has an admirer ten years older than her, called ... Papageno. Just as she is about to tell him her name, a clap of thunder sounds, she hobbles rapidly off, and Papageno determines to be silent henceforth.

Scene 16 The Three Boys enter in a flying-machine bedecked with roses. In the middle of it there is a richly set table. One Boy has the flute, another the case containing the magic bells.

No. 16 TRIO (Allegretto, A major): 'Seid uns zum zweitenmal willkommen.' The Boys greet Tamino and Papageno, and tell them that Sarastro returns their instruments to them; they are also offered food and drink. Tamino is told to have courage; his goal is near. For Papageno, silence is what matters. During the trio, which is exquisitely scored for lightly fluttering flutes, bassoons and first violins above a diaphonous accompaniment of lower strings, they set the table in the centre of the stage, and then fly off.

Scene 17 Dialogue: Papageno encourages Tamino to eat and drink, but the latter is content to blow his flute and leave the food and wine to his companion, who is enthusiastic about Sarastro's kitchen and cellar.

Scene 18 Drawn by the sound of the flute, Pamina enters. When neither of the men will speak to her, she fears Tamino has ceased to love her, and falls into despair.

No. 17 ARIA (Andante, G Minor): 'Ach, ich fühl's.' Pamina feels that the happiness of love is gone for ever; she bids Tamino see her tears, and sings that if he does not feel love's longing, she will find peace in death. This wonderful aria, frequently taken too slowly (see Ch. 6, n. 9), should be compared with no. 7 – the duet with Papageno; not only is Andante only marginally slower than the Andantino of 'Bei Männern', both numbers are in ⁶⁄₈ time and feature the rhythm ♪♪ ♪♪, initially on the tonic. At this point one may also look forward to Papageno's projected suicide (finale, bars 533–42), Andante, G minor, ⁶⁄₈, with a variant of the quaver accompanying figure, and, like Pamina's aria, accompanied by solo flute, oboe and bassoon, apart from strings.

Scene 19 Dialogue: Once Pamina has left, Papageno congratulates himself on keeping silent for once; his trivial chatter, following his greedy attention to food during the previous scene, heightens the pathos of Pamina's plight. The threefold chord (its fifth appearance) summons them, but Papageno lets Tamino go on ahead while he stays to do justice to the food ('I wouldn't go now even if Sarastro harnessed his six lions to me'). The lions immediately appear, Papageno yells, and Tamino has to come back and play his flute to rescue him. They leave together, the wind chords having had to be repeated twice more.

Ninth set

Scene 20 The scene changes to the vault of pyramids. The Spokesman and some Priests, two of whom bear a lighted pyramid on their shoulders. Each Priest holds a lantern-sized transparent pyramid in his hand. (Sarastro, though he is the first to speak in scene 21, is not specifically present for no. 18; it is possible that it is he who leads in Tamino after the chorus. Gieseke's copy of the libretto (see pp. 92–8) is of no assistance in the matter.)
No. 18 CHORUS (Adagio, D major): 'O Isis und Osiris, welche Wonne!' This solemn number is a three-part male chorus. The scoring – pairs of flutes, oboes, bassoons, horns, trumpets, three trombones and strings – might have been expected to include basset-horns. The Priests sing that the glory of the sun is dispelling the darkness of night and that the noble youth – Tamino – will soon feel new life and be worthy of admission to the priesthood.
Scene 21 Tamino is led into the presence of the Priests. Sarastro comments approvingly on his bearing so far, and warns him that two further dangerous trials await him. If his heart still beats warmly for Pamina and if he wishes in due course to rule as a wise prince, the gods will be with him. Pamina is led in, her head covered; she asks where Tamino is, and Sarastro tells her that he is present – to say a last farewell to her (reasonably enough, she interprets this pessimistically; in fact Sarastro wishes to imply – as his last words in no. 19, 'We shall meet again', indicate – that they will henceforth not be separated).
No. 19 TRIO (Andante moderato, B flat major): 'Soll ich dich, Teurer, nicht mehr sehn?' Pamina asks if she shall not see Tamino again; her grief is already sufficiently intense to cloud her reason (or so we may assume), so that she fails to comprehend the words of promise that the men utter. Nevertheless, Sarastro proclaims that the time has come for them to part. They all leave.
Scene 22 Dialogue: Papageno enters, searching for the Prince, but is

driven back by a voice behind the door through which Tamino had been led away, followed by a clap of thunder, flames and a loud chord (which Mozart did not provide). Hopelessly lost, he goes to the door by which he entered, but here, too, he is driven back. He thinks he will die of hunger and regrets having ever undertaken the journey. (Papageno's experiences in this scene, with a voice crying 'Zurück!' at each of two doors, before a representative of the temple appears and addresses him, form a comic echo to Tamino's experiences in I, 15 = no. 8, bars 68ff.)

Scene 23 The Spokesman enters, bearing his pyramid, and tells Papageno that he deserves to wander for ever in the gloomy clefts of the earth; but the gods are merciful. However, he will never know the heavenly joy of the initiates – which does not worry Papageno at all, a good glass of wine would be joy enough for him. The Spokesman leaves, and at once a large goblet of red wine appears out of the earth. He drinks, finds the wine quite excellent and feels himself almost capable of flying.

No. 20 ARIA (Andante $\frac{2}{4}$ – Allegro $\frac{6}{8}$, F major): 'Ein Mädchen oder Weibchen.' The song has three strophes; unusually, the refrain comes first, with the glockenspiel part varied each time, and the wind instruments (flute, pairs of oboes, bassoons and horns) appearing only in the last strophe. The Allegro section has different words each time; there is a brief orchestral postlude to match the introduction. Mozart may have reversed the libretto's order of the second and third strophes, perhaps preferring, in view of Papageno's forthcoming attempted suicide, to end this jolly number on a more sombre note ('or I shall really grieve myself to death'); in that case the winds convey an added irony. The bird-catcher sings that if he had a girl-friend or wife he would enjoy life again, feel himself the equal of princes; isn't there just one girl for him, to save him from an early grave? If there's not, then flames will devour him; but a girl's kiss will cure him completely.

Scene 24 Dialogue: As the song ends, the Old Woman dances in with her stick, tells Papageno she has taken pity on him, and that unless he agrees to marry her, he will remain immured in the vaults, with bread and water to sustain him. He promises to be faithful to her – until, he adds in an aside, he finds someone more attractive. She is thereupon transformed into a young woman dressed just like him. He tries to embrace her.

Scene 25 Just then the Spokesman enters and whisks her away, saying that Papageno is not yet worthy of her. He tries to follow, but is sent

back. He boldly says the earth will have to swallow him up first —
which is precisely what happens.

Tenth set

Scene 26 The scene changes to a shallow garden. The Three Boys fly
down.

No. 21 FINALE (Andante, E flat major, passing through several keys
and tempi and ending in Allegro, E flat major): 'Bald prangt, den
Morgen zu verkünden.' After a luminous little introduction for wind
sextet the Boys announce the dawn of a new day and the approaching
end of superstition (Mozart altered the libretto's words 'dark
delusion'). They pray that peace may return to men's hearts,
making earth a heaven. They see Pamina approach, driven mad
by seemingly unrequited love, and determine to comfort, but initially
to observe, her.

Scene 27 Pamina enters, half crazed, and dagger in hand, which she
apostrophizes as her bridegroom. The Boys warn her against suicide,
but they have to restrain her by force (Allegro, E flat major, ⅔),
going on to explain that Tamino would die of grief if she killed herself,
for he loves her and her alone. They may not explain the reason for
his silence, but they are allowed to show him to her. The scene ends
with a moral observation on the supreme positive power of love,
expressed with an aethereal blend of the four soprano voices and the
wind sextet, now enriched by added flute and full strings.

Eleventh set

Scene 28 The scene changes to a prospect of two large mountains,
in one of which a waterfall can be heard; the other is a volcano.
Through grilles in the mountains fire and water are visible; the horizon
must be bright red where the fire burns, and there is black mist where
the water is. The wings are rocks, and each side is closed off by an
iron door. Tamino is lightly clad, without sandals. Two men in black
armour lead him in. Fire burns on their helmets; they read him the
transparent writing which is inscribed on a pyramid centre-stage, high
up, near the grilles (Adagio, C minor). Three knocks from trombones
and strings, the first two answered by wind sextet and high cello line,
give way to a noble fugato, treated as a chorale prelude. The melody
sung by the Men in Armour is the Lutheran chorale 'Ach Gott, vom
Himmel sieh darein'. They tell Tamino that the person who walks

this difficult path is purified through fire and water, air and earth; if he can overcome the fear of death he will receive illumination and be enabled to devote himself to the Mysteries of Isis. Tamino does not hesitate and bids them open the gates. Pamina calls to him from off-stage (Allegretto), and the Men in Armour relax as they tell him she may now accompany him, and he may speak to her: a woman who is not frightened by night and death is worthy, and will be admitted to the Mysteries. She enters, and they embrace (only in this scene, apart from two bars in the Act I finale, do Tamino and Pamina sing in duet). She tells him she will now be at his side, will indeed guide him, as love leads her. The magic flute will protect them – she tells him (to the accompaniment of a noble bassoon solo) that her father fashioned it in a magic hour from the core of a thousand-year-old oak, while storms raged. The final trials are preceded by a beautiful setting for four voices, solo flute, bassoon and strings, of a couplet in praise of music, which will lead them safely through the dark night of death. To the solemn accompaniment of a march (Adagio, C major), with intricate flute line poised above pairs of horns and trumpets, three trombones and timpani, they pass slowly through the fire and the water, pausing to embrace and sing in duet between the two trials (the libretto calls for Pamina alone to sing at this point). After they have reappeared for the second time, a door opens, revealing the brilliantly lit interior of a temple. There is a moment of solemn silence. The scene must be of the most perfect splendour. A short triumphal chorus (C major; presumably sung off-stage) follows Tamino's and Pamina's realization that they have now been initiated into the cult of Isis.

(Tenth set – again)

Scene 29 The scene changes back to the garden of scene 26 (Allegro, G major, $\frac{6}{8}$). Papageno enters, blowing his panpipe and calling for Papagena. He cannot find her and blames himself for not having kept silent at the proper time. He takes a rope from round his waist and intends to hang himself from a convenient tree, but decides to wait until he has counted three, and then, since no girl appears in response to his call he prepares to take his life – the key, time-signature, tempo and scoring are, as we have seen, those of Pamina's aria. He bids the false world adieu, but is saved, as Pamina had been, by the Three Boys (Allegretto, C major). They tell him to sound his bells, which he had foolishly forgotten about, and he cheers up at once. As he plays and sings (Allegro, C major), the Boys run to their flying-machine and bring out Papagena. Mozart here deleted five lines of verse for the Boys immediately before they tell Papageno to look behind him; they fly off. At the sight of each other, Papageno and Papagena stammer out (now in G major) the syllables of their names before singing of the joys that await them if the gods grant them lots of little Papagenos and Papagenas (again Mozart omitted four lines of text). They leave the stage.

Scene 30 (There is no justification in libretto, score or words sung for a change of scene here.) (Più moderato, C minor.) Monostatos, the Queen of Night and the Three Ladies emerge from the two trap-doors; they hold black torches in their hands. They urge silence on each other as they prepare to break into the temple. But first, Monostatos repeats his demand, acceded to by the Queen (in a meeting that took place off-stage), that Pamina shall be his wife. Thunder and the roaring of water is heard, but the conspirators are unshaken in their resolve to destroy the Priests by fire and sword; Monostatos and the Ladies dedicate their act of vengeance to the Queen.

Twelfth set

A mighty chord is heard; thunder, lightning and storm. The whole theatre is at once transformed into a sun. Sarastro stands on high; Tamino and Pamina, both in priestly clothing. Near them, the Egyptian Priests on both sides. The Three Boys hold flowers. The conspirators, their power destroyed, recognize that they are being plunged into eternal night – by, as Sarastro comments, once the storm has lifted and the transformation has been completed, the beams of the sun (here, for the only time in the opera, Sarastro enters the 'Masonic' key of E flat major). The Priests hail the new initiates (Andante, E flat major, to a variant of the Adagio opening of the trials scene) and express gratitude to Osiris and Isis. A brief concluding chorus (Allegro, E flat major) tells that the strong cause has triumphed and rewards beauty and wisdom with the eternal crown; the splendour of this passage is enhanced by the delicate scoring of the dance-like figuration for flutes and violins.

4 The writing of 'Die Zauberflöte'

The traditional story

So little is definitely known about the history of the composition of *Die Zauberflöte* that the proliferation of legend is not surprising. Even basic facts are disputed − who wrote the libretto, when and in what circumstances Mozart was commissioned to set it to music, how it was staged, and how received. We cannot rely on the statements made in the early biographies of Mozart, for though in broad agreement with each other, successive writers tended to take over, and embroider, the comments of their predecessors. Before attempting to establish the facts we shall set out in chronological order the biographical information provided by contemporaries and near-contemporaries that forms the basis for the traditional story.

Friedrich Schlichtegroll's short monograph, *Mozarts Leben*, published in book form in 1794 following its appearance in 1792 in his *Nekrolog auf das Jahr 1791*, singles out 'die *Zauberflötte*' among Mozart's operas as a work that 'received such excellent and general approval that it was performed a hundred times within a space of twelve months' − a powerful exaggeration, but not grossly out of keeping with what Schikaneder was to claim in a year or two. Schlichtegroll had little information about Mozart's years in Vienna and would have been wiser to omit the precise reference to the success of the opera. Franz Xaver Němetschek (Niemetschek) in his revised and extended *Lebensbeschreibung des K. K. Kapellmeisters Wolfgang Amadeus Mozart* ('Biography of the Imperial and Royal Kapellmeister ...'), which was published in Prague in 1808 eleven years after the first of its three previous editions, contents himself with the lapidary statement: 'He wrote Die Zauberflöte for the theatre of the well-known Schikaneder, who was an old acquaintance of his' (p. 48). Later in the book, however, after mentioning *Die Entführung* and *Der Schauspieldirektor* among the German Singspiels, he asks:

What shall I say about the *Zauberflöte*? Who in Germany does not know it? Is there a theatre in which it was not performed? It is our national piece. The applause it received everywhere — everywhere, from the court theatre to the wandering troupe in a small market town, is as yet without parallel. In Vienna in the first year of its existence alone it was performed more than a hundred times. (p. 113)

Information of a different kind is vouchsafed by the musical journalist Friedrich Rochlitz. His series of articles in the *Allgemeine musikalische Zeitung* in 1798 entitled 'Verbürgte Anekdoten aus Wolfgang Gottlieb Mozarts Leben, ein Beytrag zur richtigern Kenntnis dieses Mannes, als Mensch und Künstler' ('Authenticated anecdotes from the life of W. G. M., a contribution to the more correct knowledge of this man, as human being and as artist') contains lively, interesting, though unreliable material. It is clear from her letter to Breitkopf & Härtel of 10 October 1799 that Constanze Mozart had a high regard for Rochlitz ('please give my kind regards to the intelligent ('geistreichen') Herr Rochlitz, whom I regard as the future biographer of my late husband ...'), and she seems to have encouraged her second husband, Georg Nikolaus von Nissen, to rely heavily on the anecdotes that Rochlitz published in the *AMZ* (themselves based extensively on her oral testimony).

Rochlitz claimed personal acquaintance with Mozart from the time of the latter's nine-day-long visit to Leipzig in May 1789, and it is readily demonstrable that, apart from minor changes and transpositions, Nissen's account of the commissioning and composition of *Die Zauberflöte* is taken straight from Rochlitz's articles (part 11, col. 83 to part 17, col. 147). In a later section of the 'Anekdoten' (part 19, cols. 148–9) Rochlitz talks of the physical and mental strain to which Mozart was subject during the composition of the opera ('... he, to whom day and night were one when his genius took hold of him, sank into frequent exhaustion and semi-unconsciousness that lasted for minutes at a time'), and says that his increasing debility permitted him to conduct the performances on only about ten occasions,[1] whereafter, when he could no longer even attend performances in the theatre, he listened to the music in his imagination, with his watch at his side.[2]

By the time the first full-length biography appeared, in 1828, the bare 'facts' put forward by Niemetschek had been both supplemented by research, and embroidered with further anecdotes and rumours. Nissen did not live to see the publication of his mighty work, *Biographie W. A. Mozart's*, which runs to nearly a thousand pages.

Two dozen of them are devoted to *Die Zauberflöte*, and they are introduced by a passage that takes Niemetschek's bare statement as its starting-point:

He composed the *Zauberflöte* for the theatre of Schikaneder, who was an old acquaintance of his, at the latter's request, to rescue him from his straitened circumstances. The poetry is by Schikaneder himself, who in this way was dragged to immortality by Mozart's coat-tails ...   (p. 548)

Nissen goes on to tell the tale, uncritically repeated so often since, of Schikaneder's wretched financial position, occasioned 'partly through his own fault, partly through lack of public support. Half in despair he came to Mozart, told him of his circumstances, and concluded that only he could save him.' There then follows what is presented as if it were the verbatim dialogue between theatre director and composer, depicting Mozart as a generous and helpful friend, Schikaneder by contrast as an exploiter of Mozart's good nature in that he failed to allow him to draw the sole benefit of sale of the score to other theatres. When Mozart discovered that his opera was being performed without a single copy having been obtained from him, his only comment was 'The rascal!' ('Der Lump!'), and that was the end of the matter. Even here, though, there is no hint that the text was not Schikaneder's own work – that particular refinement, to deprive him posthumously of the authorship of his own masterpiece, was not to see the light of day in book form for several more years yet. (For contemporary rumours, see pp. 89–92.)

As usual, the truth is impossible to establish, and it was assuredly less colourful than these legends suggest. If one considers the salient points in these accounts, it is easy to disprove some of them. Nothing is known about the finances of Schikaneder's theatre, in that no account-books survive. But there is some evidence to suggest that he was in financial difficulties in 1791 (see p. 144). In the two years since he took over the Freihaustheater auf der Wieden he had built up a talented ensemble and developed a popular and successful repertory. He commissioned *Oberon* from Wranitzky, already a promising composer, in 1789; in June 1790 the theatre was granted an Imperial and Royal Privilege (licence), and in the following year Emperor Leopold II attended a performance with his son and heir on 3 August. These facts do not suggest that Schikaneder was hard up (though, like any other theatre director, he was doubtless hoping that his new opera would be a box-office success). The last point from Nissen's account – namely that Schikaneder cheated Mozart of his agreed proceeds from the sale of the score to other theatres – is easily disproved. The earliest performance of the opera outside Schikaneder's theatre did not take place until nearly ten months after Mozart's death, and there is no evidence that copies of the score were in circulation while Mozart was still alive.

The next stage in the growth of the web of legends surrounding the opera is reached a dozen years later. An incomplete and undated letter by Ignaz von Seyfried to Friedrich Treitschke comments on a manuscript which the latter had sent him, in or about the year 1840. Presumably this manuscript was the draft of the anecdotal story that Treitschke – one of the librettists of *Fidelio* – published in the second number of *Orpheus. Musikalisches Taschenbuch für das Jahr 1841*, edited by August Schmidt. The story, entitled 'Die Zauberflöte. – Der Dorfbarbier. – Fidelio. Beitrag zur musikalischen Kunstgeschichte' ('... Contribution to the history of the art of music'; pp. 239–64 of the almanac), creates a typical late-Romantic fictional framework for some interesting, even valuable, comments about the three operas. Three friends meet in a tavern and agree to entertain each other with musical reminiscences. Friedrich, who speaks about *Fidelio*, is Treitschke himself; his companions are named Ernst and Adam. It is Ernst who, with help from Friedrich, tells of the origins of *Die Zauberflöte*. 'Help me, friend and Brother, or I'm lost!' are the opening words of this part of the story – reputedly Schikaneder's words to Mozart, begging him to take on the task of writing the opera that will save him from bankruptcy. The poet hands over the first act of the libretto for Mozart to begin work on, saying he will complete the rest of it shortly, even though the rest of the plot is not yet clear. Mozart good-naturedly agrees. We read of the change of plan following the première of *Kaspar der Fagottist*, of Schikaneder's hospitality to Mozart, his enthusiasm for Tamino's aria and dissatisfaction with the first two attempts at setting 'Bei Männern',[3] his prompting of the final version ('he warbled a simple, almost commonplace tune. "You'll have it", replied Mozart'), as well as many details, some of them differing from more familiar depictions, but neither the better nor the worse for that.

The suggestion that on his return from Prague in mid-September Mozart still had to compose Papageno's songs, the second finale, and orchestrate the whole score, as well as compose the Priests' march and the overture, is certainly unacceptable (see pp. 80–6). But details about the early performances, box-office receipts, and the rival productions at the Court Opera and the Theater an der Wien in 1801 and 1812, as well as about Goethe's sequel and his correspondence with Wranitzky, ring true (though they could as easily be taken from already-published sources as go back to oral traditions about the earliest years of the opera's existence). There is no question of Treitschke's having first-hand knowledge of the events of 1791, when he was fifteen; he did not come to Vienna until about 1800.

Equally, Seyfried (whose comments Treitschke solicited) can have no claim to speak with authority about the prehistory of *Die Zauberflöte*, whatever he may later have said. He, too, was just fifteen at the time of its première, and even if he had been a piano pupil of Mozart's (we have no evidence one way or the other), it is unthinkable that a fourteen-year-old would have enjoyed Mozart's friendship and the freedom of Schikaneder's theatre, let alone been entrusted with conducting rehearsals. Seyfried joined the Theater auf der Wieden as second kapellmeister in 1797; any information he was able to supply about that theatre in its earlier years was based on nothing more than oral tradition.

The 'facts' that Seyfried put forward in his letter to Treitschke are: that Schikaneder got to know Mozart, and later his business associate Zitterbarth, through the meetings of a Masonic lodge devoted to dining; that Gieseke introduced Schikaneder to *Dschinnistan*; that Mozart usually worked at the opera 'in Gerl's lodgings, or in Schikaneder's garden, just a few steps from the theatre'; that Seyfried 'often ate at the same table [as Mozart and Schikaneder], and took many rehearsals in the same salon, or to be more exact, wooden hut'. He also repeats the tales about Schikaneder's reliance on his prompter[4] for help with the versification, and about the changes to the story of the opera necessitated by the production of *Kaspar der Fagottist*; and he states that Henneberg, the young kapellmeister who took over the musical direction from Mozart after the first two or three performances, rehearsed the opera from the short score while Mozart was in Prague for the coronation. He also reports that the overture's parts 'came wet to the dress rehearsal' and that Mozart on his death bed attended performances of the opera in his imagination. There is nothing here that we can take at face value, even if some of the details sound plausible.

In 1849 – 58 years after the first performance of the opera – Julius Cornet published his account of Gieseke's claim to the authorship of *Die Zauberflöte* in his book *Die Oper in Deutschland*. We read that the libretto was the joint product of Schikaneder and Gieseke; the latter supplied 'the outline of the plot, the division into scenes, and the naïve and well-known rhymes. This Gieseke ... was the author of several magic operas, including the Zauberflöte (after Wieland's Lulu), which Schikaneder merely altered, cut, and added to, taking to himself the title of its author.' There follows a description of Gieseke's reappearance at a Viennese tavern, many years after he had left the city:

One day in the summer of the year 1818, an elegant old gentleman in a blue coat and white cravat, and wearing a decoration, sat down at the table in the tavern in Vienna at which Ignaz von Seyfried, Korntheuer, Julius Laroche, Küstner, Gned and I met for luncheon each day. His venerable snow-white head, his meticulous way of speaking, and his whole bearing, made a favourable impression on us all. It was the former chorus-singer *Gieseke*, now a professor at Dublin University; he had come from Iceland and Lapland straight to Vienna to present to the Imperial Natural History Museum a natural history collection formed from the plant, mineral and animal kingdoms. *Seyfried* was the only one to recognize him. The old gentleman's joy at being in Vienna and at the Emperor Francis's recognition (he gave him a really valuable gold snuffbox shining with solitaires and filled with brand-new Kremnitz ducats) was the recompense for many years of privations and suffering. On this occasion we learnt so much about the old days; among other things we learnt that he (who was at that time a member of the banned order of Freemasons) was the real author of the "Zauberflöte" (although Seyfried already had a suspicion of this). I relate this according to his own statement, which we had no reason to doubt. He gave us this explanation when I sang the cavatina interpolated into 'Der Spiegel von Arkadien'. Many thought that the prompter *Helmböck* had been Schikaneder's collaborator. But in this also Gieseke disabused us; Gieseke attributed to Schikaneder only the figures of Papageno and his wife.[5]

This report has much to answer for, as we shall see in the next chapter. But the demonstrable inaccuracies in points of detail probably count for less than does the fact that Cornet did not publish his account until almost all those who could have confirmed or denied it were dead, and that no one else (except in imitation of Cornet) made the same claim for Gieseke's authorship.[6]

By the time of the first centenary of Mozart's birth, and the appearance in that year of the first volume of Otto Jahn's *W.A. Mozart*, the traditional picture of the events and personalities surrounding *Die Zauberflöte* is complete. The authoritative nature of Jahn's great work, enhanced by the revised editions undertaken by Jahn himself (1867), by Hermann Deiters (1889–91 and 1905–7), and especially by Hermann Abert (1919–21; seventh edition 1955), is reflected in its continuing profound influence on Mozart studies. In many points of detail about *Die Zauberflöte* it is misleading, or quite wrong, even though a number of details have been corrected by successive editors. The shortcomings of Jahn's presentation are doubtless part and parcel of the romanticizing tendencies of his age. Lucid scholarly comment is awkwardly accompanied by gossip and rumour, much of it an elaboration of dangerously late and unauthenticated material. To the by now well-established tales of Schikaneder's penury, Gieseke's crucial rôle in the writing of the libretto, and the hasty revision of the work's plan owing to the success of *Kaspar der Fagottist*, for instance, are added new and colourful details – that Schikaneder's desperate plea to Mozart was made early in 1791 ('7 March is even given as the date'),[7] that Barbara Gerl, the original Papagena, had at least a hand in persuading Mozart to take on the commission, and that Mozart uttered the warning to the actor-manager-poet: 'If we have a disaster it won't be my fault, for I've never composed a magic opera before.'[8] We learn further of Mozart's being put to work in the little wooden hut near Schikaneder's theatre, and of the life of excessive drinking and roistering that he led under the influence of his librettist. Few of these numerous anecdotes have the ring of authenticity, and there seems to be no basis for the innuendoes that link Mozart's name with those of various women. Indeed, he could not escape the charge of hypocrisy were it otherwise, if we bear in mind the letter to Gottfried von Jacquin of 4 November 1787 in which, lightly yet firmly, he claims some of the credit for his friend's abandonment of his 'former rather restless way of life' and 'the pleasures of a volatile and capricious love'.

The evidence provided by contemporary sources

The compositions of 1791

What can take the place of the traditional stories about the origins of *Die Zauberflöte*? The short answer is that very little clear evidence survives. Our method shall be to create the context of Mozart's musical activities in the first nine months of 1791 against which to view the composition of the opera, then to examine the references to the opera in Mozart's letters and other writings, and finally to propose corroborative (or contradictory) evidence adduceable from the first edition of the libretto and from the autograph score.

It is unlikely that the details of Mozart's contract with Schikaneder (if there was one) will ever be known, or when he began to write the score. The *Catalogue*, though its entries occasionally need to be treated with circumspection, provides a clear outline of Mozart's compositional activity.[9] His principal product in the early weeks of 1791 was the series of dances for the carnival season required of him by the terms of his court appointment. He wrote his last three songs, K 596–8, on 14 January. The Allegro and Andante for mechanical organ, K 608, was entered on 3 March, an aria for bass voice, obbligato double bass and orchestra (K 612), followed on 8 March; in the same month he entered the set of keyboard variations on the song 'Ein Weib ist das herrlichste Ding auf der Welt', K 613, from *Die verdeckten Sachen*, the first sequel to Schikaneder's *Der dumme Gärtner*. The String Quintet in E flat, K 614, is dated 12 April; there are fragmentary movements for string quintet, K 515a and c, which, the paper suggests, may well date from this period. Under 20 April is entered a (lost) final chorus (K 615) for Sarti's opera *Le gelosie villane*.

Thereafter some falling-off in Mozart's productivity is apparent. 4 May saw the entry of the Andante for mechanical organ, K 616; there is also a related fragment for the same instrument, K 615a (on which leaf there are several sketches for *Die Zauberflöte*; see Tyson 1987, p. 17). Nineteen days later Mozart recorded the completion of the 'Adagio und Rondeau für Harmonica, 1 flauto, 1 oboe, 1 viola, e Violoncello'; here, too, there are related fragments, K 616a for the same combination, K 617a for glass harmonica solo. The motet 'Ave verum corpus' (K 618) was written at Baden near Vienna, on 17 June, and in the following month (no precise date is given) Mozart entered the incipit of his 'Little German Cantata', K 619. Apart from the three large-scale works that occupied him during his last months – *La clemenza di Tito*, *Die Zauberflöte* and the Requiem – and the Clarinet Concerto and Masonic Cantata of October and November, we now know that Mozart also wrote the incomplete 'First' Horn Concerto (K 412 (386b) + 514) at some time during 1791.

How is the writing of *Die Zauberflöte* to be fitted into this period of varied activity? – The legend that Schikaneder came to Mozart to commission the opera on 7 March is presumably not unconnected with Mozart's known concerns of that period. The bass aria 'Per questa bella mano' was written for two members of Schikaneder's company, Franz Xaver Gerl, the future Sarastro, and Friedrich Pischelberger, the orchestra's principal double bass player; and the keyboard variations of the same month, based on a tune by Gerl or Benedikt Schack (the first Tamino), also belong to the ambience of the Freihaustheater. Since Mozart must have received the commission to write *La clemenza di Tito* some time in July, and probably not before the middle of that month, and the opera was given as part of the coronation celebrations in Prague on 6 September, he can have had little time to work on the German opera during those few summer weeks. At least we know from Tyson's paper studies that no part of the Requiem was written down until after Mozart's return from Prague in the middle of September, though the commission, surely in fact as well as in legend, predates the journey to Prague.

Mozart's letters

The *Catalogue* laconically dates *Die Zauberflöte* 'im Jullius', with just two further items listed for 28 September, two days before the première. For information about the progress of the composition we are almost solely reliant on the letters which Mozart wrote to Constanze during the summer months of 1791 when, carrying their sixth child – the second to survive infancy – Franz Xaver Wolfgang, she was taking the waters at the spa of Baden bei Wien, whither she had travelled on 4 June.

The series of letters reveals quicksilver changes of mood and subject-matter. The predominant impression the reader obtains is of Mozart's loneliness, which can be seen as much in his affection and concern for his greatly missed wife as in the restless chronicle of his daily activities. Anxiety about his financial situation, and frustration at the problems he was experiencing in trying to finalize arrangements with an unidentified man for a large loan, strengthen still further the impression of particularly difficult working conditions. Mozart disliked sleeping alone in the apartment, even eating alone; he stayed with his old horn-playing friend Joseph Leutgeb for the first couple of nights after Constanze's departure, dined with Süssmayr one day and Schikaneder the next, travelled out to Baden to see Constanze and his son Carl at the weekends when he could, went to the theatre – and got on with the new opera. His first reference to it – and chronologically this is the earliest surviving indication of its existence – occurs in the undated letter to Constanze which from internal evidence must have been written on 11 June: 'From sheer boredom I have written an aria for the opera today – I got up at 4.30 ...' We have no way of knowing which aria this might have been; on the basis of what we know of Mozart's normal procedure when composing an opera, we would be inclined to assume that work must by then have been far advanced, since Mozart normally wrote the ensembles first and the arias later. This assumption seems to be borne out by the closing lines of this letter: 'I'm dining with Puchberg today – I kiss you 1,000 times and say in my thoughts with you: Death and despair was his reward!' This quotation of the close of the whimsical little duet for the Priests (no. 11) confirms the impression that Mozart had already composed much of the opera; further, it helps answer those who claim that the Masonic element was only introduced into *Die Zauberflöte* following the change of plan said to have been necessitated by the success of *Kaspar der Fagottist*. For the Perinet/Wenzel Müller Singspiel was given for the first time on 8 June, and by an interesting coincidence it was because he was about to go to a performance of this very work that Mozart told his wife he was obliged to write his letter in a hurry ('it is 6.45 – and the coach [to take him to the Leopoldstadt] leaves at 7 o'clock'). His letter of 12 June (it, too, has to be dated from internal evidence) continues the story of his frustrations of the previous day, when he waited in vain for the acquaintance who had promised to come and settle details of the loan, which caused him to miss dinner with Michael Puchberg, and in the evening he was even more depressed to receive a mere note of good intentions from the rich acquaintance. It was in the hope of cheering himself up that he took himself off to the Leopoldstadt Theatre for Perinet's new Singspiel (see pp. 31–2).

There are no further references to the opera until the postscript of Mozart's letter to Constanze which cannot be assigned a more accurate date than late June/early July: 'My greetings to Snai [= Süssmayr] – tell him I'm asking how he's getting on – like an ox, I suppose, – he's to write away busily so that I get my things.' In his playful way Mozart is asking his wife to make sure that Süssmayr is getting on with the copying-out of the short score of *Die Zauberflöte*. This interpretation is confirmed by Mozart's next letter, which he dated 2 July: 'Please tell Süssmayer the Stupid boy he is to send my particella ['Spart'] of the first act, from the Introduction right up to the *Finale*, so that I can orchestrate. It would be good if he could put it together today so that it can leave by the first coach tomorrow early, then I shall get it promptly at noon.' In his letter of 3 July Mozart acknowledges safe receipt of the finale (and of some clothes he had asked for), which suggests that Constanze must have sent off the last number of Act I before she received her husband's request. He repeats his injunction to Süssmayr and mentions that he had lunched with Schikaneder the previous day.

A small detail in the letter of 3 July justifies the speculation that by this time Mozart was far enough advanced with the drafting of Act II to have begun to concern himself with the scene of Papageno's attempted suicide. The words of the bird-catcher's forlorn cries for his absent Papagena read in the libretto: 'Papagena! Herzenstäubchen! / Papagena! liebes Weibchen!' ('... dove of my heart ... dear little wife'); Mozart inverted the epithets, and then revised the order of the two lines, in his autograph score. Why, one may ask. – In his letters to Constanze of 1789 and 1790 (most recently in early November 1790) Mozart had several times addressed her as his 'Herzensweibchen' ('little wife of my heart'); the letters of summer 1791 begin with variants of 'Ma trés chere Epouse' and 'Liebstes, bestes Weibchen'. I suggest that the return to the compound 'HerzensWeibchen' in the letter of 3 July may well be attributable to his having been prompted by Schikaneder's formulation in the libretto, which he slightly altered as an affectionate encoded tribute to his wife.

Hints about the progress of work on the opera continue to occur in the letters of July. On the 5th: 'Süssmayer really must send me Nos 4 and 5 [presumably Tamino's aria and the first of the Queen – unusually, Mozart's numbering begins with the overture] of my manuscript – also the other things I requested.' In a second letter written on the same day he acknowledges receipt of 'the latest packet' – the particella of Act I apart from the finale, for which he had thanked his wife on the 3rd. On the 7th he expresses his sense of deprivation, of emptiness, without Constanze: '... even my work gives me no delight because, accustomed to break off now and then and exchange a few words with you, this pleasure is now alas an impossibility – if I go to the piano and sing something out of the opera, I have to stop at once – it arouses too much emotion in me ...' In a jocular postscript to his letter of 12 July to his friend, the schoolteacher and choirmaster at Baden, Anton Stoll, he forges Süssmayr's handwriting and asks Stoll to send 'what Herr von Mozart asked you for, that is – the Mass and the gradual by Mich[ael] Haydn, or no news of his opera'. (Incidentally, the last phrase of the postscript, 'Also ein Mann hält sein Wort' – 'thus a man keeps his word' – is perhaps an echo of the famous comic touch in *Kaspar der Fagottist* where the child playing the good spirit, Pizichi, assures the comic servant: 'Und ein Mann hält Wort'; III, 10.)

The correspondence now ceases, as Mozart brought his wife and their six-year-old son Carl back to Vienna in mid-July in anticipation of the birth of the baby on the 26th. Around 25 August, Mozart, his wife and Süssmayr left for Prague (taking neither of the children with them); they arrived there on the 28th, and returned to Vienna about the middle of September after the production of *La clemenza di Tito*. It is generally accepted − though there is no firm evidence either way − that Schikaneder's kapellmeister, Johann Baptist Henneberg (who was appointed in 1790, at the age of only twenty-one), supervised the rehearsals of *Die Zauberflöte* during Mozart's absence in Prague, and took over the musical direction of the opera after Mozart had conducted the first two performances.

The *Catalogue of all my Works*

The most reliable, if necessarily cryptic, information we have about the factual details of the opera is provided by the entries in Mozart's *Catalogue*.[10] These read, literally translated:

[1791] In July
Die *Zauberflöte*. — performed the *30th September*.
− − − − − − − − a German Opera in 2 Acts. By Eman.
Schickaneder. consisting of 22 pieces. − *Ladies*. − Mad^selle Gottlieb.
Mad^me Hofer. Mad^me Görl. Mad^el Klöpfler. Mad^sell Hofmann. *Men*. Hr: Schack. Hr. Görl. Hr: Schickaneder the elder. Hr: Kistler. Hr. Schickaneder the younger. Hr. Nouseul. − Choruses.

On the opposite page Mozart notates in short score the first four bars of the *Introduzione*. There follows the entry for *La clemenza di Tito*, dated 5 September, the eve of its première. Then comes:

the 28th September.
to the opera *die Zauberflöte* − a Priests' March and the Overture.

Again, the opening bars of each are notated on the page facing, in that order.

These entries repay careful examination. '22 pieces' is correct, if one includes the overture as no. 1 (as Mozart did); and the Priests' march which, though composed only at a very late stage, was planned from the beginning, as the libretto makes clear. Mozart's indication of a total of twenty-two musical numbers does not necessarily exclude the problematical duet for Tamino and Papageno (see pp. 57−8 and 207−8), which could have been removed to make way for another number, or if a late addition to the score could have been numbered, say, 11½.

The singers named cover the rôles of Pamina, Queen of Night, Papagena, and the First and Second Ladies; and of the men, Tamino,

Sarastro, First and Second Priests, Papageno and Monostatos. The full cast (or almost the full cast) is contained on the playbill for the first night (see pp. 145–51).

The first edition of the libretto

The first edition of the libretto is probably second only to the autograph score in importance; it is also an unusually elegant production, with its two fine engraved illustrations and decorative title page. Ignaz Alberti, a master Mason in Mozart's lodge, printed the libretto, and he was also responsible for the depictions of a temple interior and of Schikaneder as Papageno ('I. Albert sc.' is the legend on both). Since the libretto was already on sale by the time of the first performance, as a note on the playbill indicates, neither illustration can be claimed as an actual representation of the first staging. Too little is known about book production in late eighteenth-century Vienna to enable us to state how long before publication, in this case how long before the première, the final manuscript would have had to be handed to the printer. What we can say is that, since the printed libretto in no. 1 has Tamino 'victim of the cunning serpent' rather than 'of the fierce lion', the autograph score with its alteration of 'dem grimmigen Löwen' to 'der listigen Schlange' pre-dates the printer's copy of the libretto.

It is unlikely that we shall ever be able to estimate precisely when Schikaneder delivered the manuscript to the printer, but we can profitably ask what the relationship is between the text of the first edition of the libretto, and that found in Mozart's autograph score. The latter, not surprisingly, contains none of the ample dialogue, nor even cues immediately preceding the musical numbers. For this reason, and also because there are no additional markings, we can reasonably assume that the autograph was not used for the musical direction of the performances (and that the score that was so used, perhaps the one copied by Süssmayr in June/July, and since lost, would have contained the definitive text as performed at the première, including for instance the wind chords at the start of the duet no. 7; see p. 123, Plate 2).

Detailed comparison of the text Mozart entered in the autograph with that of the first edition of the libretto reveals some fifty variants.[11] Many of these points are trivial, yet the pattern that emerges suggests very strongly that Mozart took from the libretto many suggestions for musico-dramatic effects. It is impossible to say to what extent Mozart influenced the text in the first place, that is before the complete version was prepared from which he and the printer independently worked. It is safe to assume, however, both from what is known of Mozart's past practice in his collaborations with Varesco on *Idomeneo* and with Stephanie on *Die Entführung*, and from the superior theatrical qualities of the libretto of *Die Zauberflöte* to Schikaneder's other libretti (as well as from Schikaneder's later tribute to Mozart for his share in the planning of the opera (see p. 89)), that the composer's influence was considerable, and probably crucial. As an instance of Mozart's observance of the librettist's instruction on a musical matter we may cite the directions appended to no. 4, the Queen's first aria: *Recitativ* (the first four lines) – *Arie* (the next twelve lines) – *Allegro* (the last four lines). Mozart, in fact, precedes the recitative with an orchestral Allegro maestoso; and the tempo for the closing fast section is Allegro moderato. Conversely, one could argue that this instance points to the libretto's taking account of Mozart's score; and certainly the fact that the bulk of the opera was sufficiently complete for Mozart to enter it in his *Catalogue* 'im Jullius' would have allowed time for the printer to incorporate the textual changes that the composer made. Correlation suggests very strongly, however, that no account was taken, in the preparation of the printed libretto, of Mozart's textual changes. Indeed, as we know from the Mozart family's correspondence at the time of the preparations for *Idomeneo*, and as abundant contemporary evidence corroborates, divergencies between sung text and printed libretto were considered unimportant.

The autograph score

The first edition of the libretto, then, can provide little or no evidence to help our inquiry into the chronology of the opera. What of the autograph score? We should perhaps remind ourselves that this treasure (restored in 1977 to its home in the Deutsche Staatsbibliothek, Berlin, after its wartime removal to a place of safety, and postwar reappearance at Kraków) was, when Mozart completed the composition, not a single large volume, but a series of separate items, capable of being reordered, added to or subtracted from. Each of the individual pieces, all of them except for the overture numbered by Mozart, and almost all of them also foliated by him, was probably stitched or conveniently gathered for ease and safety of handling; in the late 1970s the nineteenth-century binding was detached so that the facsimile edition (Bärenreiter, Kassel, 1979) could be prepared; the score has since been rebound.

In recent years there have been three differing approaches to study of the autograph score. A two-part article by the editor of the opera in the *Neue Mozart-Ausgabe*[12] studies Mozart's orthography in great detail, though the author is not primarily concerned with the dating or ordering of the various numbers in the autograph score. And Karl-Heinz Köhler[13] contributes a valuable study that applies the methods he illuminatingly brought to bear on the chronology of the autograph of *Le nozze di Figaro*. Most recent, indeed not yet published, is Alan Tyson's analysis of the paper-types and the make-up of the autograph.[14]

Karl-Heinz Köhler's article proposes a precise chronological order for the composition, based on four 'objective criteria': watermarks; rastration; the 'colour values' of the inks (nine in number) used for the first phase of composition, which established the 'contours' of the opera; and the 'colour values' of the inks (eight in number) used for completing the compositional process (instrumentation, marks of expression, etc). From analysis of the interrelationship between paper-type and the 'contour inks' Köhler distinguishes the following chronological order of Mozart's work for Act I (including one number from Act II):

1, 3, 4, 8 (to the end of scene 18, bar 440), 10 (Sarastro's first aria: Act II), 6, 7, 5, 8 (from bar 441 to end), 2

Köhler prefaces his proposed order of composition for Act II with a comment on the 'far more complex compositional process':

12, 11, 18, 21 (first and third sections), 14 (first part), 20, 13, 15, 16, 17, 19, overture ('contour'), overture (trombone parts), 1 (timpani part), Act I ('filling out' ['Füllwerk']), 21 (fourth = last section), Act II ('filling out'), then, to complete the composition, 14 (second part), 21 (second section), 8 (wind and timpani parts), 12 (wind and timpani parts), 21 ('filling out' of last section), 9, overture ('filling out'), 9ª (threefold chord)

Köhler identifies eleven phases of the compositional process (some of the distinctions here are not immediately clear):

(1) The serious parts of Act I and Sarastro's first aria in II, which are concerned with Tamino's actions, or with his characterization.

(2) The comic plane, especially Papageno, but including ironic portrayal of the Priests – the close of no. 12, and no. 11.

(3) Interruption of (2) in order to characterize the serious aspects of the Priests; then back to (2), especially to Papageno, and his forthcoming union with Papagena.

(4) The Queen's second aria (written during continuation of work on phase (2)).

(5) Serious scenes connected with the forthcoming trials of Tamino and Pamina.

(6) Outline ('contour') of overture, with its 'seven points of thematic reference': Sarastro, Priests, Tamino, Papageno, Queen, Ladies and allegorical rôle of the flute.

(7) Filling out of Act I.

(8) Composing of closing scenes of Act II finale.

(9) Filling out of Act II; completion of Queen's second aria and of Act II finale.

(10) Filling in gaps in the score and continuation of the filling out of the Act II finale.

(11) Completion of remaining parts of the composition: Priests' march, filling out of overture, and threefold chord.

Alan Tyson has identified eleven paper-types in the autograph (in addition there are three further leaves of which two contain the trombone parts for the overture, and the third − with its ten staves the only leaf in the entire score to depart from Mozart's normal choice of twelve-staff paper − contains the threefold chord. A comparison with the autograph scores of Mozart's other late operas reveals that there are seven paper-types each in *Le nozze di Figaro* and the original 1787 version of *Don Giovanni*, two main types in *Così fan tutte* (just twelve leaves are on other types), and five in *La clemenza di Tito*. The unusually large number of paper-types in the score could be attributed to several factors: Mozart was in financial difficulties and may have been unable or unwilling to purchase a large quantity of paper at one time; or perhaps his movements between Vienna, Baden and Prague (though he certainly had his hands full enough with *Tito* during his weeks in the Bohemian capital to have pushed the German opera to the back of his mind) encouraged him to have small quantities of paper with him; or − and this factor excludes neither of the previous ones − perhaps the nature of the work, with large stretches of spoken dialogue separating almost all the musical numbers, lent itself to piecemeal composition whereby Mozart would use whatever paper lay to hand (no fewer than fifteen of the twenty-one numbers are contained on six or fewer leaves, taken from nine paper-types).

Table 1A

Paper-types in the autograph score of *Die Zauberflöte*

For ease of reference the paper-types are numbered (Roman numerals) according to the order of their first occurrence in the score; the musical numbers (Arabic numerals) run from 1 (introduction) to 21 (Act II finale). One large sheet of paper, folded into four quadrants and cut, yields two bifolia or four leaves.

Type I Overture (complete); no. 16 (complete); no. 17 (complete); no. 19 (complete); no. 1 (trumpet and timpani parts for bars 40–6)

Type II No. 1 (apart from an inserted single leaf – see Type III; and the trumpet and timpani parts – see Type I); no. 3 (complete); no. 4 (first sheet = bars 1–56)

Type III No. 1 (inserted leaf with a bridge passage to replace the deleted cadenza; Tyson (1987, pp. 21 and 345 n. 18) suggests that this leaf is from the sheet on two leaves of which the 'Ave verum corpus' was written on 17 June 1791, which implies that Mozart was already revising no. 1 at this time)

Type IV No. 2 (complete); no. 4 (second sheet = bars 57 to end); no. 8 (complete); no. 10 (complete); no. 12 (first three bifolia = bars 1–103); no. 21 (two sheets, the first of which has a leaf inserted in the middle = bars 57–80, 92–134, 179–243)

Type V No. 5 (three of four sheets = bars 1–177, 242 to end); no. 13 (first bifolium = bars 1–41 [81]; no. 15 (complete); no. 21 (last two sheets and bifolium = bars 736 to end)

Type VI No. 5 (fourth sheet, inserted in middle of third sheet = bars 178–241)

Type VII No. 6 (complete); no. 7 (complete); no. 21 (inserted single leaf = bars 81–91)

Type VIII No. 9 (complete)

Type IX No. 11 (complete); no. 12 (last sheet = bars 104 to end); no. 14 (complete); no. 18 (complete); no. 21 (four sheets and three bifolia, covering four separate passages in the Act II finale = bars 1–56, 135–78, 244–438, 501–61)

Type X No. 13 (third and last leaf = bars 42 [82] to end); no. 20 (apart from glockenspiel part, see Type XI); no. 21 (three sheets and one bifolium = bars 439–500, 562–735)

Type XI No. 20 (glockenspiel part – one leaf); no. 8 (flute, trumpet and timpani parts – one leaf); no. 12 (flute, trombone, trumpet and timpani parts – one leaf); no. 21 (flute, trombone, trumpet and timpani parts – two leaves)

Sketches and fragments survive for the following numbers:

Overture (Mozarteum, Salzburg: copy of lost original; Deutsche Staats-bibliothek, Berlin: Type I paper – one leaf)

No. 8 (Uppsala, University Library: Type V paper – one leaf; Deutsche Staatsbibliothek, Berlin: Type V paper – one leaf)

No. 9   (New York, Pierpont Morgan Library: Type I paper – one leaf)
No. 11   (Uppsala, University Library: Type V paper – one leaf, containing also the sketches for no. 8 and for no. 21)
No. 21   (Uppsala, University Library: Type V paper – one leaf, containing also the sketches for no. 8, and for no. 11; Type X paper – one bifolium, containing sketches in score)

Analysis of the paper-types of which the autograph score is made up permits one to draw certain conclusions about the order in which at least parts of the opera reached their definitive form. If one begins at the end, as it were, and considers first of all the two items that Mozart entered in his *Catalogue* right at the end of the period of composition, two days before the first night, one finds that the Priests' march, no. 9, is written on paper (Type VIII) that Mozart used for most of the solo arias in *La clemenza di Tito* (Tyson 1987, pp. 52–4); and the draft for the march (which obviously precedes the fair copy) is on a paper-type that Mozart used only after his return from Prague in mid-September.[15] This paper-type also occurs in the Masonic Cantata (K 623; dated 15 November 1791), and in sketches for and the autograph score of the Requiem. In *Die Zauberflöte* it is used both for sketches for the overture and for the overture itself, and in nos. 16, 17 and 19, as well as for the trumpet and timpani parts of no. 1 (Mozart preferred twelve-staff paper – though he complained to his father about its short-comings on 20 July 1782 in the context of having the score of *Die Entführung* copied – but it did have the disadvantage that extra sheets had to be used in heavily scored music for winds and timpani). From this information one can deduce that the final revision of the introduction (no. 1) was not carried out until shortly before the first night, and that, despite the impression created by the entry in the *Catalogue* that the opera lacked only the two purely instrumental numbers which were added at the last minute, no fewer than three vocal numbers were also written, or at least only attained their final form, in that hectic period (perhaps less than a fortnight in duration) after the return from Prague: the terzetto for the Three Boys ('Seid uns zum zweiten Mal willkommen'), Pamina's aria, and the much-discussed terzetto for Pamina, Tamino and Sarastro ('Soll ich dich Teurer nicht mehr sehn?').

Useful confirmation that the Act II finale was probably completed before Mozart's journey to Prague is provided by the existence of sketches for *La clemenza di Tito* (now in Uppsala, in the University Library) on paper that contains drafts for no. 21 of *Die Zauberflöte* (Tyson 1987, p. 332, n. 9).

Working on the assumption that Mozart normally used up his supply of one paper before turning to another, we can readily see from the list of paper-types in the autograph score which parts of the score, being written on the same paper-type, probably date from the same compositional stage. What this list does not reveal is that single sheets of paper, divided into bifolia or single leaves, are shared between the following numbers of the score, which posits a closer temporal or thematic link between them. The following instances occur:

Table 1B

Type IV	No. 8, the last three bifolia, matches no. 12 (first three bifolia)
Type IX	No. 11, second and third quadrants, matches no. 18, first and fourth quadrants
Type V	No. 13, fourth and first quadrants, matches no. 15, third and second quadrants
Type X	No. 13, third leaf, probably matches no. 21, bifolium containing bars 562–97
Type IX	No. 14 matches three separate bifolia in no. 21, covering bars 135–78, 244–66 and 405–38
Type I	No. 16, first bifolium, third and second quadrants, matches no. 17, second bifolium, fourth and first quadrants
Type I	No. 16, second bifolium, fourth and first quadrants, matches no. 1, inserted leaf with trumpet and timpani parts, second quadrant

On the basis of the evidence now available there is a considerable measure of agreement between Köhler and Tyson about the ordering and interrelationship of numbers within the score, though the picture may well be modified in the light of the detailed reports that we may expect from both authors. It will be interesting to see whether Köhler can, for instance, equate his claim about the order in which the four sections of the Act II finale were composed with the layout of the score – the fact that no new section of the finale begins on a new leaf implies that at least in outline the entire number was composed consecutively (that Mozart *thought* in shorter units is suggested by his careful counting of the number of bars, the figures – ranging over his sixteen sub-divisions between 129 and [5] – being inserted before changes in tempo or time-signature (rarely at a modulation or change to Recitative)).

It is hoped that this survey of the evidence provided by nineteenth-century commentators, the casual remarks in Mozart's letters, his entries in his *Catalogue*, the first edition of the libretto, and the results of the analysis of the paper-types of the autograph score, will leave little room for doubt that the opera was substantially complete before the end of July, that rather more than has generally been thought had still to be written (or revised) after Mozart's return from Prague in mid-September – and that study of the autograph and its paper-types permits insight into the sequence in which the opera was written.

5   The libretto

The identity of the author

The debate about the authorship of the libretto of *Die Zauberflöte* should have ended in 1901, with the publication of Egon von Komorzynski's study, *Emanuel Schikaneder. Ein Beitrag zur Geschichte des deutschen Theaters* (revised second edition Vienna and Wiesbaden, 1951). Komorzynski demonstrated that there was no valid evidence to support the authorship of anyone else, and more positively that all the available evidence, internal and external, pointed to Schikaneder as the author. During the remainder of his long life Komorzynski returned to the theme many times, adducing fresh material and going over old ground – not always, it must be admitted, strengthening his arguments or avoiding speculation. Despite the force and repetitive nature of his evidence, Komorzynski's arguments were often ignored – particularly, in a British context, by Edward J. Dent, whose books *Mozart's Opera The Magic Flute. Its History and Interpretation* (Cambridge, 1911) and *Mozart's Operas* (London, 1913; revised second edition 1947) further the claims of Karl Ludwig Giese[c]ke and continue to influence generations of Mozart lovers whose language is English (Dent cites Komorzynski's book of 1901 as providing proof of the range of the librettist's borrowings, but does not mention the arguments about the authorship).

The clearest and most convincing statement against Gieseke's authorship of the libretto is contained in an appendix to Otto Rommel's magisterial study, *Die Alt-Wiener Volkskomödie* (Vienna, 1952). Rommel concludes his detailed presentation (pp. 979–91) by summarizing as follows:

(1) *Die Zauberflöte* is closely bound up with Schikaneder's artistic development;
(2) Gieseke's personal and artistic qualities are such that he could not have written the libretto;

87

(3) Gieseke cannot have made the claim to authorship which Julius Cornet reports in his book *Die Oper in Deutschland und das Theater der Neuzeit* (Hamburg, 1849), for the following reasons:

(a) this revelation was not made until two generations after the event described, and one generation after it is supposed to have been spoken;

(b) none of the other five people present ever confirmed or repeated the claim;

(c) of Cornet's witnesses, the most important, Ignaz, Ritter von Seyfried, never referred to Gieseke's claim, though he does name him as the man who drew Schikaneder's attention to Wieland's *Dschinnistan*;[1]

(d) none of the writers of memoirs, letters and other personal documents refers to Cornet's revelation or Gieseke's claim; and

(e) Gieseke's name does not occur among the lesser figures who are mentioned as possible collaborators of Schikaneder's, even though he was more prominent than the others. (For Cornet's report, see chapter 4, pp. 71–2).

It hardly helps Cornet's case that he describes the appearance of Gieseke at the time of his reappearance in Vienna in the summer of 1818 (more likely 1819)[2] as being distinguished by a 'venerable snow-white head' – Gieseke was fifty-seven or fifty-eight at the time, and as his portrait by Sir Henry Raeburn[3] (painted in 1817 and presented to the Dublin Royal Society) shows, he looked young for his years, and his almost completely bald dome is set off by dark hair around his ears.

Of all the reasons put forward by Rommel, the most productive lies within the respective œuvres and characters of Schikaneder and Gieseke. On the face of it, the latter – in his second career as a mineralogist a successful, esteemed professor at the Royal Dublin Society, and known as Sir Charles Lewis Metzler von Giesecke – is the more likely candidate for distinction (if authorship of *Die Zauberflöte* would have been considered a mark of distinction in the nineteenth century). That is one reason why it is unlikely that, in 1818 or 1819, when already secure in his new life, Gieseke should lay claim to authorship of a book that, then as now, comes in for as much censure as praise. Gieseke had not been above passing off as his own work a plagiarism of Friederike Sophie Seyler's libretto *Hüon und Amande*, which as *Oberon, König der Elfen* and set to music by Paul Wranitzky enjoyed popular success in Schikaneder's theatre from 7 November 1789 as well as in several German theatres. In the plays and libretti written during his years in Vienna Gieseke shows no sign of originality or artistic distinction. His few successes were won with adaptations and translations, and travesties. At the time of the writing of *Die Zauberflöte* the thirty-year-old Gieseke was a minor actor and occasional dramatist at the Theater auf der Wieden. Apart from

Oberon – a competent arrangement – he achieved nothing until the late 1790s that might have encouraged Schikaneder to use him as a collaborator, or even as a versifier (the burlesque *Der travestirte Hamlet* of 1794, published in 1798, contains some clever rhymes among much very ordinary doggerel). His one undoubted popular success was the farce he wrote in 1799 for his own benefit night, *Der travestierte Aeneas*. By the time this play was published in the following year, Gieseke had ceased to regard himself as belonging to the world of the theatre, as is made clear by his entry in the album of Otto Hatwig.[4] His twelve-line doggerel entry in the album is signed and dated '... Gieseke m[anu] p[ropria] Wien. 1800. d. 30 Junius k.k. priv. Mineralhändler', that is to say, he already had obtained an imperial and royal patent to trade in minerals.

The argument for Schikaneder's authorship is strengthened by the prefaces to some of his later opera librettos in which he conducts an acrimonious dispute with Christian August Vulpius, whom he castigates for the extensive, fussy and self-aggrandizing revisions he made to Schikaneder's works when preparing them for performance in Weimar.

The most important of these statements is Schikaneder's 'Vorrede' to *Der Spiegel von Arkadien* (Vienna: Ochss, 1795). This preface, dated Vienna, 14 June 1795, seven months to the day after the opera's première (the music is by Süssmayr), begins by thanking the public for its support for the work. He goes on to say sarcastically that his experiences with *Die Zauberflöte*, which was attacked by scribblers, has prepared him for animosity directed towards his latest product.

Herr Vulpius, to whom I have already said a few words on this subject, was kind enough to snip it [i.e. *Die Zauberflöte*] up into three acts. But I have already forgiven the kindly copier – for that is all he was – for this service, since, as his work shows, he hasn't any idea about music. – For if that were not the case, how could he have thought of mutilating an opera which I thought through diligently ['fleissig durchdachte'] with the late Mozart; how could he have thought of ending an act with an aria, which may have been the fashion some twenty years ago, breaking off the principal interest of the action?

Schikaneder comments further that 'a certain theatre journalist in Regensburg had the nerve to inform some actors that he had been my collaborator on my Zauberflöte. Such impudence verges on knavery.' He says further that this journalist had once sent him a totally unusable opera that showed not the slightest grasp of what works on the stage. As the figures show – 198 performances of

Die Zauberflöte in two years, as well as 73 of *Der Spiegel von Arkadien* in six months — Schikaneder's own works really do have something to them. 'For — and there are examples enough — the best musical scores have failed if the librettos are bad.' His own creed is then set out succinctly:

I write for the pleasure of the public, I don't claim to be a scholar. I am an actor — a director — and I work for my box-office; not at all to cheat the public of its money: for a sensible man is not taken in a second time.

Before concluding with compliments to his public, Schikaneder says that this is to be his last word in response to all the vexations he has been exposed to. There is no preface to the edition of this libretto that was published in the following year, but he was unable to resist prolonging the dispute in the *Pro memoria*! of 25 September 1796 printed in the libretto of *Der Königssohn aus Ithaka* (Vienna: Hoffmeister, 1797). This lengthy exercise in self-justification includes several quotations in Latin and one in Greek; its tone is again scornful of Vulpius for his clumsy and shameless plagiarism, this time of *Der Spiegel von Arkadien* (which he had renamed *Die neuen Arkadier*). His argument is backed up by several comparative examples from the two versions. The final paragraph includes the statement:

I have never pressed an opera of mine on Herr Vulpius, anyone they displease is welcome to let them lie. My Zauberflöte is already in its third edition, not counting the reprint ... It continues to please, here and elsewhere, in its original form ...

Plagiarism at the hands of Vulpius was not the only problem Schikaneder was faced with. To judge from an article in the *Wiener Theateralmanach auf das Jahr 1803* there was widespread rumour that Schikaneder relied on collaborators. Joachim Perinet, the author of this article ('Neuerbautes', pp. 66–88), which was devoted to the then new Theater an der Wien, wrote:

Here, too, a rumour must be denied, one that has unjustly become almost universal, and would have it that Schickaneder is not the father and actual begetter of his theatrical children. It has been demonstrated that the plan and dialogue are his own, and Herr Winter, who is also inspector of this theatre, will attest it; for only he, and perhaps he alone, can read Schickaneder's deliberate hieroglyphics, which he is always the first to receive for copying. That Schickaneder did not write all the verses of his opera, however, he himself does not deny.

This rumour, as we have seen, was refuted by the librettist as early as the summer of 1795, but clearly it persisted. In a period in which copyright as we now know it did not exist, and originality frequently meant no more than the ability to make good use in new ways of more or less familiar material, accusations of plagiarism were frequent, and doubtless justified. However, they become important only in the case of works which proved to be of more lasting value than the normal run of ephemera. That Schikaneder's success aroused jealousy as well as admiration is to be expected, but it is rare to find anyone bothering to doubt his rightful claim to authorship of his works other than *Die Zauberflöte*.

Whether or not he and Mozart expected the continued and indeed ever-growing popularity of *Die Zauberflöte*, we can assume that the librettist took unusual care with the book – witness the exceptionally wide and complex range of source-materials on which it is based (see chapter 1), its structural coherence and the depth of its characterization (one can even argue that the minor inconsistencies add to the work's interest and appeal). Ironically, it is precisely the literary imperfections of the book that were most often criticized, then as now; here if anywhere Schikaneder may have turned to collaborators for assistance.

If Perinet may not seem the most unbiased witness for the defence in a case of plagiarism, since he himself was principally an adaptor of the material of others (see pp. 31–4), at least he was in the right place and at the right time to give his comments a plausibility lacking in the pronouncements of others. On the face of it, the testimony of Ignaz Castelli, noted poet, dramatist, translator and man of letters, might be considered more reliable. He is, however, among the commentators who were either too young at the time, or then living elsewhere, to have authentic first-hand knowledge of the events they purport to describe. His memoirs, the bulk of them not written until late in his long life, contain a number of reminiscences about Schikaneder and the Freihaustheater. Castelli (1781–1862) admired Schikaneder as a natural poet, and claimed some familiarity with his theatre and company by virtue of having stood in for his violin-teacher at performances in the Theater auf der Wieden, where he also appeared as a monkey in the Act I finale of *Die Zauberflöte*. This is what Castelli had to say about the help Schikaneder was rumoured to receive in the writing of his plays:

A priest, a friend of Schikaneder's, is said to write his plays for him, and the latter then published them under his own name. About this I can say what follows with certainty: There was at that time a priest called Wüst, attached to St Stephen's, who was a regular visitor to my grandmother's house and was addressed as 'Cousin'. The man busied himself with dramatic works, especially magic plays, for which he usually made models of the necessary stage machinery. I know that Wüst was acquainted with Schikaneder and often visited him. It may well be that he was his collaborator; but from my knowledge of Wüst, he was certainly a man who could give advice and practical help in the matter of scenery, but I never saw a trace of fantasy or originality in him.[5]

The most important objection to our taking Castelli's comments at face value is that most of the activities and persons he refers to — his standing in for his violin-teacher in the Freihaus orchestra and the names he gives for the singers in *Die Zauberflöte* — demonstrably date from a period between five and ten years after the opera's première.

Gieseke's copy of the libretto

An important and little-known copy of the first edition of the libretto of *Die Zauberflöte*[6] deserves careful examination, puzzling as some of its features are. It is leather-bound and elaborately tooled, and lacks the two engraved illustrations. The printed pages have been interleaved with a rather heavier paper. The title-page bears the signature 'Gieseke'; the name ends in a flourish which was the contemporary contraction 'mp', i.e. *manu propria*. Tradition has it that Karl Ludwig Gieseke was stage-manager for the first production of the opera; the playbill for the première lists him in the speaking rôle of First Slave. Some of the manuscript stage-directions inserted into this copy of the libretto accord ill with our assumptions and knowledge of the production. A problem is that much of the writing on the interleaved pages, and some of it on the printed pages, was cut away when the volume was trimmed for binding. Most of the manuscript stage-directions are written in black ink; some, along with the signature on the title-page, are in a paler brown ink; the writing tends to be firmer on the interleaved pages which, being of better quality paper, have absorbed less surplus ink.

The great majority of the handwritten stage-directions are shortened paraphrases of the familiar directions from the printed libretto; they were clearly cues to the stage-manager to facilitate his control over the essentials of the performance: scene-changes, entrances and exits, properties. For instance, the first manuscript note (in brown ink) reads 'Act I. Sc. 1. Felsentheater' (i.e. 'rocky theatre'); the second (in black ink) reads: 'Tamino mit Bogen, ohne Pfeil, die Schlange verfolgt ihn' ('Tamino with bow, without arrow, the snake pursues him'). The student hoping to gain insight into technical or interpretative details of the first production from this libretto will on the whole be disappointed − there are no indications as to how the stage-machinery worked, no instances that show that details of the production were changed in the course of the long run of performances (except perhaps for ones in II, 2 and 20, which are discussed below).

The first scene-change − that at I, 6, for the first appearance of the Queen − is headed: '*Verwandlung*. Sternproskekt' (*recte* 'Sternprospekt'; 'Transformation. Starry backdrop'); for the following scene the legend is 'Verwandlung. *Scena VII. Felsentheater*'. At I, 9 the trimming of the leaves has removed part of several words, but there is no difficulty in reconstructing the full text (editorial emendations are in square brackets); the fact that the first five words (underlined) are written in brown ink, the following lines in black ink, points clearly to two different stages in the insertion of stage-directions: '*Scena 9*. / [Ägy]*ptisch Zimer, Seitenthür* / Verwandlung. Die Sklaven / [tr]agen die Tisch, Pölster und / [Te]ppich heraus welche sie aufbreit[en]' ('Scene 9. / Egyptian room, side door / Transformation. The slaves / carry in the table, pillows and / carpet which they spread out.') At Papageno's entrance in I, 12 the essentials are again brought out: 'Papageno approaches the window from outside, then he enters with the glockenspiel. Has the portrait suspended from a ribbon round his neck.'

The next points of note in Gieseke's manuscript jottings occur right at the end of the act. The published libretto has as the last direction before the curtain: '(Two [Priests] bring a kind of sack, and cover the heads of the two strangers.)' The handwritten direction here glosses the passage as follows: 'die 2. Priester komen. d[er eine] / hat einen grünen Sak vo[r den] / Tamino, der andre hat [eine] / [Kas ?]-perlhaube vor den Papageno. / Sie sezen ihnen selbe auf, und / nehmen ihnen die Flöte und / das Glockenspiel ab.' ('the 2 priests come. One has a green sack for Tamino, the other has a Kasperl bonnet [?] for Papageno. They put them on them and take from them the flute and glockenspiel.') Trimming has removed some details, most tantalizingly the prefix to the description of the headdress that is placed on Papageno; it is difficult to think of any other syllable of the appropriate length that would make sense than one that equates his headgear with that favoured by Kasperl La Roche, the comic star at the rival Theater in der Leopoldstadt – in one extant picture, a large, floppy, broad-brimmed hat rising to a point.[7]

The handwritten production notes for Act II are even more informative than those for Act I. The first, which might well be considered to have been entered some twenty-seven pages too early, reads: '*NB The food, the flute* [and] *glockenspiel must be put in the Boys' flying chariot* [which] *they bring in sc. 16.*' An interesting minor detail, which may well reflect on the number of choristers available for the production, and/or on the space available on stage, is entered in brown ink opposite the first stage-direction of the act. It will be recalled that the printed text calls for '18 leafy seats' for the priests. Gieseke's note (the trimmed right-hand margin calls for some imaginative reconstruction) reads: 'Act II. Sc. 1. Palm grove, 14 seats, 14 horns, 14 pyramids.' The implication is that, for practical reasons, the number of participating priests was reduced from 18 (3 x 6, including Sarastro) to 15 (3 x 5, i.e. 14 plus Sarastro).

The first major puzzle posed by the handwritten production notes occurs at the start of II, 2. This is the scene in which Tamino and Papageno are led into a dilapidated forecourt of the temple. Although the trimming has here removed even more than usual of the additional material, the word 'Quodlibet' is clearly visible. At this period the term quodlibet was commonly used in three distinct ways in the Viennese theatre: it could be (a) a collection of plays, or of loosely connected items, (b) a pasticcio and (c) a pot-pourri or musical switch (e.g. the wind serenade that accompanies Giovanni's last supper in Mozart's opera). There is no indication either in the printed text or in the manuscript notes as to the meaning of the term; the same is true when the term is used again, this time spelt 'Quod libet', in II, 20. Were the word intended to indicate replacement of the next musical numbers (the duet 'Bewahret euch' in II, 3 and the chorus 'O Isis und Osiris' in II, 20) by pot-pourris, the words of the familiar numbers would probably have been struck out and the incipits of the replacement numbers written in; nothing of the sort occurs. And no musical or textual quodlibet copies or sketches in any way connected with *Die Zauberflöte* are known to me.

A possible explanation may, however, be put forward. If the term quodlibet is here interpreted quite literally, meaning 'what you will', 'whichever pleases', then the direction could point to a choice between two numbers. An early tradition has it that some variety was introduced into performances of the opera by the use of alternative numbers (see p. 209). It has been asssumed that an earlier version of no. 7 ('Bei Männern') was sometimes substituted, for instance. The hypothesis that I now put forward is that Gieseke's copy of the libretto may throw some light on the matter, namely that the term 'Quodlibet' at the opening of II, 2 indicates that in this scene-sequence either no. 11 ('Bewahret euch vor Weibertücken') or the unauthenticated duet for Tamino and Papageno ('Pamina, wo bist du?') was to be performed, but not both; and that 'Quod libet' before II, 20 meant, say, that either no. 18 ('O Isis, und Osiris, welche Wonne') or the terzetto no. 19 ('Soll ich dich Teurer nicht mehr sehn?') was to be performed.

It might be objected that, since the Tamino/Papageno duet was reputedly not performed until 1802, by when Gieseke was no longer in Vienna, his copy would not contain such an annotation. However, the libretto as a stage-manager's copy would have remained theatre property; and the different colours of ink, and the differing hand-writing, would certainly support the assumption that the copy remained in use for a number of years.

Scene 13 (transformation to a hall in which the Boys' flying machine can operate) is for no obvious reason headed 'Mondtheater' (i.e. 'Moon theatre', 'lunar landscape'?). The printed stage-direction at the opening of this scene contains a rare deletion to Schikaneder's original wording: the last six words of the following sentence are crossed out in pencil: 'Das Flugwerk ist mit Rosen und Blumen umgeben, wo sich sodann eine Thüre öfnet.' ('The flying machine is bedecked with roses and flowers, in which a door then opens.') Whether this deletion was because the actual flying machine had no door, or whether Gieseke – if it was he who made the deletion – was reacting against the contorted syntax, can only be a matter for speculation.

The handwritten notes for the next few scenes contain no surprises; they follow the normal pattern of highlighting for the benefit of the stage-manager the entrances, with the appropriate props, the exits, and the off-stage music and sound effects ('Accord' or '[3. maliger] Posaunenton', i.e. 'Chord' or '[Threefold] trombone call', and '[starker] Donner', i.e. '[loud] thunder').

The inserted directons at II, 20, apart from the 'Quod libet' already discussed, are a shortened paraphrase of the original text. The additional directions in II, 22 are of interest, pointing up as they do a generally unremarked symmetry between Papageno in this scene, and Tamino in I, 15, just after his arrival at the temple. 'A voice cries: Stand back! (then a thunder-clap; flames burst from the door; a loud chord.)' The thunder, flames and chord are an intensification of the moment when a voice twice stopped Tamino in his tracks in the first finale; and, of course, they also provide a comic element in that they frighten Papageno. Gieseke's gloss here reads: 'The voice from the right side. Loud *thunder*. Flames burst from the door. Chord.' At the other door, the one by which he entered, the extra direction indicates: 'On the left, as above, etc.' Schikaneder's libretto only indirectly conveys that, like Tamino in I, 15, Papageno tries the right-hand door first, then the left-hand door, before being accosted by the Spokesman. The practical nature of Gieseke's production notes is again borne out by the entry concerning the appearance of the glass of wine which Papageno requests. It comes 'out of the ground' according to the printed text, 'up through the trap-door' in the manuscript note.

II, 26, like II, 13, is on the interleafed page headed '*Mondtheater*' (both times written in brown ink). Since the hall in which scenes 13 to 19 play is not stated to be illuminated by moonlight, and the garden of scene 26 is by implication lighted by the pale glow of early dawn ('Bald prangt, den Morgen zu verkünden, / Die Sonn auf goldner Bahn ...'), the obvious explanation that 'Moon theatre' merely means that the stage is moonlit, is unsatisfactory, the more so as II, 7 (Pamina asleep in the garden, with the moonlight falling upon her face), a much stronger candidate for this interpretation, has the manuscript heading 'Garten, *Mondsc*[hein]', with the second word firmly crossed out (the fact that a pencil scrawl lower on the same page is a copy of these words suggests that a child has at some stage got hold of the volume rather than that a production detail was reinstated). The one obvious link between II, 13 and II, 26 (cf. also II, 29) is the presence in both of the Boys' flying machine; it would be far-fetched to suggest that a stage-director in 1791 saw the *Flugwerk* (*Flugwagen* in Gieseke's notes) as a kind of lunar module after the analogy of the vessel that supposedly transports gullible mortals to the moon in the various settings of Goldoni's *Il mondo della luna* (e.g. that by Haydn, Eszterháza, 1777).

II, 28 (the trials by fire and water) is headed in the handwritten notes '*Feuertheater*. / Verwandlung. / Tamino wird von den / Geharnischten mit dem Sak / hereingeführt.' ('Fire theatre / Transformation. Tamino with the sack [over his head] is led in by the Men in Armour.') Pamina's entry a page later is likewise accompanied by a handwritten note specifying that she, too, is brought in 'with the sack'. The covering of the heads in this scene is not called for in the printed libretto; indeed, the description of Tamino ('lightly clad, without sandals'), and the implication that Pamina enters alone, rather than is led in, bear out the implication that the lovers at this stage are not blindfolded. On the other hand, the last of the six coloured engravings of scenes from the opera made by the Schaffer brothers, which shows Tamino and Pamina awaiting their trials, and which includes two priests who are called for neither by the music nor the text, has one of the two priests carrying over his arm what look uncommonly like two head-cloths, or 'sacks' (see Plate 8, p. 188). Since neither the Gieseke annotations (which do not mention the priests here) nor the Schaffer illustration (which shows Tamino wearing ankle-boots, and anything but lightly clad) tally with the printed libretto in these details, one is no nearer to an informed opinion on the validity of the manuscript production notes or on the identity of the production represented in the Schaffer pictures.

The next manuscript note of interest occurs at the opening of II, 29; it amplifies the description of the garden given at the opening of scene 26: '*Garden, moon, grassy bank*' (brown ink), and 'Papageno with pipe and a rope' (black ink). When the Boys descend in their flying machine a note specifies that they have Papagena with them, and when they ascend, that fact is made more obvious in the handwritten addenda. Gieseke's notes do not have a separately numbered scene for the last attempt of the Queen and her entourage to destroy the temple; instead, '*Scena XXX. / Soñentheater.*' (i.e. 'sun theatre') is appended at the point where darkness gives way to light (conversely, the printed text numbers the Queen's last appearance as scene 30 and does not number the final tableau). Gieseke's abbreviated (and in the binding more than usually harshly trimmed) notes here contain one of very few mistakes, neatly corrected – in place of 'Tamino and Pamina are in [priestly] attire ...' he originally wrote 'Tamino and Papageno ...'.

What light does this copy of the libretto throw on the old controversy about the authorship of the text? If one accepts that the signature on the title-page is genuine (there is no reason to doubt it), might one not have expected some explicit assertion from Gieseke of his own claim (if he felt himself to be the true author, deprived by Schikaneder of all credit) and his disapproval of Schikaneder's proprietorial attitude? As we have seen, there are a number of minor unclarities in the handwritten additions but the principal purpose of the notes is clearly to draw attention to the stage-directions as they affect the progress of the performance, functioning as the stage-manager's cues for directing entrances and exits, and indicating the props and lighting required for the coming scene. None of the handwritten notes can be considered critical of the work or its author. I conclude that this copy of the libretto provides further evidence against the claim that Gieseke was its author.

The figure of the bird-man

The best-known and most lovable of operatic bird-men has a broad-spreading family tree. A recent acquisition by the Getty Museum at Malibu, California − an Attic red-figured vase of two dancing men dressed as birds, perhaps an illustration of Aristophanes' *The Birds*[8] − may remind us of Papageno.

A late French prose romance, *Le Chevalier du Papegau*, may be remotely linked with Schikaneder's bird-man. A parrot, borne in an elaborate golden cage on the back of the eponymous knight's horse (the knight is in fact King Arthur), sings to encourage its master despite its own cowardice. Though this romance does not seem to have been translated into German, common elements occur in it and in Wirnt von Grafenberg's epic *Wigalois* (*c.* 1204−9). Hendricus Sparnaay detects 'striking resemblances' between it 'and the *Chevalier du Papegau*; in both, for instance, the prize of the beauty contest is not a sparrow-hawk [as in other versions of the story] but a parrot'.[9] *Wigalois* was known in the eighteenth century, mainly through a frequently reprinted late fifteenth-century *Volksbuch* retelling that keeps the essential details of the original: the prize is a talking parrot in a golden cage, along with a magnificent horse. A version was included in Reichard's *Bibliothek der Romane* (1778), and a travesty was published at Leipzig in 1786.

A more central branch of Papageno's family tree points to the Italian theatre. Egon Wellesz in his contribution to the *Festschrift Otto Erich Deutsch zum 80. Geburtstag*, 'An ancestor of Papageno', exhumes a comic intermezzo from the Pariati/Conti opera *Teseo in Creta* that was performed at the Vienna court on 28 August 1715. The comic figure, Pampalugo, disguises himself as 'Papagallo' in his efforts to gain the love of Galantina ('little chicken'; cf. 'gallina', 'a hen'); they sing together in duet with 'papaga' calls and with the same rising demisemiquaver run (here in the violins) that is familiar from Papageno's pipes.[10]

The eighteenth-century Viennese theatre can show numerous instances of bird-men and bird-catchers. In Heinrich Rademin's

Plate 1   Act I, scene 17: 'Das klinget so herrlich' – Papageno (with dulcimer), Pamina and Monostatos

Runtzvanscad, König deren Menschenfressern (printed in 1732) the comic servant Hanns-Wurst uses his magic golden horn to win the love of the initially unenthusiastic Babiccia; when she, later thinking that she has lost him, soulfully strokes a swan, Hanns-Wurst pops out of the swan, and they sing a merry duet. The surviving collection of *Teutsche Arien* – song-texts for the popular comedies performed at the Kärntnertor-Theater – includes *Bernardon Zettel-Trager ... und betrogener Vogel-Jäger-Junge* ('Bernardon bill-sticker ... and deceived birdcatcher's apprentice'). In 1783 a carnival farce, *Der Haushahn* ('The domestic cock'), by M. von Schönborn with music by Hofmeister, was performed in the Kärntnertor-Theater: it was a parody of *Der Hausvater*,[11] Lessing's translation of Diderot's *Le Père de famille*; it was performed some thirty times in the Court Theatre between 1770 and 1805 and was later revived. Included in the same vogue was Baron Gemmingen's sequel, *Die Familie*, which from 1781 in Schröder's arrangement was even more popular than the Diderot/Lessing original. Since these works were in the repertory at the time when Schikaneder was performing in Vienna in the mid-1780s, there is no need to look far to find a predecessor for the bird-man strutting about on the stage. Further, in 1784 Barbara Fuhrmann staged a play in the small theatre 'beim Wasen', close to the River Wien, that included swans and peacocks in its dramatis personae.[12] Marinelli staged Hensler's *Kasperl' der glückliche Vogelkrämer* ('Kasperl the happy bird-seller') for the first time on 3 March 1791; by the time of the première of *Die Zauberflöte* it had already been given thirteen times.

Another and then living link between *Die Zauberflöte* and the Italian stage is Carlo Gozzi. Mozart's first recorded contact with the plays of Gozzi was brought about by a request from Schikaneder.' K 365ᵃ (Anh. 11ᵃ) is the lost (recitative and) aria 'Warum, o Liebe, treibst du jenen grausamen Kurzweil' which Mozart, then in Munich preparing for the production of *Idomeneo*, wrote for insertion into *Peter der Grausame, oder Die zwei schlaflosen Nächte*, an adaptation of Gozzi's *Le due notti affanose* that Schikaneder staged during his winter season at Salzburg in November/December 1780. Just over a year later, on 15 December 1781, Mozart discussed Gozzi's *Il pubblico segreto* ('das öfentliche geheimnüss') in the course of a letter to his sister; there were four Gozzi plays in the repertory of the Burgtheater in the 1780s, including *Die zwei schlaflosen Nächte*, and Schikaneder took over into his *Der wohltätige Derwisch* (1793) the motif of a cabinet of silence from a fifth, *Il re cervo*, and a further motif from a sixth, *Il mostro turchino*. *Il re cervo* was not at that time staged in Vienna, though it is probably nowadays one of Gozzi's better-known plays, thanks in part to Henze's opera of 1956, *König Hirsch*. From *Il re cervo* Schikaneder may also have derived something of the figure of the bird-catcher, who appears under the old *commedia dell'arte* name of Truffaldino. The stage-direction (I, 5) describes him as follows: 'Truffaldino, in oriental fashion, dressed as a bird-catcher in green, carrying many little pipes [i.e. panpipes] in a ridiculous and comic way.'[13] Apart from his similarity in appearance to Papageno, Truffaldino goes on to claim that he had slain a stag found dead, so as to secure a reward (cf. Papageno's acceptance of the credit for someone else's feat of slaying the serpent).

The qualities of the libretto

Language and prosody

It has long been fashionable to decry the libretto of *Die Zauberflöte*, to express amazement that Mozart agreed to set such a text to music and to make apologies on his behalf that he did so. The truth, as Goethe saw, is rather different:

> The text ... is full of improbabilities and jokes that not everyone is capable of understanding and appreciating; but one must in any case grant the author that he has understood to a high degree the art of making effective use of contrasts and of producing grand theatrical effects.[14]

Schikaneder, unlike Varesco, one of Mozart's other operatic collaborators (*Idomeneo*, the abandoned *L'oca del Cairo*), was an experienced man of the theatre: actor, singer, dramatist, composer, producer and manager. When we read Mozart's letters in which he discusses his problems and concerns in setting *Idomeneo*, *Die Entführung* and *Figaro* we come across numerous statements about the primacy of music and the need to adapt and alter the libretto in the interest of dramatic coherence and musical impact. There is abundant evidence that Mozart himself took a major part in the shaping and reshaping of the text. That he had a hand in the final stage and in points of detail of *Die Zauberflöte* can be demonstrated not only by the divergencies revealed by a close comparison of printed text and autograph score,[15] but also by the superior quality of the libretto to any of Schikaneder's numerous other products – as well as by Schikaneder's statement in his foreword to the printed text of his *Der Spiegel von Arkadien* (1795) that he had diligently discussed the opera with Mozart (see above, p. 89).

The finished product is admirably suited to its purpose. One does not demand that a libretto, especially one written for the popular theatre, should have literary quality. Certainly there are banalities in it – 'Wo ist sie denn?' ask the Second and Third Boys, after the First Boy has said that Pamina is tormented by despair; 'Sie ist von Sinnen!' the First Boy replies ('Where is she then?' – 'She's out of her mind!'). The rhymes, too, are weak, even bathetic, at times, as when Papageno on his entry in the terzetto no. 6 produces the tortured 'Leute ... Kreide'. Attempts to improve the linguistic qualities of the libretto (it is in the verses, if anywhere, that Schikaneder accepted help) have not achieved notable success, even if the version of the text found in the first full-score edition of the opera[16] contains improvements in points of detail. Criticisms of inconsistency, even of absurdity, in the plot are common (for some examples, see chapter 9); they are rarely raised by people who are thoroughly familiar with the spoken dialogue – which is all too frequently cut or rewritten for theatrical purposes, or ignored in the concert-hall and recording studio. The balance between spoken dialogue and music, their inter-relationship, is exemplary; Schikaneder tells the story with skill and economy – hardly a line lacks point. There is pathos in the spoken words of the Queen, dignity (and a not unattractive touch of human frailty) in the dialogue of Sarastro, ardour in Tamino, simple good humour and a sense of fun in Papageno (his speech tinged with Austrian German inflections, but entirely free of the specifically Viennese language of Perinet – or of Schikaneder himself in his *Lokalstücke*). We cannot expect to comprehend Monostatos unless we pay attention to his spoken utterances (which should be kept free of such traditional instrusions as 'Herr ... ich bin unschuldig!' – 'Sir ... I am innocent!' in II, 11). The simple fact is: however sympathetically we may respond to Mozart's appellation of 'German Opera' and Schikaneder's of 'Grand Opera', the work is a very superior Singspiel.

Schikaneder was no poet, which is not to say that his libretto for *Die Zauberflöte* is anything other than well suited to Mozart's musical intentions. The rhymes may creak from time to time, the images be banal, but the metric control is masterly almost throughout, and well varied (not least by variation between masculine and feminine line-endings). The basic pattern is of iambic four-beat lines (for instance, throughout no. 2, Papageno's entrance-song); iambic three-beat lines are also quite common, both within a longer number, and for instance in the first four lines of each strophe of Sarastro's second aria (no. 15, 'In diesen heilgen Hallen') before a return to the much commoner four-beat lines of the closing couplet. Five-beat iambs are the metre of the Queen's second aria (no. 14, 'Der Hölle Rache kocht in meinem Herzen'), with telling interspersion of stressed syllables at the start of the second, third and eighth lines, the broken dactylic contrast (— ◡◡) suggesting barely controlled anger; comparison may here be made with the pathos of the same character's narration in her first aria (no. 4) of the kidnapping of her daughter. Schikaneder intended a dactyl at 'Nŏch sĕh ĭch ĭhr Zĭttĕrn', but Mozart set it amphibrachically (ᵕ—ᵕ | ᵕ—ᵕ); the last four lines again show a difference between Schikaneder's intended iambs, and Mozart's incisive trochaic accentuation, with added dactyl ('... sie zŭ bĕfreiĕn ...') and – at the start of the last two lines – triple upbeat subtly strengthening the blandishments of the injured, emotionally disturbed Queen.

Many of the ensembles are rich in metrical and rhythmic changes, which frequently point up progression from one dramatic situation to the next; this can naturally be most clearly discerned in the long and complex finales, but the opening ensemble (no. 1) provides a good example. The dactylic stabbing cries for help of Tamino are set as four amphibrachs, immediately followed in score as in libretto by three dactyls and a trochee (—ᵕ) for the second line. The setting of this passage provides an excellent early example of what one may term the productive tensions between words and music: Schikaneder's iambic 'Ach rettet mich! Ach schützet mich!' become trochees in Mozart's frenetic repetitions. The dramatic entry of the Three Ladies (for which Mozart decided to hold in reserve the trumpets and timpani in a late revision; see pp. 131–2) is metrically irregular, though they soon settle into four-beat iambs, which persist until the reduction to three-beat iambs at 'So geht und sagt es ihr'. The modulation to G major with change of tempo and time-signature to Allegretto ⁶⁄₈ briefly suggests a dactylic beat, though alternating four-beat and three-beat iambs are quickly re-established, a pattern that persists to the end of the number.

Not surprisingly, we find that most of the solo numbers are metrically simple and straightforward. Papageno's no. 2 consists of four-beat iambs, albeit set by Mozart with the opening phrase as an anapest (ᵕᵕ—); his no. 20 has three-beat iambs, though the varied refrain has two dactyls to the line ('Dann schmeckte mir Trinken und Essen'). His suicide scene (II, 29) reads on the page as four-beat trochees, though Mozart introduces rhythmic variety by setting 'P̆ăpăgĕnŏ frisch hĭnauf! Ĕndĕ deinĕn Lĕbĕnslauf!' anapestically, effectively producing three-beat lines. Monostatos' aria (no. 13) is in four-beat trochees, given variety by Mozart's preference for irregular phrasing and accentuation. Pamina's aria, no. 17, reads on the page as regular four-beat trochees, with alternating feminine and masculine line-endings, but Mozart extends and varies the simple pattern with his longer and shorter repetitions of phrases. Sarastro's no. 10 is also simply structured – perhaps deceptively so, in that it might at first glance be read strophically. However, the differing rhyme-scheme of the two quatrains (*a b a b / c c d d*) and the move from iambic four-beat lines in the first to dactyls followed by what read as trochees in lines 3 and 4 (following the dactylic effect of the enjambment between lines 1 and 2) reveal a subtler touch, one that doubtless helped shape the musical setting – for after the first two lines there is no upbeat, and all four lines of the second quatrain begin dactylically. Not the least interesting feature of this famous aria with chorus is that, at least as late as the preparation of the printer's copy for the first edition of the libretto, it was headed 'Chorus'.

The two duets are also direct and unaffected in their verse. No. 7 ('Bei Männern'), like no. 10, say, which could not have been set strophically, and unlike no. 17 which might have been, has a varied metrical pattern in its two halves, not in the four solo lines (which rhyme *a b a b / c d c d* and could have been set strophically), but in the duet refrain, which has two lines (set by Mozart in six bars) the first time round and four (set in twenty-two bars) the second time round. Apart from repetitions, the other verbal features of this number that stand out in Mozart's music are the alternation between note-for-syllable setting and the varied use of slurs (for instance the melismatic treatment of 'Creatur' in contrast to the directness of its rhyme, 'Natur'); and the productive tension between Schikaneder's implied iambic metre in the refrain, and Mozart's enriching departure from it:

Schikaneder 'Wir wollen uns der Liebe freun, | Wir leben durch die Lieb allein.'
Mozart   'Wir wollen | uns der Liebe | freun, Wir leben | durch die Lieb al|lein.'

Even more remarkable in this number is Mozart's revision of his barring, carried out when he had composed as far as the final measure. Moving the bar-lines back by half a bar produces some unexpected accentuations (the emphasis now falls on 'welche' rather than 'Liebe', for instance); however, the musical gains outweigh the losses, and here presumably lies the reason for Mozart's second thoughts.[17]

By comparison the second duet, that for the two Priests, no. 11, is metrically uncomplicated, with alternating feminine and masculine four-beat iambs (set by Mozart with insistent three-quaver upbeat in its first three lines, asymmetrically answered by amphibrachs ('Er fehlte') and the weirdly emphasized 'und versah sich's nicht' (here for the first and last time in the number the flutes, oboes and bassoons move in thirds with the voices) before a new rhythmic pattern is established (twice repeated): 'Verlassen sah er sich am Ende' etc., before the startling incursion of the trombones to accompany bassoons and lower strings for the jocular *sotto voce* march rhythm of 'Tod und Verzweiflung war sein Lohn', sung twice, then eerily hammered out *piano* by virtually the entire *Zauberflöte* orchestra.

The terzetto for the Three Boys (no. 16) reads as doggerel four-beat iambs; the composer's procedure is to score it magically (with fluttering violin, and more sparingly flute and bassoon, figuration, and high cello line supporting the Third Boy), and to create the impression of a dactylic opening to each line (and phrase), which has the effect of turning the succeeding iambs into trochees, until (and it is here that the woodwinds re-enter the texture) the men are directly addressed; even now it is only in the phrase 'Du, Papageno ...' that the dactylic rhythm is challenged.

The finales are superb achievements not only in musical respects – the librettist has played a full part in constructing and versifying the verbal content. In one important respect the two finales are very different: the first, which observes unity of place (the grove in front of the temples), is continuous; the second, which includes three scene-changes, is in four musical sections. Schikaneder introduces sufficient variety into the basic four-beat iambs of both finales, most obviously with a move to trochees ('Schnelle Füsse ...', 'Könnte jeder brave Mann ...'; 'Wahnsinn tobt ihr im Gehirne ...', 'Klinget, Glöckchen, klinget ...', 'Heil sei euch, Geweihten ...'). Dactyls are used sparingly and effectively – to help convey curiosity (Tamino's 'Es zeigen die Pforten ...') and excitement ('Das klinget so herrlich ...') as well as, at times, doubtless for variety or convenience. Line-lengths range between three and six beats; the chorale of the Men in Armour alternates between six-beat and five-beat lines, introducing further variety by means of a dactyl ('Der, welcher ...') and the swing between iambs and trochees. Other metres (perhaps surprisingly, hardly ever a spondee ($- -$)) are sufficiently uncommon as to catch the attention when they do occur – anapests suggest themselves for 'Wer viel wagt' or 'Papagena!', amphibrachs for the closing chorus ('Es siegte die Stärke ...'); the first finale opens with the unusual structure of amphibrach plus trochee plus cretic ('Zum Ziele führt dich diese Bahn').

The fact that Mozart from time to time deliberately ignores the expected rhythmic pattern and chooses to emphasize words or syllables that would strike the reader as unimportant could, of course, be held to imply his dissatisfaction with the work of his librettist. The desire to 'correct' misaccentuation in part lies behind the anonymous revision of the libretto for the Simrock full-score edition of 1814. Had Mozart considered misaccentuations to be important he could have corrected them himself, or given the task of revision to his librettist. Certainly he altered Schikaneder's text in points of detail in numerous places, for instance the phrase describing Tamino's attacker in no. 1 (from 'dem grimmigen Löwen ...' to 'der listigen Schlange ...' − 'fierce lion' to 'cunning serpent').[18] Instead, for purely musical reasons he sets the unimportant words 'O [so eine Flöte]' in the quintetto no. 5 to a semibreve, and 'sonst [erwischen sie uns noch]' ('or [they'll catch us]') to a *sforzato* minim in a crotchet-and-quaver context in I, 16 ('Schnelle Füsse').

Of course, from the earliest years the libretto of *Die Zauberflöte* was not sacrosanct. Long before the first edition of the full score the text had been printed as a word-book and in vocal score with more or less far-reaching alterations. Of these the Vulpius version (Leipzig, 1794), at times hopelessly unmatched to the music, is the best-known and most useless,[19] but it has numerous rivals, including the libretto published at Passau in 1795[20] and those used at Mannheim in 1794 and at the first production of the work at the Vienna Court Opera in 1801.[21]

The motivation of the action

A recurrent problem for audiences and students of *Die Zauberflöte* is whom or what to believe. In the world of the fairy-tale − into which we find ourselves conveyed at the very start of the opera − normal standards of objective truth hardly apply; until we can perceive the basis of the moral and aesthetic standards that are to be the norm, we incline to accept the validity of statements that are made by characters whose truthfulness we see no reason to question. Thus when a young Prince in disarray is pursued by a serpent, and saved in the nick of time by the intervention of Three Ladies, we assume that they are on the side of good, an assumption that is only lightly thrown in question by the ensuing rivalry between them for the task of standing guard over the handsome stranger while the others report to their Queen. The case of Papageno is different. From the start − both the music and the words of his entrance song leave us in no doubt − we recognize that he is an engagingly sympathetic figure; beyond that, he is our principal source of information about the world into which the as-yet unnamed Prince has strayed (and into which we have strayed with him). Appropriately, he has limited knowledge of this world, even of his own identity, and none of the wider world; yet he cheerfully reveals what he does know, and because we already know the truth about this particular event we are disinclined to judge him over-harshly for accepting the credit, when it is offered to him, for rescuing the Prince from the serpent; and we furthermore feel sympathy for him at the punishment meted out by the Ladies.

With the gift to Tamino of the Queen's daughter's portrait the plot takes on a new depth. The tenderness and growing passion of Tamino's aria tell us of the genuineness of his love for the girl in the miniature portrait, yet this emotional commitment lays him wide open to the schemings of the Queen. It is, of course, not quite so simple − at this stage there is little justification for his or our questioning her sincerity. A parent who gives a bachelor a portrait of a beautiful daughter is conventionally employing a mild form of blackmail (as the more modern example of Count Waldner's enclosure of Arabella's portrait in his letter to his old friend Mandryka in the Hofmannsthal/ Strauss opera confirms); but in the case of the Queen of Night, we learn that her daughter has indeed been taken from her − even if the circumstances and the motives turn out to be subtly different from those her Ladies and she adduce. Even before her first appearance, the Queen has won Tamino to her cause (see his last speech in I, 5); the rhetoric of her first aria (flattery, underplaying of her own power, pathetic pleas, stirring encouragement of the rescuer-victor) leaves him confused in all else save his commitment to carrying out the task imposed on him;

TAMINO (*after a pause*) Is what I saw reality? Or do my senses stupefy me? − O, ye gracious Gods! Do not deceive me! or I shall fail your test. − Defend my arm, steel my courage, and Tamino's heart will beat in eternal gratitude to you. (I, 7)

His confusion reaches its height in the opening scene of the first finale (I, 15); ours, too, has been fuelled not least by the rôle of the Three Boys. They were invoked as the Prince's guide by the Three Ladies in the final section of the quintet no. 5 and characterized in the aetherially beautiful Andante in B flat with pairs of clarinets and bassoons accompanied at first only by unison violins *pizzicato* (bars 214ff.); Papageno has already told Pamina that, despite the Three

Ladies' promise, he and Tamino have seen no sign of the Three Boys who were to guide and instruct them (I, 14). Since the Prince had sent Papageno ahead to report his arrival to Pamina, it is perfectly reasonable to argue that the Boys do indeed fulfil the rôle accorded to them by the Ladies, but do so only within the precincts of Sarastro's temple, that is, the Boys no longer serve the Queen (whose moral lability is implied by her late husband's dying instruction that the sevenfold circle of the sun was to be handed over to the initiates: II, 8) – they only serve the cause of good. Their words of instruction to Tamino make a deep impression on him; yet the paradoxical nature of his quest does not escape him: 'This path leads thee to thy goal', the Boys have told him (that is, Pamina is held prisoner here); but he senses the majesty and righteousness of his surroundings ('Is this the seat of the gods? The portals and columns show that wisdom and labour and arts have their dwelling here; where industry is enthroned and idleness has no place, evil cannot readily maintain its dominion.').

Tamino's inherent moral uprightness and open-mindedness are now in conflict with the quest he has undertaken ('The purpose is noble, and pure and chaste. Tremble, cowardly villain! To rescue Pamina is my duty.') The conventional wisdom imparted by the Boys has been followed by the aesthetic impact made on him by the beauty of the temple; yet, as is immediately perceived by the Old Priest who challenges him at the entrance to the Temple of Wisdom, his response to the question what he seeks in the sanctuary ('The properties of love and virtue') is at odds with his inner turmoil ('Thy words are of exalted import. Only, how wilt thou find these qualities? Love and virtue do not lead thee, because death and vengeance inflame thee.'). It is the function of the Priest to question Tamino as to his motives, as well as to answer some – but not all – of the young man's questions: an intellectual exchange, following the Boys' instinctual advice and the aesthetic appeal of the beautiful temple. The Priest interrogates Tamino as to the reason for his hatred of Sarastro, and on learning that the young man is relying on the testimony of 'an unhappy woman, oppressed by grief and woe', warns him against accepting such evidence as the truth – even though the basic fact is, as the young man says, that Sarastro did abduct Pamina. Tamino's fear that Pamina may already have been sacrificed is not stilled until after the end of his interview with the Priest; for the moment he has to be satisfied with the assurance (nobly enunciated, to a 'knocking' Masonic rhythm) that his veil of doubt will be lifted 'As soon as thou art led by the hand of friendship into our sanctuary in an eternal bond'. For the moment, though, he is left alone to ask (though the audience asks with him): 'O eternal night, when shalt thou disappear? When shall mine eye find the light?' Off-stage voices comfort him with the information that Pamina is alive. From this time forth Tamino's resolve is clear and, despite his passing grief that the obligation of silence imposed on him causes Pamina to suffer deeply, it is unshaken.

Pamina's situation is very different (though she, like Tamino, faints on her first appearance on stage). We have no indication as to how long she has been held by Sarastro, but it is clear that she has equivocal feelings towards him. She tells Papageno that, if Sarastro were to see him in the temple precinct, his death would be an agonizing one (I, 14). Earlier, however – as the Third Slave reports – Pamina had saved herself from Monostatos' lustful intentions by invoking Sarastro's name. And when, in the first finale, the chorus hail his imminent entry, Pamina again fears the worst ('O friend, all is now lost for us!'). But she will not hear of lies or evasions when Papageno asks what they shall tell him: 'The truth, the truth, even if it were a crime.' And the reality turns out to be far more benign, even loving, than the reputation had led us to expect. In the priestly assembly at the start of Act II Sarastro explains that the gods have destined Pamina, 'the gentle, virtuous maiden' for the 'goodly youth'. But it is not made clear to Pamina either that she is being tested, or that Tamino is – whereas Tamino and Papageno are told by Sarastro at the end of the first finale that they are to be led into the temple of examination to be purified (in a performance the director must decide whether Pamina is meant to hear this instruction). The ignorance in which she is kept, and the implication that she is the first woman to be admitted, make her ordeal even more taxing than is that of the male initiates; and furthermore, she is torn between love and loyalty towards her mother, love for Tamino, fear of Monostatos and respect for the man whom her mother is trying to persuade her to kill (II, 8–12). In view of this inner conflict, which is sharpened by her conviction after II, 18 that Tamino no longer loves her, it is understandable that she fails to perceive the veiled message of hope in Sarastro's spoken and sung words in II, 21 (no. 19) and attempts suicide in the first section of the Act II finale (scene 27). It is only after the Three Boys have saved her and brought her comfort that she regains the serenity that will enable her to lead Tamino through the perils of fire and water ('A woman who does not shun night and death is worthy, and will be initiated', as the Two Men in Armour sing with Tamino).

With *Die Zauberflöte* as with Michael Tippett's libretto for *The Midsummer Marriage*, or Hofmannsthal's for *Die Frau ohne Schatten*, the reader's initial sense of bewilderment gradually gives way to understanding and appreciation. The more one re-reads, ponders and reads about Schikaneder's libretto, the more impressed one becomes at its depth, breadth, charm, humour and mysteriousness.

6 *The music*

ERIK SMITH

Mozart in 1791

The completion of *Così fan tutte* in January 1790 was followed in Mozart's output by a relatively fallow period of over a year.[1] He was forced to make his living in such unpromising ways as orchestrating Handel to sound more up-to-date, or composing for glass-harmonica and mechanical organ (admittedly producing some masterpieces). It may have been that work was not available − he made a desperate and useless journey to the imperial coronation in Frankfurt from September to November 1790 in search of patronage − rather than because of the exhaustion brought on by the pace of the last years (one might say of all the years) of his short life and by the early stages of the illness that was to carry him off in December 1791. At all events, there was little to prepare us for the incredible six months beginning around April 1791 in which he composed, beside some smaller works, the Requiem (a good part of it), the clarinet concerto and two operas which differ fundamentally from their predecessors.

They stand at the start of a new century, which may be said to open a decade early in the arts, as it does politically with the French Revolution. Compared with the baroque richness of *Idomeneo*, *La clemenza di Tito* shows neo-classical austerity. This essay sets out to reveal the new characteristics (taking a few examples from the many available) to be found in *Die Zauberflöte*: in its structure it broke free from the bonds of the eighteenth century, in its harmony it found simplicity for the sake of classical nobility but also to please its popular audience − appropriately enough at a time when the French Revolution was abolishing the age of the aristocrat. And, alone among Mozart's works, it contains the facets of German Romanticism − the fairy-tale, the symbolical and, in a sense, religious meaning, the closeness to folk-song and the exotic setting. It has certainly left its mark, until our own time, on Parisian Grand Opera, on Wagner's allegorical fairy-tales and right up to Tippett's *The Midsummer Marriage*.

Mozart's letters to his father from the time of the composition of *Idomeneo* and *Die Entführung* tell us about his views on dramatic construction and librettists, but there is little to be learned from the letters to his wife at Baden written in 1791. He alternately advised her to take good care of herself, and to be less flirtatious. He mentions a meal with Schikaneder on 7 June, but it seems likely that he had begun work on *Die Zauberflöte* after the completion of the Quintet K 614 in mid-April, because so little new music is entered in the *Catalogue* after that. On 11 June he wrote to Constanze, 'out of sheer boredom I have written an aria for the opera'. By 2 July he was asking her to get Süssmayr to return 'meine Spart'[2] of Act I up to the finale so that he could fill in the instrumentation. He entered the opera in his *Catalogue* as being completed before the end of the month. By then he had received the commission for *La clemenza di Tito*, which he composed and put on in Prague before returning to Vienna to write the overture and march for *Die Zauberflöte*, entered in his *Catalogue* on 28 September. The première took place two days later.

A new public

In composing for Schikaneder's Theater auf der Wieden, Mozart was writing his first opera for a popular audience. (His previous German operas, *Die Entführung* and *Der Schauspieldirektor*, had been written for the court.) His librettist was the experienced actor-manager Schikaneder himself, who well knew the ingredients to whet his public's appetite – humour, magic, stage machinery and more action than meditation. These factors were to have a radical effect on the musical structure.

Mozart's views on the Singspiels by his contemporaries were not complimentary. In 1781 he saw Umlauf's *Die Bergknappen* (very successful in its day) and commented: 'He took a year to write it, but you need not think that it's any good because of that. Entre nous, I should have taken it for a 14 to 15 day job.' And in June 1791, as we heard above (see pp. 31–2), he went to Müller's *Kaspar der Fagottist* and thought that there was nothing to it.

The new opera was to be quite different from these. For one thing there was a serious side to the story, with a musical depiction of the ideals of the Freemasons. For another there was that classical balance and homogeneity which distinguish Mozart's music perhaps above

that of all others and which would still reign over the new elements
brought in by Schikaneder and the demands of the popular audience.

Innovations in musical form in *Die Zauberflöte*

Mozart's earlier operas followed the contemporary practice of
combining arias, in binary or da capo form, usually on the sorrow
or fury of unrequited love, with recitatives and, in the case of *opera
buffa*, ensembles to advance the story. By the time of the da Ponte
operas sonata and ternary forms were the basic pattern: two examples,
'Dove sono' in *Figaro* and 'Per pietà' in *Così*, include a complete
return of the opening words and music. Most ensembles, for example
the quartetto and terzetto of *Don Giovanni* (analysed in Julian
Rushton's book on the opera in this series) or the Act II terzetto in
Figaro, are also in a kind of sonata form, though there are subtle
variations at the return of the opening to suit the developing situations
and words. Like the arias mentioned above, each of these ensembles
concerns a single more or less static situation with each character in
one prevailing mood, which makes the return of the opening music
at the recapitulation quite appropriate. The finales consist of a chain
of movements of this sort, each concerned with only one step of the
story.

But how did Mozart construct an aria or an ensemble out of
a sequence of events and out of changing situations and moods?
In the Act I finale of *La finta giardiniera* he had composed a busy
rondo, in which different characters entered with the same theme,
but with entirely different texts (see Ex. 1). This procedure is musically
effective (and was very commonly practised amongst Mozart's
contemporaries), but it hardly shows the composer's art of fitting
exactly the right music to every piece of the text at its most exalted
level.

Example 1

In *Figaro* Mozart departs from formal structure with its demand
for a recapitulation of the opening melody on several important
occasions. In 'Porgi amor' we get entirely new music instead of a
recapitulation: the text is actually the same as at the start, but the

Countess has now abandoned the controlled sorrow of the opening for a mood of greater despair, which calls for different music. Only the orchestral coda returns to the calmer music of the intro-duction. 'Deh vieni' has no melodic recapitulation, though the mood and rhythm of the opening are always with us. Mozart again rounds off the aria with the orchestra repeating the end of the introduction. The sextet predicts most clearly the structures of *Die Zauberflöte*. After the opening subject (Figaro reconciled to his parents) and a new section (Susanna's arrival and fury) the recapitulation is due: but Marcellina needs a new tune to explain to Susanna that she is Figaro's mother, so she is *accompanied* by the opening subject now played by the woodwind. This use of what we might call a vestigial recapitulation becomes the norm in *Die Zauberflöte*.

Whatever freedom he allows himself in the return of melodies, Mozart always adheres to the *harmonic* pattern of sonata form — the move to the dominant or relative major, the so-called develop-ment in various keys (which may be more concerned with *new* subjects than with development, depending on the demands of the libretto), the recapitulation and often a coda in the tonic.

Five pieces become strophic songs, a form more common in the Singspiel than in *opera buffa*. Each one is about a single subject: Papageno's nature and aspirations in nos. 2 and 20, love in no. 7, the lust of Monostatos in no. 13 and the ideals of the temple in no. 15. (There are variations in the melody of the second verse of no. 7 and in the accompaniment of the later verses of no. 20.)

But in the other arias and ensembles, the text, in developing new emotions and situations, will not permit a repeat of the same music. In 'Dies Bildnis', Tamino is led through admiration of Pamina's portrait (first subject) and the awakening of love (second subject in the dominant) to the thought of finding her (development ending on the chord of the dominant seventh). The thought is almost too much for him (a whole bar's rest). What would he do then? Well, (although he is back in the tonic key), certainly not go back to mere admiration of a portrait, as sonata form would demand. The violins lead him on with a tender phrase, while he expresses with gradually increasing confidence his hopes of embracing Pamina. The vestigial recapitu-lation occurs in bars 52–6 to the words 'und ewig wäre sie dann mein' ('then she would be mine for ever'), to the melody originally heard in bars 10–14 to the words 'mein Herz mit neuer Regung füllt' ('fills my heart with new emotion').

Apart from formal considerations, there is an emotional effect in hearing a melody for the second time, never more so than in those quintessentially Mozartian moments when a melody first heard in the major returns in the minor. In 'Ach, ich fühl's,' which fits into the harmonic pattern of sonata form, neither words nor music are recapitulated, except for that magical phrase (bars 12–13 'meinem Herzen') which returns (in bars 30–1 'so wird Ruhe') but now with the poignant sweetness of the B flat major phrase turned to the heartbreaking sorrow of G minor.

The Queen of Night's aria no. 14 has the appearance of an *opera seria* piece, but here again the recapitulation is only suggested. The return of the tonic D minor at bar 73 coincides, not with a repeat of the opening (which never reappears at all), but with a one-bar coloratura phrase taken from the second subject at bar 30. Apart from that, only the strikingly dramatic exclamation 'flammet um mich her' ('[death and despair] flame around me') in bars 8–10 (see Ex. 2) reappears in bars 80–2 and again, with modified rhythm, in bars 90–3.

Example 2

The system of the vestigial recapitulation, used occasionally in earlier operas, becomes the rule in *Die Zauberflöte*. Even in the overture, where he was not dependent on the demands of the text, Mozart used a truncated recapitulation, cutting the first twenty-three bars of the Allegro and beginning with the first *forte*.

Papageno's suicide aria in the Act II finale is in rondo form, but only the four-bar refrain (Ex. 3) returns. Its jolly nature is in amusing contrast to the woeful words.

Example 3

The ensembles are built on the same sort of principles as the arias. The quintet no. 5 could be described harmonically as a sonata rondo with coda, but not in the normal sense of a recurring melody, for Mozart constantly finds new words and new situations requiring new music. There are, however, a few phrases, sometimes very slight, which reappear to give the listener a faint feeling of unity. Here is the plan of the quintet:

> Bars 1–33 in B flat. Tamino commiserates with the padlocked Papageno. A perfunctory modulation brings
> Bars 34–77 in F. The Ladies release Papageno and they all moralize: a short modulation leads to
> Bars 80–132 in B flat with entirely new music. The Ladies present Tamino with the magic flute. More moralizing and another short modulation to
> Bars 133–71 in G minor. Papageno is ordered to accompany Tamino.
> Bars 172–83. A short E flat section in which Papageno is presented with the glockenspiel.
> Bars 184–213 in B flat. The new treasures are admired. After saying good-bye, the men remember to ask the way.
> The Andante in B flat forms the coda. The men are told of the Three Boys who will accompany them and they again take their leave.

Harmonically, then, this appears to be a rondo, but in fact the constant stream of melody has few repeats and no recapitulations. The phrase for 'O Prinz, nimm dies Geschenk' ('O Prince, accept this gift') in bars 80–4 (see Ex. 4) is used later for 'sind zu eurem Schutz vonnöthen' ('they are necessary for your protection') in bars 188–91: in both places the Ladies refer to the gift of the flute.

Example 4

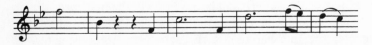

Also, the descending legato scales of the violins, accompanying the general admiration for the flute in bars 109–16, become descending staccato scales for the woodwind in bars 185–7 where both of the magic instruments are praised. Papageno's section (bars 133–83) is pervaded by his fluttering motif in the violins (Ex. 5) which becomes a fainter flutter during the farewell (Ex. 6). The whole ensemble is built with great economy and brevity: the text is only repeated in the

Example 5

Example 6

way one might expect of a repeat in a play, that is where Tamino
tells Papageno he is sorry he cannot help him, in the little moralizing homilies that are dotted through the entire opera, or in the
farewell.

The next encounter between Tamino, Papageno and the Three
Ladies, the quintet no. 12, shows a similar construction. Here,
however, there is a single situation throughout: that of the Three
Ladies trying to deflect the steadfast Tamino and the gullible
Papageno from their new duties. Mozart, therefore, binds the
first half of the quintet with a recurring instrumental phrase (Ex. 7)
which at first represents the sweet blandishments of the Ladies.

Example 7

When Tamino adopts it by singing his rather platitudinous refusals
to it, the Ladies drop it altogether and begin a new sweet strain at
bar 112. When this, too, fails, they all join in singing of the resolution of men who will not speak foolishly. In the end the Three

Ladies are driven off by the threatening cries of the Priests (off-stage) — an anticipation, both dramatic and musical, of the routing of the forces of night at the end of the opera.

The finales

The finales bear little relation to the tight constructions of those in the da Ponte operas. In each new section of the latter, predicament was heaped upon predicament to lead to the greatest excitement of the greatest number of people before the curtain came down. The Act II finale of *Figaro* is a perfect example, and the type lives on in Rossini. The finales of *Die Zauberflöte* are more episodic, for the libretto presented Mozart with a number of separate scenes not necessarily connected with those that follow. This is particularly true of the finale to Act II, which consists of four virtually separate and self-contained pieces:

1. In E flat, scenes 26 and 27, in which the Three Boys rescue Pamina from her suicide-bid.
2. In C minor (ending in C major), scene 28, in which Tamino passes the Two Men in Armour and is finally united with Pamina. Together they undergo the trials of fire and water. A hidden chorus hails their triumph.
3. In G major, scene 29, in which Papageno, disconsolate without the promised Papagena, is only saved from suicide by the Three Boys, who urge him to play his magic bells. This conjures up Papagena and they rejoice together.
4. In C minor (ending, with the same key-signature, in E flat), scene 30, in which the Queen and her Ladies, now joined by Monostatos, are foiled in their attempt to destroy the temple and are routed. Sarastro and the chorus celebrate the triumph of light over darkness.[3]

The Act I finale presents a continuous sequence of events in the normal fashion, with just one complete break in the middle, when the stage is left empty for a moment between the departure of Tamino at the end of scene 15 and the entry of Pamina and Papageno. Even then, these two scenes are cleverly linked, for in scene 15, with Tamino on stage, we hear the off-stage pipings of Papageno, and then in scene 16 when Papageno and Pamina have entered, we hear the off-stage flute of Tamino. The marvels of this finale cannot be fully described, but something must be said about the long scene in recitative, in which Tamino finds the Temple of Wisdom and meets the Old Priest, perhaps the most influential scene Mozart ever wrote in respect of later opera composers.

In Italian accompanied recitatives, the words were sung to that unmelodic so-called approximation to dramatic speech which had become a convention. It was left to the orchestra to intervene with a musical characterization of events and emotions. (French recitative, especially Gluck's and, of course, Italian recitative in the operas of Monteverdi, had already shown far greater musical expressiveness.) In Tamino's great scene, he often (and the Priest occasionally) breaks into highly expressive *arioso*. The orchestra performs several functions, in providing rhythmic impetus as it punctuates Tamino's short phrases (bars 39–49), in depicting his actual movements on the stage (bar 58, for example, and bars 68–71), and in describing feelings – not so much the ones spoken of but those as yet unperceived. Thus, when Tamino tells the Old Priest that he has come to seek the realm of love and virtue, his melodic phrase (bars 88–90) is intertwined with a short melody on the clarinets which anticipates the march of the Priests at the start of Act II, though at this early stage Tamino is far from believing that he will find love and virtue among the Priests. More remarkable still is the wistful little phrase (Ex. 8) (bar 102, and then bars 103–4 and 106–7) which contradicts Tamino's stern refusal, sung in these bars, to have anything to do with Sarastro;

Example 8

it also contradicts the Priest's rather cool behaviour. This phrase expresses the germ of Tamino's conversion to the goodness and truth of the temple. The Priest does not say much to help Tamino, yet at his exit we hear that falling sixth (bar 139) once more and a falling diminished seventh in the next bar. Tamino now prays for conversion to the faith of light (bars 141–3); the mysterious off-stage chorus, setting his mind at rest about the fate of Pamina, brings it about. Music and mystery are used as in Masonic ritual.

In the intermingling of recitative and melody, of discussion and emotion, of solo voices and chorus, the old division between the recitative and the 'musical number' is at last broken down. This is one of the important ways in which *Die Zauberflöte* pointed forward to the much freer construction of nineteenth-century opera.

When there is a text a composer can allow the music to be shaped by the words alone without the need to impose a form of the kind required by instrumental music. But the great composers have rarely been content to accept this solution. Wagner's formal solution was, of course, in the leitmotif, which, though directly related to the text of the moment, had its cross-references in the rest of the music. Even twentieth-century opera composers continued to demand some kind of musical structure. Berg and Britten both used such forms as variations and the passacaglia in their operas; admittedly these structures are not perceptible except to the prepared listener, but they must represent a useful loom, as it were, on which to weave the music. In *Die Zauberflöte* Mozart predicts this approach, for his form, sonata or rondo, has a harmonic plan which is hidden because it lacks the melodic landmarks.

Perhaps the most striking feature of all about *Die Zauberflöte* is the economy and brevity of each episode.[4] Words are not usually repeated. There are very few musical repeats, apart from the five strophic numbers: a 14-bar section in no. 1 ('Du Jüngling schön und liebevoll'), the two halves of the march, and very little else. If one asked an opera-lover brought up on Wagner and Verdi but not familiar with *Die Zauberflöte* to guess how long a duet Mozart had provided for Tamino and Pamina at the end of all their trials, the last music they sing in the opera, what might he guess? The answer is: two bars! *Die Zauberflöte* had no influence on the nineteenth century in this respect.

The setting of the text

We have seen that Mozart did not allow traditional concepts of form to impede him from telling the story in the most direct way and with exactly the right musical equivalent. More than that, he did not even allow the *text* to get in the way of the right musical expression. One might have thought that in at last setting an opera in his own language and after his own heart, he would have paid the greatest attention to reflecting the natural stresses required by the meaning of the words. But his opinion of librettists was not high: during the time of *Die Entführung* (when he had admittedly not yet met his two best librettists) he put them on a par with trumpeters – and his opinion of *them* is reflected in the very simple parts he trusted them with. He sometimes composed before he had received the actual libretto; he said of Osmin's aria: 'I have described the aria to Herr Stephanie

completely – and the essentials of the music were complete before
Stephanie knew a thing about it.'

Die Zauberflöte is full of wrong stresses, permitted by Mozart
because he regarded the character of the music as more important.
The very first words in the opera are a case in point. Why does
he put such weight on 'bin' in 'Zu Hilfe! Zu Hilfe! sonst bin ich
verloren'? when the accent would fall correctly on 'verlōren'.
('Help! or I'm *lost*', not 'I *am* lost'). The answer is partly in order
to stretch out what would be a rather banal two-bar phrase (Ex. 9)

Example 9

into something suitably irregular for Tamino's panic. And the
repeated high 'i' of 'bin' underlines that feeling of panic. Mozart
often makes Tamino sing his higher notes on that vowel, usually
considered to be so awkward on high notes. In fact, it appears
in our next illustration.

> Dies Bildnis ist bezaubernd schön,
> Wie noch kein Auge je gesehn!

The musical accents fall on 'Bildnis' and 'noch', while the sense
demands that they should fall on 'be*zau*bernd *schön*' and '*kein
Au*ge'. Yet the outburst on the top G, as Mozart wrote it, exactly
expresses the release of pent-up emotion, which was more important
to him. If the matter of the wrong accents had really worried
Mozart and Schikaneder, they might have changed the text here
to, say, 'Wie schön ist dieses Zauberbild' or to 'so reizend hold,
so zaubrisch schön' as in the Simrock full score of 1814, which
had the text re-arranged throughout to overcome these 'errors'.[5]

There are many other instances. Pamina sings 'Ach, ich fühl's, es
ist verschwunden' with the main accent on 'ist' (where it does not
belong, unless the sense was 'yes, it *has* vanished, whatever you may
say!'). Mozart's indifference to the matter of accented words is proved
by the fact that he sometimes made changes which put accents in the
wrong places when they had been right before. There is a sketch
correctly set as 'Pamina *ret*ten' (Ex. 10),[6] which in the final version
becomes 'Pa*mi*na retten' (Ex. 11), as though to say that he must rescue

Example 10

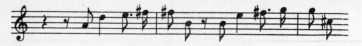

Example 11

Pamina and nobody else. Yet the latter version is musically the more interesting and also allows Tamino to dwell lovingly on the name of Pamina. He rebarred the duet no. 7 when he had nearly finished writing it, so that it now starts:

> 'Bei Männern *wel*che Liebe *füh*len,' instead of the
> original correct 'Bei *Män*nern welche *Lie*be fühlen.'[7]

A different case of Mozart flouting the sense of the words is in the chorus in the Act I finale:

Es lebe Sarastro, der	sotto voce
göttliche Weise,	f
er lohnet und strafet in	sotto voce
ähnlichem Kreise.	f

The dynamics make something mysterious and disturbing out of music that might otherwise have been a little banal, but they certainly have nothing to do with the words.

Mozart's music is in *Die Zauberflöte* always the perfect expression of the *meaning* of the words and the emotion behind the text. In no other opera does almost every phrase express the meaning in an unmistakeable manner. Two passages which do so more clearly than almost any other are actually songs without words – Papageno's humming through his padlocked mouth, and the 'pa-pa-pas' of the two bird-people's wooing.

There is also instrumental music vividly expressive for mime, as when Papageno first spies Pamina and cautiously enters her room (no. 6). Is there anything so descriptive in the earlier operas apart from the duel in *Don Giovanni*?

Every page of the score has examples of musical phrases which

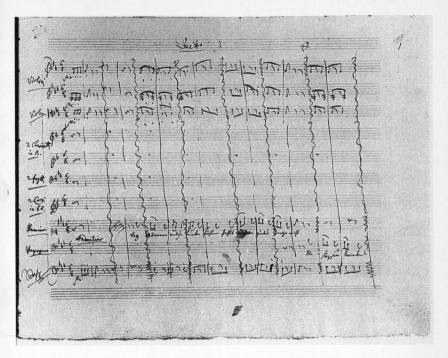

Plate 2.   Act I, scene 14: opening bars of the duetto 'Bei Männern, welche Liebe fühlen'

conjure up the characters: for example Pamina's gestures in her suicidal mood with its broken phrases finally healed by the courteous intervention of the Three Boys, in the restraining gesture that precedes 'Sollte dies dein Jüngling sehen' ('If your youth should see this') (Ex. 12).

It is, of course, in the nature of opera that the music should express the meaning and the emotion of the moment. Mozart had long practised the fine art, a particularly interesting exercise being in the

Example 12

entr'actes of *Thamos* (*c*. 1776–7), where the autograph bears explanations in the hand of Leopold Mozart ('the false character of Pheron', 'the honesty of Thamos', 'the treacherous conspiracy of Mirza and Pheron', etc.).

We know what emphasis Mozart laid on the character of Osmin's aria of rage in *Die Entführung*. Surely *Die Zauberflöte* shows the illustrative capacity of music at its most complete. But he did not easily arrive at that perfection. He owed much to da Ponte and Schikaneder. It is not by chance that *Idomeneo* and *Die Entführung*, for all the great beauty of the music, do not approach *Figaro* and *Die Zauberflöte* in popularity. In *Die Entführung* Mozart and Stephanie decided, presumably together, to set neither Selim's words nor the actual abduction and capture of the Europeans to music. In this way they eliminated most of the potential for drama, avoiding a true dramatic confrontation between Constanze and the Bassa in favour of the comic tiffs between Blondchen and Osmin. Apart from that, some of the music really does not fit the character of the text, for example that of the quartet no. 16. So much the worse for the text, since this is one of the most beautiful ensembles ever composed, none of it more so than the gentle *Siciliana* to which the ladies sing most unsuitably about their lovers' intolerable suspiciousness.

By contrast, the music of *Die Zauberflöte* not only mirrors the meaning of the text, but illustrates all the important actions and emotions of the opera. The dialogue is only needed for explanations, ritual and extra comedy.

The language of melody

It has been suggested that Mozart's melodic invention was drying up at this time and that he was consequently forced to borrow more than usual from his earlier works. Both A. Hyatt King (*Mozart in Retrospect* (Oxford, 1955)) and Jean Chantavoine (*Mozart dans Mozart* (Paris, 1948)) provide many examples of thematic relationships between parts of *Die Zauberflöte* and other works. It is a fascinating pursuit, though in the nature of the limitations of diatonic music there are bound to be many similarities. Mozart does seem to have connected particular emotions with particular phrases. There is surely the same kind of exultation in 'Dies Bildnis ist bezaubernd schön' (Ex. 13) as in Pamina's 'Tamino mein' in the Act II finale (Ex. 14) (and several times more in the scene that opens with it and in the flute solo that follows). There is exultation of a very different kind,

Example 13

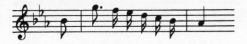

Example 14

but exultation nonetheless, in the Queen's 'Sarastro Todesschmerzen' ('Sarastro [must feel through you] the pangs of death') (Ex. 15).

Example 15

The same phrase in the minor illustrates revenge, as in the Queen's 'Der Hölle Rache kocht in meinem Herzen' ('Hell's vengeance boils in my heart') (Ex. 16) or in the Old Priest's 'weil Tod und Rache dich entzünden' ('because you are fired by death and vengeance') (Ex. 17).

Example 16

Example 17

One can also find melodic similarities with other works of the same period, such as Papageno's trembling 'motif' 'O wär' ich eine Maus' ('If only I were a mouse') (Ex. 18) to the 'Quantus tremor est futurus'

Example 18

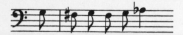

('What trembling there will be') in the Requiem (Ex. 19). And there are echoes of music of another period, such as the lovers' farewell 'Ach, goldne Ruhe' ('Ah, golden peace!') in the terzetto no. 19 (Ex. 20) to Ilia's 'Peggio è di morte' ('It is worse than death'), *Imeneo* no. 21 (Ex. 21) (the quartet, another parting of lovers).

Example 19

Example 20

Example 21

The phrase which opens the final chorus 'Heil sei euch Geweihten' (Ex. 22) had also appeared in the final chorus of *Idomeneo* ('Scenda Amor, scenda Imeneo') and in the reconciliation scene of *Figaro* ('Contessa, perdono' – an expression of 'All's well that ends well').

Example 22

Yet, the same phrase (admittedly introduced by a stern *unisono*) played in C minor by the woodwind and cellos at the opening of the scene with the Two Men in Armour, sounds full of foreboding and desolation.

None of these can be described as a 'leitmotif', but we do find that Mozart attached more or less the same meaning to a phrase wherever it occurs. A curious example, hard to explain in this sense, is in the striking phrase that opens the quintet no. 5 (Ex. 23). It also appears three times as Tamino tries the temple doors (when the third door opens, there is, in contrast to this descending arpeggio, a *rising* triad).

Example 23

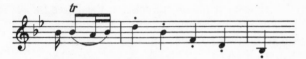

The same theme appears about twenty times in the *Idomeneo* recitative (no. 23) in which the High Priest describes the terrors inflicted by the monster. What have these serious moments got to do with Papageno's comic predicament? Perhaps the answer is that to Papageno the predicament was not comic at all and that Mozart, true dramatist that he is, sees things through his characters' eyes. When at last Papageno is united with Papagena and they foresee the arrival of a numerous family, the violins play this motif with a *rising* arpeggio (Ex. 24).[8]

Example 24

Musical characterization

If Mozart characterized every moment's thought and feeling, he also had a musical view of each character as a whole – the Queen alternating pathos with spitting venom, or Monostatos, small surely (the opposite of his colleague Osmin), always neurotically jingling (the accompaniment illustrates this more than his vocal part) except for the moment when he complacently cocks his ear to hear what his reward shall be. The expression of Tamino and Pamina is normally in the long, noble, legato line. The feminine wiles of the Three Ladies, sentimental and spiky by turns, are beautifully displayed, but the mere fact of having to write in harmony for three more or less equal voices makes it difficult to differentiate strongly between the Three Ladies, the Three Boys, the Slaves in no. 8 and the Priests in no. 18.

Papageno is usually seen as a totally simple merry fellow, but his suicide attempt should prevent a heedlessly merry interpretation of the rest of the part. Mozart brings Papageno's lugubrious side to our attention with surprising excursions into the key of G minor (the 'key of suffering'; see p. 130), not only in the suicide scene but also in no. 5, bar 134, where he tries to get out of the mission the Three Ladies have imposed on him and, more briefly in no. 12, bar 71, where he remains unconvinced by Tamino's steadfastness. Perhaps he is a less simple fellow than Tamino.

Of course, each character, except the Queen, also enters the musical styles of the others when taking part in ensembles. Sometimes one is not sure whose world it is: the duet 'Bei Männern', no. 7, seems to have the simplicity of Papageno's folk-tune-like melodies, but it is Pamina who starts it. In fact its long-spun melody, the legato aspect of which is emphasized in the decorated second verse, may be more appropriate to Pamina than to Papageno after all.

Sarastro is the most difficult character to assess, both dramatically and musically. His rôle in the story is strangely ambivalent: he turns from the supposed ogre of the opening scenes to the supposedly godlike leader of the later parts. He seems to have abducted Pamina on account of his own passion, which is hinted at in their encounter in the Act I finale. He calls her 'O Liebe' and admits 'du liebest einen andern sehr. Zur Liebe will ich dich nicht zwingen, doch geb ich dir die Freiheit nicht' ('O love, you love another very much. I will not force you to love, yet I do not give you your freedom'). If this is not the behaviour of an ogre, it smacks more of a Bassa Selim than of a wise priest. And why does he employ the unsuitable Monostatos and punish him so mockingly? We are concerned with the music here, not with the problems of the libretto, but did Mozart himself show ambiguous feelings about Sarastro and his establishment? The weird dynamics of the hymn of praise to Sarastro were mentioned above. Gerl obviously prided himself on his low notes, so Mozart − to the despair of many a bass-singer since − allowed him to display them rather ostentatiously, especially the unaccompanied low F on 'doch'. Is this to be taken entirely seriously?

The strange little duet, no.11, in which Two Priests sing of the dire consequences of heeding women's wiles, seems to be comic in intention. The perky setting of the words 'Tod und Verzweiflung war sein Lohn' ('His reward was death and despair') and Mozart's jocular quotation of them in his letter of 11 June strengthen this view.

It is difficult to love Sarastro's music quite as much as the rest of the opera. One reason may be that much of the opera is often performed too slowly.[9] 'O Isis' is a fine if slightly sanctimonious air. But 'In diesen heilgen Hallen', though full of excellent sentiments, shows in its melody a curious regular repetition of the same pattern, as though Sarastro pacing around felt himself hemmed in by the 'sacred walls' at every second bar (Ex. 25).

Example 25

etc.

The harmonic scheme

Mozart chose the keys for the pieces that make up an opera for three entirely separate reasons. He observed a general rule that each opera as a whole and, from *Die Entführung* onwards, each finale, though consisting of many pieces in different keys, should begin and end in the same key. In the later operas elaborate patterns become noticeable in the keys of successive pieces: thus, for example, *Figaro* has the succession E flat – B flat – G – C at the end of Act I, again at the start of Act II and almost immediately again at the start of the finale to Act II. In *Così* there are other patterns: the first five pieces of Act I move down a third at a time – G – E – C – A – F minor. The key-signatures of the first nine numbers in Act II are based on triads: G – B flat – E flat, D – F – B flat, E – G – C minor. In *Die Zauberflöte* there is no real pattern of this sort (another superfluous sophistication to be cast aside when dealing with essentials), but all the pieces of Act I before the finale are in the keys of the triad of E flat – E flat (or its relative minor), G or B flat.

The second reason for choosing a key is in the inherent character of that key. We shall come to the Masonic significance of keys later, but there are emotions and subject-matters which Mozart tended to attach to a particular key (as he did to a particular melodic phrase). This was partly on account of the wind-instruments that were at home in a particular key, often for purely practical reasons. So music of pomp and battle was normally in D and C, the keys for trumpets and timpani (though they were also played in B flat and E flat, especially in the later works). The clarinet, which conveyed tender feelings, took over the key of E flat more and more, though also happy to perform in B flat and A, but never in G.[10] D major is also a *buffo* key, G major a rustic key and so on.

Hermann Abert in his great biography claims that 'the key of the mystical basic idea is E flat, that of the world of the Priests is F, that of the dark hostile powers is C minor, while G major is reserved for the cloudless world of the comic figures. The key of suffering is G minor. At the most important points the representatives of the opposing powers leave their sphere to enter sharper keys, the Queen D minor and Sarastro E Major.' But, alas, the exceptions are often discovered almost before the rules! One must ask, for example, what Papageno (no. 20) and Monostatos (in no. 8, scene 19) are doing in the Priests' F major.

Mozart clearly did associate particular keys with particular subjects, though probably in an instinctive rather than in a schematic way. For instance, the key of C minor throughout *Die Zauberflöte* is nearly always connected with death or the threat of death:[11] the opening scene in which Tamino is pursued by the serpent, two phrases in the scene with the Old Priest 'weil Tod und Rache dich entzünden' ('because you are fired by thoughts of death and vengeance') and 'Wenn du dein Leben liebst so rede, bleibe da' ('If you love your life, speak, stay!'). In the second finale there are Pamina's thoughts of suicide, the chorale of the Armed Men with its reference to 'Todesschrecken' ('death's terrors'), the invasion of the temple by the forces of evil. Less obvious is the rôle of the key of A flat, a rather rare key in Mozart. In *Die Zauberflöte* it nearly always denotes rescue or relief after danger: the rescue of Tamino by the Three Ladies, the appearance of the Old Priest, the approach of the Three Boys to the demented Pamina, the passage after the chorale when Tamino is about to be joined by Pamina for good. Though the contrast is generally with the threatening C minor, it is interesting that Mozart turns for relief not to the relative major,

E flat, but to its subdominant A flat (strictly speaking, the first two of these examples are in A flat as the subdominant in E flat sections). But these recurring keys, like the recurring themes mentioned above, seem to be due to a subconscious procedure. If he had set out to use keys schematically, he would surely have differentiated between the grief of Pamina and that of her wicked mother, instead of using G minor for both.

The third reason for the choice of key is so obvious that it is rarely commented on: when Mozart invented a melody (to a given text and situation) to be sung by the voice available (he always composed with particular singers in mind) only one key was possible. For Tamino's glorious outburst at the opening of the Bildnis aria his top note had to be G – and that automatically made for an aria in E flat. Likewise, he had to modulate into F for Pamina's cry 'Tamino mein' for the sake of the soprano's radiant A. No other note would have done.

The orchestration

The accompaniment is always subservient to the main idea, the telling of the story, the depiction of the emotions. It never serves a purely decorative function as did the wind obbligati in *Idomeneo*, *Entführung*, *Così*, and even the contemporary *Clemenza di Tito*.

If this was partly because the orchestra of the Theater auf der Wieden was markedly inferior to that of the Nationaltheater, Mozart, as always, makes a virtue of a necessity and creates a score which could not be more ideally suited to its purpose. The only obbligati are of the two magic instruments, and these are used sparingly. The magic flute is only played twice (not counting the stage-direction that Tamino plays it in the dialogue of Act II, scene 17) and even then Mozart soon interrupts the rondo with flute obbligato to get on with the story (with just enough time to charm the wild beasts).

The chorus, too, is confined to essentials. In its first appearance in the Act I finale and at the conclusion of the trials it is not permitted a full-length melodic piece like the chorus in a similar position in *La clemenza* but has little more than a few bars of a glorified fanfare.

The accompaniment is kept as simple as possible.[12] An article by Gernot Gruber in the *Mozart Jahrbücher* of 1967 and of 1968–70 states that of the changes of instrumentation made by Mozart in the autograph, thirty simplified or reduced the scoring while only seven increased it. Most of the changes are very slight. Two of the most striking changes occur in no. 1. Originally there were trumpets and

Plate 3.   Act I, scene 1: opening of the *Introduction* in Mozart's autograph

timpani playing from the start (see Plate 3). They do add to the tension
of the scene. (Roger Norrington and Kent Opera included them at
one performance in Bath in 1980.) But Mozart must have decided to
cut them to avoid anticipating the brilliant trumpet entry as the Ladies
kill the serpent.[13] The other change occurs at the end of the piece,
where Mozart originally had a $^6_4$ chord followed by a full cadenza
for the Three Ladies, rather an amusing idea in view of their boastful
behaviour. But he crossed it out (see Plate 4).

When an instrument does have an independent line, not merely
a doubling part to support a voice, it must have a special significance.
The bassoon does in two awe-inspiring moments: in no. 4 (doubled
by the viola), as the Queen describes Pamina's terror at her abduction,
and in no. 21, as Pamina recounts the mysterious origin of the flute.

The encounter of Pamina and Sarastro in the Act I finale can serve
to illustrate Mozart's use of the accompaniment. In earlier works,
or in *La clemenza di Tito*, this confrontation would probably have
taken place in recitative, possibly in *recitativo accompagnato*.

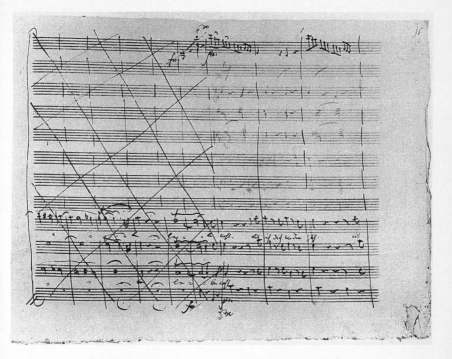

Plate 4. Act I, scene 1: last six bars of the deleted cadenza for the Three Ladies in the *Introduction*

But in *Die Zauberflöte* Mozart opened the frontiers between recitative and ensemble, so that this scene fits quite naturally into its surroundings. Pamina opens calmly and nobly 'Herr, ich bin zwar Verbrecherin' ('Lord, though I am guilty') with long notes over slow chords, but at the thought of 'der böse Mohr' ('the wicked Moor') her indignation becomes evident in the accompaniment figure in the violins (see Ex. 26). Sarastro replies with long notes and dignity,

Example 26

but when he begins to speak of love the flute joins him and leads him over his hesitation to a rather embarrassed repetition of the words 'einen andern sehr' ('you greatly love another'), and now, as he thinks of his own love for her, his heart-beats make themselves heard in the strings (Ex. 27) before he calmly tells her that he will not free her.

Example 27

At this, Pamina's thoughts of her poor mother make her more agitated than ever, as the violins indicate (Ex. 28). Sarastro answers sternly in unison with the dotted rhythm of the strings and, as Pamina calms down, the scene ends in conventional accompanied recitative.[14]

Example 28

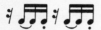

Most of the next scene is pervaded by the motif of the busy, neurotic Monostatos (Ex. 29). It is a beautiful irony that Tamino and Pamina first meet, as it were, under his auspices. For a moment the strings change to a smoother figure for this encounter (Ex. 30).

Example 29

Example 30

Immediately the chorus cry out 'Was soll das heissen?' ('What does this mean?'), the only time they abandon their formal duties, to create the most vivid tension – with just five notes in unison (Ex. 31). The effect is closer to 'Hagen, was tust du?' ('Hagen, what dost thou?') at the death of Siegfried in *Götterdämmerung* (Ex. 32) than to anything else in Mozart.

Example 31

Example 32

The scoring, though enormously varied, never exists for the mere sake of its own colour, as it does, for example, in the late dances for the Redoutensaal, but always, as in the greatest music of Wagner and Verdi, for the specific purpose of giving the right dramatic and emotional colour to the scene or to the moment.

As in all of Mozart's greatest operas, almost every piece has its unique tonal colour. Only five orchestral combinations are used for two pieces, none for three. For the Priests, basset-horns and trombones are present as a colour, not as solos (no. 10 even omits violins and double-basses for a special twilight effect). But Sarastro speaking informally, as it were, in nos. 15 and 19, does without them.

Mozart especially favoured the clarinet in his late years, perhaps because of its Freemasonic association, or his affection for the brilliant virtuoso Stadler, or just because he liked its sound. Clarinets appear, of course, in the tutti pieces – the overture and the end of the opera. They are naturally omitted from all pieces with basset-horns since they were played by the same musicians. If we exclude the C clarinets, which rather lack the warmth of the B flat and A clarinets and are principally used in pieces of a more military band-like character, nos. 11 and 13, the use of the clarinets indicates a subject of special importance, not specifically Masonic, in fact usually that of love – when the Three Ladies fall head over heels in no. 1, in Tamino's aria no. 3 and the duet no. 7 (all these in E flat). But it also characterizes the first mention of the Three Boys in no. 5 and the important announcements by the Three Boys at the opening of each finale. The most telling example is at Tamino's words 'Der Lieb und Tugend Eigentum' ('The realm of love and virtue') in his scene with the Old Priest. In the autograph we can see that Mozart, after writing four notes for the flute (which he used in the whole of this scene), crossed them out and

Plate 5.   Act I, scene 15: revised scoring in the scene for Tamino and the Old Priest

rescored them for the clarinets (see Plate 5) – which make no appearance apart from these two bars, if we discount the C clarinets mentioned above, between the beginning of the first and the second finale. The melody they play (referred to above as a sort of leitmotif) suggests the opening of the Priests' march no. 9 (where it is played by a flute and basset-horns). This detail of scoring must have been important to him, but seems to stem rather from the musical dictates of his inner ear than from a system of symbolical use of instruments (see 'Masonic symbolism' below).

The Three Boys sing for the most part without double-basses, which gives them a suitably air-borne effect. When they appear at the start of the Act II finale it is with a wind-band, like the one in *Così* suitable for a twilight serenade (here it is an aubade).[15]

Mozart is very conscious of the subtlest details of scoring: he calls on the first violins to play on the fourth string at 'schon nahet sie sich' in no. 1; he used trumpets and timpani both *con sordini* at the opening of finale I. The scoring for the trial by fire and water by no means attempts to depict those elements realistically but achieves a mysterious solemnity: under the flute's lonely melody, the brass chords followed by the timpani introduce a threatening gesture. Another subtle effect is the 'sempre pianissimo' (apart from two *sforzato* chords) in Monostatos' aria, giving a dream-like effect.

Masonic symbolism

There is no doubt about Mozart's strong links with the Masonic movement even before he was admitted into it in December 1784, for he had had Masons among his friends and had set Masonic texts. But the matter under investigation here, the musical effect of the Masonic influence, admits of less certainty. There are a number of musical characteristics to be found in Mozart's specifically Masonic works and partly in Masonic music by other composers. The problem is that all these characteristics also appear in other non-Masonic works: one could infer from this that even the instrumental music of the last years was composed very much with Mozart's Masonic ideals in mind. Let us examine some of these traits.

1. The harmony. Because of the Masonic significance of the number three, the key signature of 3 flats (and to a lesser extent of 3 sharps) had a special importance: so did C major, the key of light. In fact, Mozart does use these keys frequently but by no means exclusively in *Die Zauberflöte* and in his Masonic works, yet Sarastro only sings in E flat in his last few bars, while a character most opposed to light, Monostatos, has a C major aria.

There are also harmonic progressions said to have a special Masonic meaning, such as I – V – VI that opens the march of the Priests (no. 9) among many other examples in *Die Zauberflöte* (and appears in much non-Masonic music besides).

2. Rhythmically, three chords, as used in a specifically ritual manner in the opera, are obviously Masonic. Moreover, dotted rhythms are said to signify the resolution of the Mason and a dotted knocking rhythm to denote the candidate seeking admission. These are frequently present, but so they are in *La clemenza di Tito* (in such moments of firm resolution as no. 6, bar 4, no. 18, from bar 30, the end of no. 23 and the start of no. 24).

3. Certain melodic figures are supposed to have a Masonic meaning, for example a chain of pairs of legato notes, as in the accompaniment to the final chorus (Ex. 33), those moving in thirds and sixths, those associated with rising scales and arpeggios and so on. All these are present in *Die Zauberflöte* (and in the Masonic cantatas) but scarcely less so in the music of the Three Ladies than in that of the more enlightened circles.

Example 33

4. Counterpoint symbolized an order of equality rather than of general subservience to one melody and was therefore appropriate to the brotherhood of the Masons. Though its use in *Die Zauberflöte* is striking, it is, of course, even more widely used in eighteenth-century Church music.

5. Clarinets and basset-horns were favourite instruments in Masonic music. Mozart used the basset-horn in *Die Zauberflöte* quite specifically for solemn occasions (not, though, in the Priests' chorus, no. 18), yet he also used it in *Die Entführung* and *La clemenza di Tito*, but not in the Masonic cantatas.

The subject has been examined most thoroughly by J. Chailley in *The Magic Flute, Masonic Opera* (English translation London, 1972) and by Katharine Thomson in *The Masonic Thread in Mozart* (London, 1977). Professor Chailley believes that almost every melody, rhythm, key, harmony and detail of orchestration in *Die Zauberflöte* has its place in an immense system of Masonic symbolism. Though the beliefs and sentiments of the Freemasons were increasingly present in Mozart's mind, in a way which could not but affect his music, it goes against what we know about Mozart from the rest of his music to believe that his musical invention began to be based on forces other than purely musical or dramatic ones, in the way Schumann used cryptograms.

The musical style

It has been observed that Mozart combines a great variety of styles with perfect homogeneity in *Die Zauberflöte*, with its Viennese popular songs, Italian coloratura arias and *buffo* ensembles, accompanied recitatives and ariosos, hymns, chorales and fugues. The simple Singspiel style, derived from folk-songs, appears especially in Papageno's rôle and in the earlier parts of the opera. The frequent thirds which inevitably result from the three-part writing for the Three Ladies (and also the Three Boys) tend to lead to the 'somewhat melancholy character of German folk music' as Hermann Abert wrote of 'Du Jüngling schön und liebevoll' in no. 1.[16] Apart from the music for the Queen, Tamino's aria with obbligato flute and a few bars of Pamina's in no. 7, and her aria, no. 17, the opera is free of coloratura.

Die Entführung had been very different in that respect. 'Too many notes, my dear Mozart,' the emperor had been said to remark of it. By 1791 Mozart might have come to agree with him.

He still composed music suited to his singers, of course, but it had to fit the situation. He had admitted to 'sacrificing to Mme. Cavalieri's nimble throat' when composing the rôle of Constanze in 1781. He now wrote coloratura music of far greater virtuosity still for Josepha Hofer in the part of the Queen. This was in her line, since she had, according to some accounts, dazzled Vienna with her high coloratura in Wranitzky's *Oberon* in 1791, though one witness had called her 'a very disagreeable singer without the high notes for this rôle which she squeaks her way through' (Abert, *Mozart*, p. 646, note). The point is that her music is absolutely appropriate for two distinct reasons: *opera seria* is traditionally the vehicle for kings and queens; and the weird sound of stratospheric coloratura emphasizes the mysterious and sinister nature of the Queen.

The high-point of Mozart's assimilation of counterpoint into his own style came with the 'Jupiter' symphony in 1788. After his renewed acquaintance with the music of Bach (instigated by the visit to Leipzig in 1789) and of Handel (through his work on Handel's oratorios in 1790) he showed a special affection for counterpoint in a style by then archaic, in his fantasias for mechanical organ K 594 and 608 and in the Requiem. The Masonic Funeral Music K 477 of 1785 had been composed on a *cantus firmus* – perhaps the Protestant form was suggested by the English origin of Freemasonry in the eighteenth century – but now the scene of the Men in Armour begins as a full chorale prelude; the *cantus firmus* (taken from the old chorale 'Ach Gott, vom Himmel sieh darein' ('O God, look down from Heaven')), sung in octaves and doubled in the wind, is accompanied by a four-part fugato in the strings. It is a scene of great power and earnestness, in remarkable contrast to the mellifluous Allegretto that follows it 'Was hör ich? Paminens Stimme?' ('What do I hear? Pamina's voice?'), when the Two Men in Armour, who had seemed so inhuman, reveal themselves as really good fellows after all with 'Ja, ja, das ist Pamina's Stimme' ('Yes, yes, it is Pamina's voice'). Here again is that incongruous but delightful mixture of the supernatural with the informal, which is so beautifully reflected in Mozart's music.

Tradition has it that Schikaneder constantly urged Mozart to keep the music simple for his popular audience. When the composition of the overture could be put off no longer (it was always an eleventh-hour procedure), one can imagine Schikaneder, having reluctantly swallowed the counterpoint of the chorale prelude, saying with a nervous laugh, 'I suppose you're going to write a fugue and frighten the audience away before we've even begun' and Mozart drumming his fingers with a far-away look saying slowly, 'Schikaneder, you've given me an idea ...'

If one agrees with the claim made above that *Die Zauberflöte* shows the illustrative capacity of music at its most complete, the question still remains why we should regard as a supreme achievement a setting, however perfect, of a Singspiel text which, but for Mozart's music, would have been forgotten long ago like the rest of Schikaneder's output. There is, of course, the intrinsic beauty of the music. This also exists in his instrumental music, but the achievement of *Die Zauberflöte* is something more. If, then, it is not to be found in the music alone, still less in the libretto, it must have been produced by the reaction between the two.

How does the music of Mozart's operas relate fundamentally to his libretti? *Figaro* lives in the essentially eighteenth-century realm of irony; first of all the irony of comic or slightly dubious situations set to celestial music, then the irony of the situations in themselves. How often do the most moving moments arise from the laughter over a comic or somehow false situation – Susanna's retorts to the Count in their duet, the absurd dénouement revealed in the sextet, even 'Deh vieni', sung (at least to start with) to tease the over-suspicious Figaro. The hilarity releases the flood-gates of our emotion. *Don Giovanni* is all irony, in being about divine retribution in an age which had ceased to believe in it and about a man who set out to love all women and was incapable of loving even one. In *Così*, most of all, every emotion, however sublime the music that expresses it, is mocked by some irony.

Irony was not Schikaneder's strong point. (Sarastro's facetious remark to Monostatos on ordering his bastinado 'Don't thank me. It's my duty', proves this.) Nor was irony required by the opera or by the audience. How does the music for the genuine innocence of Pamina, Papageno and the Three Boys differ from the mock innocence of Susanna emerging from the closet to tease the Count with 'Signore! Cos'è quel stupore?' ('Sir, why so amazed? Take your sword and kill the page')? Not at all, really, it is the relationship between words and music that has changed.

In *Die Zauberflöte* the hidden meanings below the surface are no longer the ironical ones of da Ponte, but those of allegory, not just the Masonic allegories, but the central allegory of our journey through life and in the shadow of death. The characters are not depicted as vividly and naturally as those in the da Ponte operas. But this very failing helps to give Pamina and Tamino their universal quality, which perhaps provides the clue to the puzzling question – why is *Die Zauberflöte* capable of moving us most of all the operas?

For once, there is a truly happy end, not the improbable bliss promised in *Figaro* and *Così*. It is a victory of light in a dark world, a victory which Mozart sincerely desired. And it can never be far from our minds when hearing this uniquely rich view of life, as full of humour as of humanity, that Mozart had only a few months to live. It is our story set to the music of the spheres, though Shakespeare (*The Merchant of Venice*, V, i) thought it impossible that mortals should hear it:

> Such harmonie is in immortall soules,
> But whilst this muddy vesture of decay
> Doth grosly close it in, we cannot heare it.

7 *Performance and reception*

The Freihaus auf der Wieden and its theatre

The history of the 'Freihaus' goes back to 1647, when Conrad Balthasar von Starhemberg acquired the estate as a freehold property and was granted exemption from taxes (hence the name: 'free house'). The Starhemberg family from time to time added to their acquisition, and the huge complex was frequently extended and improved. The most famous member of the family was probably the diplomat Georg Adam von Starhemberg who, born in London in 1724 (where his father was Austrian ambassador), became Maria Theresia's ambassador to Paris, and was created prince in 1765.

From Joseph II's register of property in the late 1780s we learn that the Freihaus had ninety-three dwellings; there were also thirteen shops, eight workshops, and extensive gardens with fruit-trees, vines, vegetables and flowers. The complex had its own chapel; and at the latest from 1776 (when the Keess troupe is recorded as having performed there) there was a simple theatre. The number of residents is variously given as 600 or 800; according to the census of 1857 there were then 1,125 inhabitants.[1]

In January 1787 Christian Rossbach applied for permission to build a more permanent theatre in the Freihaus, and following his renewed request the next month, accompanied this time by plans of the intended structure, permission was granted. The theatre was a long, rectangular building; initially it had two galleries in addition to the stalls area, but it was extended by a further gallery in 1794. The stage, like the whole building, was rather longer but narrower than that of Marinelli's Theater in der Leopoldstadt. The building was of brick and stone, with tiled roof; only the interior was of wood. It is estimated that it held nearly one thousand spectators.

As permission to erect the theatre was not given until 16 March 1787, and the first performance took place on 14 October of the same

142

year, no time was lost. Christian Rossbach, an experienced man of the theatre, had overstretched his resources, however, and within five months he was obliged to move out. The new director was Johann Friedel, novelist, dramatist and actor, who ran the company with his mistress, Schikaneder's estranged wife, Eleonore. Comedies, tragedies and spectacular dramas were given, and also operas by Paisiello and Dittersdorf; however, Friedel died suddenly at the end of March 1789, and the new theatre required its third director in less than eighteen months. Eleonore Schikaneder lacked the resources to run the theatre, even if she had been granted the licence, so she invited her husband to take over the direction, and they re-established their marriage. Financial support was provided by a rich army officer, Joseph von Bauernfeld; within two years he, too, was bankrupt.

With a company consisting of some members from the previous ensemble and some whom Schikaneder brought with him from Germany, the theatre reopened on 12 July with a new work that pointed towards the genre that would provide the staple fare of the repertory. It was *Der dumme Gärtner aus dem Gebirge, oder Die zween Anton* ('The stupid gardener from the mountains, or The two Antons'), a so-called 'comic opera' by Schikaneder himself, with music by two members of his company, Benedikt Schack and Franz Xaver Gerl. It enjoyed thirty-two performances in the next six months and ran to no fewer than six sequels over the following five-and-a-half years. However, if Schikaneder had hoped with his comic gardener figure to create a character to rival in longevity and popular appeal the Kasperl of Marinelli's Leopoldstadt Theatre, the rôle taken for well over twenty years by Johann La Roche, he was to be disappointed.

The pattern that Schikaneder established proved very successful: operas (for the most part light Singspiels) alternated with comedies and tragedies; military and knightly plays and other spectacular stagings were a feature, and melodramas, concerts, and in due course ballets, were also given. A high proportion of the offerings were written by Schikaneder himself. But the leading names of the theatre of the time also occur: Lessing, Schiller and Goethe, Iffland, Schröder and Kotzebue; and the composers represented include Franz Teyber, the young Johann Schenk, Georg Benda, Guglielmi (*La sposa fedele*, under the title *Robert und Kalliste*), Dalayrac, and in later years Haydn, Süssmayr, Mozart (with several operas), Gluck, Grétry, Umlauf and Winter, as well as Wranitzky, whose *Oberon* provided Schikaneder with his first more widely significant success – and who, like Mozart, composed music for Vienna's lodges in the 1780s. There were also English and French dramas in what must be regarded as a distinguished repertory.

1790 was a year of consolidation for the Wieden Theatre: the repertory continued to grow, with spoken plays outnumbering new musical works; Schikaneder with his financial backer Bauernfeld successfully petitioned the emperor for an imperial and royal licence for the theatre, which from June was proclaimed from the playbills; and for the first time Schikaneder published his own theatre almanac. The most significant première of the year was probably that of the incompletely preserved *Der Stein der Weisen, oder Die Zauberinsel*, a heroic-comic opera book by the impresario himself, with music by Schack and others (including Mozart, who at the very least orchestrated the comic duet 'Komm liebes Weibchen', K 625/592a). This work was given on 11 September, and the duet was sung by the couple who were to sing Papageno and Papagena just over a year later. Here, too, the influence of Wieland is felt — though Wieland as adapter and editor rather than poet: the opera takes more than just the first part of its name from the penultimate story, 'Der Stein der Weisen oder Sylvester und Rosine', of volume I of the collection *Dschinnistan* (discussed in chapter 1).

For Schikaneder and his theatre, 1791 was a year of mixed fortunes. Dittersdorf conducted one of his Singspiels; Schiller's *Don Carlos* was staged; one of Haydn's newest symphonies was performed in a benefit concert; the third of Schenk's new Singspiels to be premièred in the Freihaus Theatre entered the repertory; Leopold II, accompanied by his heir, Franz, and Archduke Alexander, attended the first night (on 3 August) of a revival of Schikaneder's ten-year-old play *Ludwig Herzog von Steiermark, oder Sarmäts Feuerbär*; and in November Peter von Winter's heroic-mythological opera *Helena und Paris* was produced. Before Christmas a new entrance to the theatre, enabling carriages to drive to the doors, was constructed. Above all, on 30 September the first night of *Die Zauberflöte* took place. This catalogue of activities appears to be in stark contrast to the story that Schikaneder had begged Mozart to write him a magic opera to save him from insolvency. Yet recent discoveries have shown that Schikaneder did seek, through a public announcement in the *Wiener Zeitung*, to silence rumours that he was in financial difficulties.[2] Further, the appearance of Schikaneder's name on the imperial and royal audience lists for 28 July and 1 August,[3] a few days before the court's visit to his theatre, suggests that he felt the need for official recognition that he was free from the suspicion of impending financial embarrassment. So perhaps Schikaneder really did need the box-office success that Mozart could bring him. That Mozart was himself in financial difficulties in 1791 finds further corroboration in another discovery of Hans-Josef Irmen, namely that Mozart anonymously advertised an organ for sale in the *Wiener Zeitung* on 26 and 29 January.[4]

By this time Schikaneder's company, many of whom lived in apartments in the Freihaus, was quite large. As Leopold von Sonnleithner's records show, the theatre orchestra consisted of thirty-five musicians in the early 1790s.[5] The set of 'Instructions and rules' drawn up by Schikaneder makes it plain that he insisted on good discipline. Fines could be imposed for minor offences (arriving late for rehearsals or performances, powdering wigs or cleaning shoes in the green room, for example) the funds were to be used for the benefit of poor itinerant actors and actresses.[6] Contemporary opinion on the standard of the company's performances differed widely, but it seems likely that jealousy or prejudice were responsible for some of the unfavourable comments. One can say with confidence that Mozart would not have associated himself with the Freihaustheater troupe, or been on friendly terms with several of its members, unless he had been satisfied with its artistic standards.

The cast for the first performance

The playbill for the first night, 30 September 1791, identifies almost all the singers for whom Mozart wrote. It was a distinguished cast, mainly young. Let us take each in order of his or her appearance on the playbill (which is the order of the rôles printed in the first edition of the libretto).

The librettist, director and the first Papageno was one of the outstanding men of the German theatre of the time. Born at Straubing on 1 September 1751, Emanuel Schikaneder was educated at the Jesuit Gymnasium at Regensburg, where he was a chorister at the cathedral. In the mid-1770s he became an itinerant actor, having taken part in a court ballet at Innsbruck in 1774, where his Singspiel *Die Lyranten* (for which he wrote both words and music) was performed in 1775 or 1766. In 1777 he married his colleague Eleonore Arth (born 1752), and appeared with success as Hamlet at the Munich Court Theatre. By the next year he was director of a troupe that performed in many central and southern German as well as Austrian towns. In autumn

1780 he began a lengthy season in Salzburg, and the Mozarts' friendship with Schikaneder dates from this time.

In the mid-1780s Schikaneder and his partner Kumpf were summoned to Vienna by Joseph II to perform in the Kärntnertor-Theater, and he also appeared with the Burgtheater company. In 1786, after his wife had left him for the writer and actor Johann Friedel, Schikaneder founded a new company with which he again toured the Austrian provinces and southern Germany, spending much time in Regensburg. Here in the spring of 1789 he learnt of Friedel's death, and gave up his provincial licence so as to move to Vienna (taking talented members of his company with him), reconstitute his marriage and take over the Freihaustheater auf der Wieden. He remained there until his magnificent new Theater an der Wien was built, which opened on 13 June 1801 with his own latest opera, *Alexander*, set by Franz Teyber. Despite some successes, Schikaneder's fortunes were by now on the wane; in 1806 he left Vienna for Brünn, and though he returned to the capital in 1809, he failed to re-establish himself. On the way to take up an appointment at Budapest as director of a new German theatre company in 1812 he went mad, returned to Vienna, and died there in poverty on 1 September.

He was a remarkable all-round talent: actor in the comic and the serious genres, singer, composer (of vocal chamber works as well as of Singspiel scores), theatre manager and director, and author of over a hundred plays and librettos. Though no other work of his has had a success remotely comparable with that of *Die Zauberflöte* he was in his day, and for at least a generation after, one of the most frequently performed of dramatists. Some of Schikaneder's comedies – *Das abgebrannte Haus* and *Die Fiaker in Wien* (both 1792), *Der Fleischhauer von Ödenburg* (1794) and the comic opera *Der Tyroler Wastel* (1796) – helped establish the genre of the *Lokalstück*. The grandiose opera-books in which he failed to emulate the success of *Die Zauberflöte* lack the happy blend of fantasy, mysteriousness, high drama and cheerful comedy which, thanks to Mozart's guiding genius, that opera shows. All the same, *Der Spiegel von Arkadien* (1794), *Babylons Pyramiden* (1797) and *Das Labyrinth* (1798) enjoyed a popularity that almost any contemporary author would have envied.

How good a singer was Schikaneder? Writing in 1782, Abraham Peiba, the author of *Gallerie von Teutschen Schauspielern und Schauspielerinnen der ältern und neuern Zeit*, says of him: '... In the Singspiel he usually takes the comic rôles, at times falling into the exaggeratedly coarse comic vein. His voice is pure, melodious; he sings with insight and taste.'[7] That was nine years before he undertook the rôle of Papageno, and it seems clear that he was by 1791 losing the elegance of bearing and comeliness of figure for which he was earlier praised. Though he had been a competent composer of theatre music, there is no evidence that he invented Papageno's melodies. There is, however, no reason to doubt that he was still a very able singer (Papageno's vocal line, though predominantly simple, requires a singer with some agility who can manage trills) – and his is the longest rôle in the opera, both in terms of the number of solos and of the ensembles in which he is involved.

The Sarastro was Franz Xaver Gerl, then twenty-four years old. A former chorister at Salzburg and student of philosophy and physics at the university there, he joined a theatrical company in Bavaria in 1785, in the following year moving on to the famous company of G. F. W. Grossmann and specializing in 'comic rôles in comedies and Singspiels'. By 1787 he was a member of Schikaneder's troupe at Regensburg, making his début in a German version of Sarti's *Fra i due litiganti*, and singing Osmin in *Die Entführung*. In the spring of 1789 he came to Vienna with Schikaneder, and on 2 September of that year he married the soprano Barbara Reisinger (born 1770) who, after several years as a child star (singer, dancer and actress) touring with provincial troupes, had joined Schikaneder's company at Regensburg in early 1789. Gerl was a fine singer – Friedrich Ludwig Schröder, who had been recommended to hear him, did so and thought him 'very good'[8] – and the music Mozart wrote for him bears this out (the taxing aria 'Per questo bella mano', K 612, as well as Sarastro's music). He was the talented composer or part-composer of some fifteen Singspiel scores. After he and his wife (who sang 'Ein altes Weib', i.e. Papagena, in the première) left the Freihaus company in 1793 they performed for some years in Brünn, and then at the Court Theatre at Mainz, where he was admired as an actor in straight drama and also as a singer.

Benedikt Schack, the Tamino, was thirty-three at the time of the première. Bohemian by birth, he was a fine all-round musician: flautist and oboist, composer of stage and sacred music, and an outstanding tenor singer – on 26 May 1786 Leopold Mozart told his daughter in a letter: 'He sings excellently, has a beautiful voice, easy and flexible throat, and beautiful method ... This man sings really very beautifully.' Schröder, too, referred to him as 'a good [German: ein braver] tenor', though he commented adversely on his 'Austrian accent and suburban declamation'.[9] He had been a chorister at

Prague Cathedral before studying medicine, philosophy and singing in Vienna. From 1780 he was kapellmeister to Prince Heinrich von Schönaich-Carolath in Silesia, and in 1786 he joined Schikaneder (just before Leopold's report to Nannerl about his singing). His first recorded theatre score was performed in the Theater in der Leopoldstadt in 1784; by the time he came to Vienna in 1789 he had enjoyed several successes with his Singspiels, almost all of them settings of libretti by Schikaneder. The first of more than local interest was *Der dumme Gärtner aus dem Gebirge, oder Die zween Anton*, on which, as several times in the following years, his musical collaborator was Gerl.

His most talented collaborator was Mozart who, as Constanze's letter to Schack of 16 February 1826 states, looked on him as a close friend and occasionally wrote pieces for his Singspiels (for Mozart's share in 'Nun liebes Weibchen', K 625/592a, see p. 144). Schack's skill as woodwind player makes it possible that he played Tamino's flute himself. His wife Elisabeth (née Weinhold) sang the part of the Third Lady in the production. The Schacks left Schikaneder in 1793. After three seasons in Graz they moved to Munich in 1796, where he was a member of the Hoftheater until about 1814, when he lost his voice and retired. He seems to have abandoned writing for the stage before he went to Munich; his later compositions were mainly Church music, and as readers of *A Mozart Pilgrimage* may recall, Vincent Novello was so impressed by a mass by Schack which he heard in Munich in 1829 that he obtained a copy and in due course published it, convinced (surely misguidedly) that parts of it were by Mozart himself.[10]

It is uncertain what parts were actually sung and spoken by those designated as Priests. The playbill reads:

Sprecher.		Hr. Winter.
Erster		Hr. Schikaneder der ältere.
Zweiter	} Priester.	Hr. Kistler.
Dritter		Hr. Moll.

Winter, who was stage-manager ('Inspizient') of the theatre, is not recorded as having been a singer; in the *Wiener Theater-Almanach für das Jahr 1794* (which covers the season after the one that saw the première, i.e. 1792–3) he was identified as taking 'gesetzte Rollen' – sober, or middle-aged, characters. This points towards his having taken one of the purely speaking rôles, probably that of the Spokesman in II, 1. Both autograph score and first edition of libretto identify the Priest who instructs Tamino in the Act I finale as 'ein alter

Priester' rather than as 'Sprecher' (a word not used by Mozart anywhere in his score), which suggests a long-established error in performance practice.[11]

Schikaneder's elder brother, Urban (born in 1746), a bass singer, is called 'First Priest' on the playbill; it is likely that he sang the Old Priest's part in the first finale. The dialogue in II, 3 is spoken by the 'Sprecher, und der andere Priester' ('Spokesman, and the other Priest'); after the opening stage-direction the latter is designated 'Zweyter Priester' (Second Priest). The confusion is made worse by Mozart's autograph, in which reasonably enough, though misleadingly, the tenor Priest is called 'First', and the bass one 'Second' in the duetto no. 11. For the reason already given, it is unlikely that Winter took part in this duet; Deutsch identifies 'Hr. [Johann Michael] Kistler', Second Priest according to the playbill, as a tenor, thus presumably Mozart's 'First Priest' in no. 11; and 'Hr. Moll', Third Priest on the playbill, as a bass, thus presumably Mozart's 'Second Priest'.[12]

An unregarded inconsistency in the libretto is that in II, 6 and 13 the Spokesman is Tamino's interlocutor, whereas in II, 23 and 25 he has become Papageno's guide, the rôle previously given to the 'Second Priest'. Moll is not named among the singers in Mozart's *Catalogue*, though Kistler is: both had left the company by the time the lists were compiled for the *Theater Almanach* for 1794, so no further information is forthcoming from that source. It is to be assumed that these two singers also took the parts of the Two Men in Armour (not mentioned on the playbill) in the Act II finale.

The Queen of Night was written for Mozart's sister-in-law Josepha Hofer, the eldest daughter (born in 1758 or 1759) of Fridolin and Caecilia Weber. Her husband was the violinist Franz de Paula Hofer, a friend of Mozart's and his travelling-companion on his visits to Prague in 1787 and Frankfurt in 1790. Josepha was a member of Schikaneder's theatre from 1789, and Mozart aimed to exploit her high soprano voice in the (not-quite-completed) aria 'Schon lacht der holde Frühling', K 580 (17 September 1789). Friedrich Ludwig Schröder, hearing her in the title-rôle of Wranitzky's *Oberon* on 23 May 1791, was most uncomplimentary about her (see p. 139). Certainly Mozart had hardly been one of her admirers ten years earlier: '... a lazy, coarse, perfidious woman, as cunning as a fox' (letter to Leopold Mozart of 15 December 1781). However, both the nature of the music and a surviving anecdote[13] suggest Mozart's satisfaction with Hofer's singing; and she continued to sing the part almost throughout the long run in the Freihaus-Theater. Eighteen months after the death of her husband in 1795 she married Friedrich Sebastian Mayer, fourteen years her junior, who created the rôle of Pizarro in *Fidelio*; he took over the rôle of Sarastro on 9 September 1793, his house début.

The singer who created the rôle of Pamina was Anna Gottlieb who, on 1 May 1786, two days after her twelfth birthday, had sung Barbarina in the first performance of *Le nozze di Figaro*. Her parents were both Burgtheater actors, and she and her sisters were from a tender age used to appearing on stage. She joined Schikaneder's company in 1790 and performed mainly in Singspiels. In 1792 she moved to Marinelli's Theater in der Leopoldstadt, becoming a very popular and versatile member, praised for her singing and acting as well as for her readiness to take minor parts – essential in a theatre with an immense repertory. In May 1791 Schröder had found her 'not bad in her acting and singing, only her hand movements are somewhat wooden.'[14] Later in her career she was admired for her parodistic skills. After her retirement in 1828 she became increasingly eccentric, as well as poor, and must have had good cause as well as abundant time to contrast her early fame with her long decline; she died shortly after the centenary celebrations of Mozart's birth.

The playbill identifies the Three Ladies as having been sung by Mlle Klöpfer, Mlle Hofmann and Mme Schack. The first of these was a soubrette; Schröder heard her as Fatima in *Oberon* four months before the first performance of *Die Zauberflöte* and found her 'singing adequate, hand movements wretched'.[15] Even less is known about Mlle Hofmann, though in the 1794 *Wiener Theater-Almanach* she is listed as taking 'young lovers, naïve rôles, and sings', and she was still with the company in 1796. The singer of the Third Lady, Elisabeth Schack, has already been mentioned.

The Papageno and Papagena – 'Herr Schikaneder, Junior', to distinguish him from his elder brother, and Barbara Gerl – have already been discussd, 'Monostatos, a Moor', was taken by (Johann) Joseph Nouseul who, then approaching fifty, was the oldest member on the cast list. Nouseul, born in 1742, was primarily an actor rather than a singer, and had for a while been director of a company in Germany, then in Graz (1783–5); like his wife, the distinguished actress Rosalie Nouseul, he was for many years a member of the Burgtheater, both before and after his engagement at the Freihaus-Theater. Contemporary comment mentions his exaggerated and unnatural manner 'in all passionate, declamatory rôles', and his 'soft tone' and restricted vocal range.[16] This was in the context of his performance in spoken drama – his singing abilities are not mentioned – but it may be reasonable to see here the cause of the marking against Monostatos' aria 'to be sung and played as *piano* as if the music were at a great distance'. Nouseul, identified in the 1794 almanac as portrayer of 'traitors, exaggerated rôles and comic old men in comedies, sings', was no longer listed as a member two years later.

Of the designated Three Slaves, speaking rôles confined to I, 9–10, Herr Gieseke, the First Slave, has been discussed above (p. 92). Herr [Wilhelm] Frasel, the Second Slave, is listed in the almanac for 1794 as playing 'young heroes in tragedies, comic parts in comedies'; he, like Nouseul, is listed in the 1796 edition as having left the company (likewise Dem. Klöpfer). Herr Starke, the Third Slave, is listed as taking minor rôles.

The Three Boys are not included on the playbill for the première. Tradition has it that Urban Schikaneder's daughter Anna (born 1767) sang First Boy; she, like Anna Gottlieb, whom she outlived by six years, was later to become a member of the Leopoldstadt Theatre, singing the Queen of Night when that company staged the opera in 1811. Castelli informs us that the Second and Third Boys were sung by trebles: Handelgruber, who later became parish priest at Hainfeld, and Franz Anton Maurer,[17] who went on to enjoy a distinguished career as a bass, making his début as Sarastro in the Freihaus-Theater on 8 October 1795, at about eighteen. We should treat Castelli's memoirs, like so much other comment about the early history of *Die Zauberflöte*, with caution: he was only ten at the time of the première, and the singers he names as having sung two of the Three Ladies are demonstrably of a later generation;[18] however, a selection of surviving playbills confirms that the Three Boys were normally taken by one or two women, and two or one boys.

The other names on the playbill for the first night are those of 'Herr Gayl, theatre painter', and 'Herr Nesslthaler as designer'. Nesslthaler is not listed among the members of the company in the earliest surviving list, that for the season following the première, but Joseph Gayl (or Gail) is listed each year until 1796, and the bill for the first night of the opera in the new Theater an der Wien on 4 January 1802 names Vinzenz Sachetti and Herr [Mathias] Gail the Younger as responsible for the sets.

Though not named on the playbill, Johann Baptist Henneberg deserves to be mentioned: he had been appointed kapellmeister to the theatre in 1790, when still only twenty-one, and he is said to have taken the rehearsals for *Die Zauberflöte* in August and September when Mozart was in Prague preparing *La clemenza di Tito*, and to have taken over musical direction after Mozart had directed the first two or three performances. As Alan Tyson has pointed out, Henneberg's song 'Das Veilchen und der Dornstrauch', one of the same collection of *Frühlingslieder* from the *Liedersammlung für Kinder und Kinderfreunde* (Vienna: Alberti, 1791) that included Mozart's songs K 596–8, uses a tune that we associate with the closing section of the Act I quintetto; it is unclear whether Mozart was paying tribute to the young kapellmeister, or – as would appear more likely – Henneberg was recalling Mozart's opera.[19]

Early reception of the opera

The earliest report we have on *Die Zauberflöte* in performance is contained in Mozart's letter to his wife (who had returned to Baden in the first days of October) written on 7 October, a week after the première:

friday at half past 10
at Night

dearest, best little wife! –

I've just got back from the Opera; – It was just as full as always. – the Duetto *Mann* und *Weib* etc.: and the Glöckchen Spiel in the first Act was as usual encored – also in the 2nd Act the boys' Terzett – but what pleases me most, is, the *Silent approval*! – one can see well how much, and increasingly so, this opera is gaining esteem ...

He tells his wife that their Prague friends know of the opera's success, and that on the same night as the German opera was given for the first time 'with so much applause', *La clemenza di Tito* was performed in Prague for the last time, 'with extraordinary applause ... all the numbers were clapped'. The next letter, dated only 'Saturday night at half past 10' and traditionally ascribed to 8–9 October, reports the continuing success story:

the Opera, although Saturday is always a bad day, because it is a post day, was performed to a packed house and with the usual applause and encores; – it will be given again tomorrow, but not on Monday – so Siessmayer must bring Stoll in on *tuesday*, when it will again be given for the *First time* – I say for the *First time*, because it will presumably again be given several times in succession ...

He goes on to say that his horn-playing friend Leutgeb had asked to be taken to the opera again, and on the next day he was to take his mother-in-law, to whom Hofer had already given the libretto. 'But with Mama it will be the case that she *sees* the opera, not she *listens to* the opera.' He then returns to the evening's performance and mentions an annoyance:

The ....s [a name deleted by Nissen] showed their approval very strongly of *everything*, but he, the know-all, showed himself to be such a true *Bavarian* that I couldn't stay, or I should have had to call him an ass; – unfortunately I was with them just when the Second Act began, and thus for the solemn scene. – he laughed at everything; at first I had patience enough to try and draw his attention to certain speeches, only – he laughed at everything; – that was too much for me – I called him *Papageno*, and left – but I don't think the fool understood. – so I went to another box where *Flamm* was sitting with his wife; there I enjoyed myself hugely, and there I stayed until the end. – only I went into the wings at Papageno's aria with the GlockenSpiel because today I felt such an urge to Play it myself. – then I played the joke, when Schickaneder has a pause at one point, I played an Arpeggio – he jumped – looked into the wings and saw me – when it came the 2nd time – I didn't do it – then he stopped and absolutely refused to continue – I guessed what he was thinking and played another chord – then he hit the Glöckchenspiel and said *shut your mouth* – then everyone laughed – I believe that many people learned for the first time from this joke that he doesn't play the instrument himself. – Furthermore you can't think how charming the music sounds when you sit in a box close to the orchestra – much better than in the gallery; – as soon as you return you must try it. –

In a P.S. he quotes three phrases from the terzetto no. 19.

Mozart's very last surviving letter is the one to his wife of 14 October. Again his delight in the success of *Die Zauberflöte* shines through:

Yesterday at 6 o'clock I picked up Salieri and la Cavalieri in the carriage and took them to the box – then I quickly went to fetch Mama and Carl, whom I had meanwhile left at Hofer's. You cannot think how charming they both were, – how greatly not only my music but the libretto and everything about it pleased them. – They both said it was a true *Opera*, – worthy to be performed before the greatest monarch at the greatest festivity, – and they would certainly see it very often, for they had never seen a more beautiful and agreeable piece. – He listened and watched with the greatest attention [,] and from the Sinfonia to the final chorus there wasn't a single number that failed to draw from him a bravo or a bello, and they could hardly stop thanking me for this kindness [;] they had always intended going to the opera yesterday. But they would have had to be sitting there at 4 o'clock already – as it was they saw and heard everything in peace. – After the theatre I had them driven home, and I supped with Carl at Hofer's. – Then I drove home with him, where we both slept splendidly. I gave Carl no little pleasure by taking him to the opera ...

This last little series of letters by Mozart throws light on a matter about which almost nothing is known, namely the duration of a contemporary performance of *Die Zauberflöte*. The fact that Mozart was back in his apartment in the Rauhensteingasse and writing to his wife by 10.30 p.m. on 7 and on 8 October is relevant to this question. The performances began at 7 p.m., as is clear from the playbill. Since it would presumably have taken Mozart a good twenty minutes to walk the mile or so back from the Freihaus (and we know from the letter of 7 October that he walked that evening, rather than going by carriage) over the Glacis, via the Kärntnertor and on to his dwelling, we can assume that the performances were over by very soon after 10 p.m. – or rather earlier if, as seems likely, Mozart did not leave the theatre the moment the curtain fell. Since, in contrast to modern practice, there is no evidence to suggest that the dialogue was shortened, it is reasonable to assume that rapid delivery of the spoken scenes, and fast tempi in most of the musical numbers, were the practice (the more so since three numbers, or part-numbers, were normally encored, as we know from this same letter). Certainly the implication of rapid tempi – Norrington, or (with some exceptions) Toscanini, rather than Furtwängler or Böhm – is in keeping with what is reported about tempi in Mozart's day (see chapter 6, pp. 129 and 228–9, n. 9).

By early November other comments on the work were beginning to appear, both in private correspondence and diaries, and in public print. A report that was published in the *Musikalisches Wochenblatt*, Berlin, in early December but has the date-line 'Vienna, 9th October', comments sourly:

The new comedy with machines, *Die Zauberflöte*, with music by our Kapellmeister *Mozard*, which is given at great cost and with much magnificence in the scenery, fails to find the hoped-for success, because the contents and the language of the piece are altogether too wretched.[20]

On 6 November, that inveterate attender of musical events, Karl, Count Zinzendorf, entered in his diary:

At half past 6 to the *Théatre de Starhemberg* in the Wien suburb to the box of M. and Me d'Auersperg to hear the 24th performance *of the Zauberflöte*. The music and the sets are pretty, the rest an incredible farce. An immense audience.[21]

During November the earliest announcements of publication of music from *Die Zauberflöte* began to appear in the *Wiener Zeitung* – a trickle that was soon to turn into a stream, as competition grew among Vienna's publishers of music, both in manuscript copies (Lausch and Traeg) and engraved and printed. Laurenz Lausch gave notice on 5 November that 'various pieces, to be sung at the piano-forte, may be had'.[22] On 23 November Artaria advertised the duet 'Bey Männern welche Liebe fühlen' and the aria 'In diesen heil'gen Hallen', engraved and with piano accompaniment, at twenty kreuzer each. Three days later Leopold Kozeluch's house, the Musikalisches Magazin, announced the same two numbers, the latter under the first words of its second strophe, 'In diesen heil'gen Mauern'; the prices were ten kreuzer for the aria, fifteen for the duet (by 3 December Kozeluch had added the terzetto no. 16; a fortnight after that, he was offering twelve numbers, a milepost that Artaria had reached on 7 December). Kozeluch's edition was completed in 1793, but the Artaria one, like Hoffmeister's (which was announced on 14 January 1792 and appeared between February and May 1792), remained incomplete. An interesting additional offering from Kozeluch was announced on New Year's Eve: '12 German dances from the opera die Zauberflöte by the late Herr Mozard, with all the parts, 1 fl. 30 kr., in piano score, 40 kr.'; the arrangements were the work of Stanislaus Ossowsky.

On 14 January 1792 Joseph Haydenreich [Heidenreich] announced a wind arrangement of 'that well-loved opera, *die Zauberflöte*, the last work of the great Mozart', for eight wind instruments ['Harmonie'], to be published by subscription at 6 fl. 40 kr.; issue of an additional arrangement for wind sextet would depend on sufficient subscribers coming forward. On the same day Johann Traeg repeated an offer he had made a few weeks earlier with music from *Le nozze di Figaro*: 'Duetti for 2 violins. (From *die Zauberflöte*.) 3 fl.' Lausch also inserted an advertisement that day, listing no fewer than thirteen numbers (including sections of the first finale) as being available, and string quartet versions of the same were offered for subscription. And in an attempt to play on his readers' emotions he added: 'N.B. This is the last work of this world-famous composer; lovers of the art of music, shed a tear for him! – Wolfgang Amade Mozart – the darling of the Muses – is no more. – ' F. A. Hoffmeister also climbed aboard the band-waggon on 14 January, stating that twelve numbers from the opera were available in vocal score from his establishment, as well as '6 Minuets, with all the parts, from the opera Die Zauberflöte, 1 fl.'

The sheer quantity of published music from *Die Zauberflöte* is strikingly indicated by *The Catalogue of Printed Music in the British Library to 1980*, in which no fewer than twenty-nine columns are devoted to editions of and excerpts from this opera (by comparison, *Le nozze di Figaro* covers twenty-two columns, *Don Giovanni* thirty-and-a-half). Within five or six years there were vocal scores from Rellstab in Berlin, Hummel in Berlin and Amsterdam (1792–3), and Hummel again under the Amsterdam imprint (1792), Simrock in Bonn, Götz in Mannheim, an Italian edition from Breitkopf in Leipzig (1794), a German one from the same firm in the following year, and one by Schott in Mainz – apart from the ones already mentioned from the Viennese houses. That list is certainly not comprehensive – Stegmann (Bonn), Richter (Dresden), Albrecht (Prague), Fischer (Leipzig) and Heckel (Mannheim) were also early in the field. All the same, there was surely a measure of exaggeration in the report that appeared in the Chemnitz publication *Teutschlands Annalen des Jahres 1794*:

Mozart's *Zauberflöte* in piano score published in Mainz, Mannheim, Offenbach, Leipzig, Berlin and Brunswick: that is, six times in one and the same year: an hitherto unexampled occurrence in the history of music literature, and one which sufficiently justifies what was said above about the general enthusiasm for Mozart's works.[23]

This is an enthusiasm without parallel, in that Mozart provides the first instance of a composer whose fame continued to grow, whose works continued to be performed with increasing frequency, after his death.

Little is known about the size of the print-runs of these early editions, though some of them were certainly large – Constanze Mozart in her long letter to Breitkopf & Härtel of 27 October 1798, part of her campaign to secure as much as she possibly could from the publishers of many of her late husband's works, throws back at them their own remark that they had sold more than three thousand copies of *Die Zauberflöte* (in a mere three or four years).

As A. Hyatt King has pointed out, the enormous popularity of *Die Zauberflöte* in the 1790s, as measured by the number of printed editions, did not continue to such a marked extent into the first three decades of the nineteenth century: '*Die Zauberflöte* with nine editions takes third place to *Don Giovanni* and *La clemenza di Tito* with fifteen and ten respectively.'[24] Of course, one reason could be that the market was still flooded with the editions from the first decade of the opera's existence. And it should be mentioned that in the history of our opera the major publishing event of the early nineteenth century was the first edition of the full score, issued by Simrock of Bonn in 1814, with German and Italian words – the German version being that for which claims of priority have been advanced by Michael Freyhan.[25]

The unreliable nature of much of the surviving 'contemporary' material about *Die Zauberflöte* is most strongly brought out by the fact that it was not actually contemporary at all. Those who were of an age to have the opportunity to write about the opera at the time of its creation and slow progress towards popular success were perhaps too busy with other concerns, or perhaps they doubted that the work was going to survive long after its composer's death. The reminiscences on the basis of which the legends have grown are on the whole those of people either too young to have been closely connected with the work, or who, for one reason or another, delayed writing down their memoirs until so long after the events that they could not recall them accurately, or – which perhaps comes down to the same point – were contaminated by the intervention of the genuine or putative memories of others.

Ignaz Castelli's *Memoiren meines Lebens* are a case in point. He was only ten years old at the time of the première, and his memoirs did not appear in a definitive form until some sixty years later. Nevertheless, he is frequently cited as the authority for the anecdote he attributes to Friedrich Sebastian Mayer (who joined the Freihaus-Theater only in 1793) about the composition of the duet for Papageno and Papagena:

Hey, Mozart! That's no good, the music must express more astonishment, the two of them must first look at each other dumbly, then Papageno must begin to stutter: Pa – papapa – pa – pa; Papagena must repeat this until finally both of them bring out the full name. Mozart followed this advice, and the duet constantly had to be repeated.[26]

Even less likely, because specifically contradicted by the stage-direction in the first edition of the libretto, as well as by the entry in Mozart's *Catalogue*, is Castelli's suggestion that the Priests' march was written at Schikaneder's request during the dress rehearsal, the composer writing each player's part straight into his folder.

Franz Gräffer was even younger than Castelli (he was six at the time of the opera's first performance), though in his case the memoirs were at least published comparatively early, in the 1820s.[27] His recollection of the 'wonderfully beautiful voice of the Pamina, a certain Anna Gottlieb', and of the absurdly unsuitable Papageno of Schikaneder ('Just think of a Papageno six feet tall, a fathom across the middle, with a huge and very fat neck!'; vol. i, pp. 243–4) might be thought to have the ring of truth. The trouble is, he mentions in the same paragraph the impending move from the Theater auf der Wieden to the new Theater an der Wien – which took place a good eight or nine years after Anna Gottlieb left Schikaneder's company to become a permanent member of the rival Theater in der Leopoldstadt. In view of this, it is wise to ignore completely Gräffer's detailed account of the supposed meeting at which the manager commissioned the score from Mozart, and the conversation between the two of them on stage at the end of the first act at the première (vol. ii, pp. 5–6).

However plausible some of these anecdotes may seem, they tend to present what later generations wanted to regard as the truth, and to reflect the love of gossip typical of a society like that of Vienna in which everyone is interested in the goings-on of its favourite adopted sons, especially those whom it largely ignored during their lifetime. Not surprisingly, Mozart is the foremost of these adopted sons, and it is seldom easy to state precisely what the original source is that lies behind the first appearance of a particular 'reminiscence', or to sift the occasional grain of truth from the chaff of wishful thinking.

What information do we have about early performances of the opera? – Music criticism was then in its infancy, and most of the reports that have come to light tell very little about the musical standards achieved. Even the few that there are cannot be regarded as free from prejudice. What is clear is Mozart's own satisfaction with the performance in Schikaneder's theatre, though the joy he shows in his letters may well have been tempered by his recognition that ideal standards were unobtainable. The one long and fairly detailed 'review' that has so far come to light – it is here republished for the first time – contains obvious errors and some padding, as well as clear evidence of antagonism towards the librettist, and veneration for the composer.

'Das Theater auf der Wieden. The interior of the house is well fitted out, the stage-machinery well appointed, so that large-scale transformation scenes can be carried out ... The orchestra is well manned.' Schikaneder – the anonymous writer informs his readers – knows what is good for business:

He employed the clever device of elevating his own inferior products by means of skilful composers and by using their talents so as to win the taste of the public for his farces; this was the case with the *Zauberflöte*. – This ridiculous, senseless and stale product, faced with which understanding must stand still and criticism blush, would but for the composition of the great Mozart be forgotten and scorned, yet through the talents of this genius, which he displayed therein in all their strength, the whole work triumphed, people disregarded the nonsense harangued by a Moor, a bird-catcher and a witch even as they gave themselves over entirely to the delightful melodies, they laughed at the caricatures and took delight in the magic of the music, regretting only that such great talents had not been put to a more worthy and nobler subject. Not content with grouping together the most far-fetched beings and bringing on a Queen of Night with her female servants, Zoroaster with his priests, initiates and profane persons, spirits, monsters and furies, the director has attempted to deceive the eye by means of sixteen different transformations and, in baroque fashion, conjured up the scenes of nature. However ridiculous and absurd the representation of this farce is, so excellent is the music in which the late Mozard shewed himself in his greatness; the genius of the musician shews itself in the overture – the chorus of the Priests of Zoroaster 'in diesen heiligen Mauren etc.' is solemn, the arias 'bei Männern, welche Liebe fühlen' are excellent. The duets and trios, and the recitatives, worthy of a Mozart in their invention, expressiveness and art, whom the genius of humanity mourns. He is no more! This opera, too, has to thank this enchanting harmony for its so often repeated performances and its large receipts – all classes hastened to see the *Zauberflöte*, and one constantly discerned new musical beauties, the more often one saw it: it must be said in praise of the orchestra that it worthily performed this masterpiece, for its creator himself directed it at its first performances.[28]

There is quite a lot of evidence that changes in the style of performing Mozart's operas set in within a very few years of his death. Erik Smith gives examples in chapter 6, taken from the vitally important area of tempo (see pp. 159 and 228–9, n. 9). The subject of ornamentation is also important, and well documented. Schikaneder's nephew, Joseph Carl (son of Urban Schikaneder, 'First Priest' in the première), and himself a member of the Freihaus company from 1790 to 1793, reports an incident that presumably happened during a rehearsal of Sarastro's second aria. 'As he ['Basist Gerl'] tried to ornament ['variieren'] this song Mozart called out: "Stop, Gerl! If I'd wanted to have it like that, I'd have written it like that. Just sing it as it's written." '[29] By the summer of 1812, when rival productions of *Die Zauberflöte* were running at the Theater an der Wien and at the Kärntnertor-Theater, stylistic integrity had evidently disappeared. At the Court Opera the rôle of Tamino was taken by Anna Milder-Hauptmann, and the Queen of Night – Therese Rosenbaum – was long past her best and had the music simplified and lowered in pitch.

At Schikaneder's old theatre there was an excellent young Tamino in Franz Wild, and Antonia Campi was a fine Queen, 'but we cannot exactly find it worthy of praise that she overwhelmed even the recitative "o zittre nicht" with embellishments'.[30] And three-and-a-half years later a violinist from Mannheim, Michael Frey, who was in Vienna for the winter, commented in his diary on the performance of *Die Zauberflöte* that he attended at the Theater an der Wien on 15 December 1815; he singled out the famous Giulio Radicchi, the Tamino, for his special displeasure:

H. Radichi sang the aria 'Diess Bild' etc. with such execrable embellishments that one could no longer recognize the beautiful melody. He vexed me every time he appeared on stage by ruining many passages with his wretched mannerisms.[31]

On the same occasion the bass Anton Forti, another renowned singer, sang Sarastro

with very noble delivery; he sang the aria 'in diesen heiligen Hallen' with particular beauty, the first time quite simply, the second time [i.e. the second strophe] with unexaggerated embellishments.

Frey had similarly criticized members of the cast of *Don Giovanni* in the same theatre on 30 November: 'Mme Campi ... sang gloriously, apart from the unnecessary embellishments she made in the quartet in the first finale, and in her aria';[32] the same reservation was expressed about Mme Forti (= Henriette Teimer) who liberally decorated Zerlina's line in the duet with Giovanni – despite the fact that she had been singing Mozart rôles in Prague since at the very latest 1793, when the Mozart performing tradition was still very much alive there.

That over-embellishment was something of a family failing of the Campis is borne out by a report published in the *Allgemeines Europäisches Journal* in 1794 concerning opera performances in Prague; the Italian-language performances of *Die Zauberflöte* given by Guardasoni's company included Antonia Campi and her husband, Gaetano. 'Hr. Campi as Sarastro sings with dignity; more simplicity and the omission of the unnecessary ornaments ['Schnörkel'] in Mozart's simple vocal line would yield yet greater dignity.'[33]

Early performances of *Die Zauberflöte* outside Vienna

Though *Die Zauberflöte* quickly settled down as the greatest draw in Schikaneder's repertory, it was comparatively slow to be taken up by other theatres. By the time it was staged in Prague, on 25 October

1792, Schikaneder was shortly to announce the hundredth performance in his theatre (he was exaggerating: it was the eighty-third performance that took place on 23 November that year).[34] It was almost a decade before any of the other Viennese theatres mounted it – and when the time came, the Court Opera production was something of a disaster.

Mozart's great popularity in Prague was assuredly the reason why that city was the first after Vienna to see his last opera. Its première in the Nostitz Theatre in October 1792 by Mihule's company was followed by a run of performances – twenty in the first six months. In the 1793–4 season it was staged by Franz Spengler's company at the Thun Theatre in the Malá Strana, proving with twelve performances the second most popular work in the repertory, and being given with an enlarged orchestra of some thirty players, and around twenty specially hired extras, including children dressed as apes and tigers.[35] In the carnival of 1794 the opera was also performed in Italian there, as *Il flauto magico*, translated by Giovanni de Gamerra and with recitatives composed by J. B. Kucharž. In October of that year *Die Zauberflöte* was also given in Czech. Tomislav Volek has established important details about the production, which took place in the Patriotic Theatre in the former monastery of the Irish monks. Surviving police records make it clear that a Masonic or pseudo-Masonic society, the so-called 'Mathias Brethren' ('Mathias-Brüder'), was behind the venture. Few of the performers were artists of significance, though the then twenty-year-old Vincenc Tuček, the Tamino, went on to enjoy a successful career as composer and conductor, and Antonín Volánek, who conducted the performance (as he had the first German-language production two years before), was a well-known music director and composer for the stage.[36]

Frantisek Xaver Němeček (better known under the spelling Niemetschek as author of one of the first biographies of Mozart) reported in the *Allgemeines europäisches Journal* that, even if the repertory of the Patriotic Theatre included 'much [that is] tasteless and all too popular ... every true Bohemian must rejoice that his all-Bohemian fellow-countrymen have a nobler entertainment than animal-baiting and the beer-tavern, and can educate their perceptions!'[37] That the performances were not of a very high standard is suggested by a report in the same periodical in 1798:

What wretched casting! Would it be a wonder if at performances like this Mozart's offended shade were to return from the spirit realm and take his revenge by changing some of these bunglers, who distort his divine tones into hyena howls, into monkeys and wolves?[38]

Despite the imperfections of these Bohemian performances, *Die Zauberflöte* becamj ever more widely known and loved in Czech lands (not least in those curious transformations that saw numbers from operas reappearing in sacred guise with texts adapted for ecclesiastical use).

A strict chronological listing of productions of *Die Zauberflöte* would have required interruptions in the section devoted to the opera's early fortunes in Prague.[39] For 1793 witnessed the beginning of the work's triumphal progress through Germany's opera-houses great and small: Augsburg, Leipzig and Passau saw productions in January; Graz, Brünn, Bad Godesberg, Munich, Dresden, Frankfurt am Main,[40] Linz and Hamburg followed suit before the end of the year; and it was also staged in Pest and Ofen in March, and in Warsaw in July, each time in German. The list of stagings in 1794 is even longer: Weimar, Königsberg, Mannheim, Brunswick (in German first, and later in French), Freiburg, Stettin, Hanover, Olmütz, Berlin,[41] Amsterdam, Nuremberg, Elbing, Mainz, Cologne, Altona, Lauchstadt, Aachen, Dessau, Rudolstadt, Bautzen, Halberstadt, Erfurt, Bremen, Danzig, Düsseldorf, Lübeck and Schleswig. So extensive is this list that it comes as some surprise to note that audiences in Stuttgart and Kassel, for instance, had to wait until 1795 and 1796 respectively for the chance to see *Die Zauberflöte*. In the latter year it was given in Temeschburg (Timişoara) by a local company in German, and in Hermannstadt and Eisenstadt. It reached St Petersburg in 1797, and Moscow in 1801. A mutilated version reached Paris in that year (discussed in more detail below), and London first heard it in Gamerra's translation on 6 June 1811 in the King's Theatre; the first reasonably complete production in the British Isles seems to have been the one staged at Norwich, in an English translation, on 1 June 1829.[42] Theatres outside Germany tended to prefer to hear the opera in the vernacular – it was given at Amsterdam in Dutch in 1799, the 1801 Moscow production was in Russian, in 1802 and 1805 it was given in Polish in Warsaw and Poznań, in 1812 in Stockholm in Swedish, in 1816 in Copenhagen in Danish, and it was in 1816 that it finally reached Italy, being staged in Milan in Italian.

Some of these productions deserve detailed attention, either because they are remarkable for the version in which they were given, or because the staging was in some way remarkable. The fact that every manager wished to stage it meant that, even when as in Spengler's Prague production extra players and singers were drafted in, there was often a marked gap between ambitious intention and actual achievement; many of the smaller companies, especially touring ones, had to make do with modest sets, costumes and transformations, whereas larger houses treated the work as a grand opera, sometimes turning it into an Italian piece even in resolutely German centres. It was Guardasoni – remembered as the man who commissioned *Don Giovanni* – who staged the Italian performances in Prague in 1794, and his troupe also gave it in Dresden and Leipzig in the same year. As befitted a *dramma eroicomico*, the dialogue was replaced by Italian verse, set as recitatives by Kucharž, thus materially altering the balance and nature of the work. The positioning, and even the apportioning, of individual numbers was altered – the Queen's first aria was given to Pamina, to precede her duet with Papageno; and the Queen's second aria was brought forward to follow her opening recitative.[43]

Changes of a more insidious kind are typified by the libretto that Christian August Vulpius, Goethe's future brother-in-law, cobbled together for the production at Weimar.[44] *Die Zauberflöte* in his hands was subjected to a curious bowdlerization, which proceeded from the claim, expressed in the preface to his three-act perversion, that 'it was absolutely impossible to bring *Die Zauberflöte* in its original state before our delicate public in this theatre'. The changes he made are at once clumsy (frequently they cannot be fitted to Mozart's vocal line) and fussy – minute alterations are often introduced for no good reason. Vulpius employs the apparatus of scholarship in annotating his changes and accounting for them, yet time and again he smudges details in Schikaneder's text. The serpent is turned into a dragon that breathes smoke and flames, and the Three Ladies chase it back into its lair instead of killing it with their spears. Vulpius clearly did not work with Mozart's music, or with a musician, at his side. He usually leaves out the same lines that were erroneously omitted from the first printing of the Viennese libretto (even 'Stirb, Ungeheuer, durch unsre Macht!' at the climax of the rescue of Tamino in the opening number), and mindlessly keeps lines that Mozart did not set. Among his few original contributions are to make Sarastro the Queen of Night's brother-in-law, and to have Sarastro retire from his office of high priest in favour of Tamino.

Sequels and parodies

Despite the feebleness of Vulpius's adaptation *Die Zauberflöte* was staged a record eighty-two times at the Weimar Court Theatre between 16 January 1794 and the end of Goethe's directorship in 1817. A by-product of Goethe's involvement with this opera is his own unfinished sequel, on which he worked intermittently between 1794–5 and around 1800.[45] *Der Zauberflöte Zweiter Teil* was intended to make use of the same characters and sets as the original, but the failure of Goethe's negotiations with the Vienna Court Opera seems to have diminished his enthusiasm. Paul Wranitzky, then the leader of the opera orchestra and presumably also a member of the administration, wrote to Goethe on 28 November 1795 to request from him a libretto that he himself would set to music. Goethe's reply on 24 January 1796, offering to complete his sequel to *Die Zauberflöte* and requesting an honorarium far in excess of what the Opera was prepared to pay, drew a negative response from Wranitzky, who clearly did not relish the challenge of vying with Mozart's score. By 1802, when he published his fragment in an almanac, Goethe seems to have given up the intention of completing his sequel.

The one passage in Goethe's text that enjoys any currency is a lyric, intended for Papageno and Papagena, that begins 'Von allen schönen Waren' ('Of all beautiful wares'). Under the title 'Wer kauft Liebesgötter?' ('Who'll buy Cupids?') it was set by Schubert (D 261) on 21 August 1815 – surely in ignorance of its original context in a sequel to the opera which Schubert must have had in his mind when writing 'Heidenröslein' just two days earlier.

Schikaneder's clever and successful local comedies and Singspiels of the 1790s give the lie to the claim sometimes made that the rest of his career was a series of failed attempts to emulate *Die Zauberflöte*. Nevertheless, in quite half a dozen works, set to music by a series of more or less minor composers, he reused and varied stock characters, situations and jokes that can be traced back to the Mozart opera. The most important, as well as closest, sequel was *Der Zweyte Theil der Zauberflöte unter dem Titel: Das Labyrinth oder Der Kampf mit den Elementen* ('Part Two of the Magic Flute under the title: The Labyrinth, or The Battle with the Elements'). It was first performed on 12 June 1798, with music by Peter Winter; it was given a full-scale revival by the Bavarian State Opera (Cuvilliés-Theater) on 18 November 1978, under Wolfgang Sawallisch.

Despite powerful reinforcements for the forces of darkness, light again triumphs, with Tamino hurling his adversary in single combat into the depths of a volcano. There is no sign of consistency, balance, even of an overall plan – partly at least because this time Schikaneder had no Mozart to guide, cajole and inspire him.

Some of the versions in which *Die Zauberflöte* was staged must have been as remote from the intentions of composer and librettist as are the sequels just mentioned. A curiosity is the anonymous text published at Passau in 1795, presumably made for the theatre of that town, with its limited resources. The opera was given there on 31 January 1793.[46] From this edition the Egypto-Masonic elements have been removed and some of the music has been deleted or transferred to another character; the dialogue has also been shortened. In keeping with the changing cultural atmosphere of the mid-90s Tamino has become 'a wandering knight', given to swearing by the attributes of King Arthur;[47] his thoughts are solely concentrated on the rescue of Pamina. Oddest of all is the fate of the Queen of Night. Here named Karmela, 'a magician through music', she does not appear until the second finale; her first aria is sung by the First Lady, with the familiar words transposed to the third person, and the second by Pamina, as if repeating the instructions her mother had given her in a dream.

A more famous – indeed, infamous – version was staged at the Paris Opéra on 20 August 1801. With text rewritten by E. Morel de Chédeville and score arranged and provided with recitatives by Ludwig Wenzel Lachnith it was undoubtedly successful (134 performances in twenty-six years), but *Les Mystères d'Isis*, to give it its Parisian title, was stylistically such a disaster that it thoroughly deserved its local soubriquet of *Les Misères d'ici*.[48] Music was pillaged from *Le nozze di Figaro*, *Don Giovanni*, *La clemenza di Tito* and Haydn's 'Drum-Roll' symphony. Even the music that was retained from *Die Zauberflöte* was cut, recomposed, transposed, and altered as to order and dramatic function. No wonder that Berlioz commented, despairing of a city renowned for its musical murders, 'Mozart a été assassiné par Lachnith'.[49] The changes were not confined to the score – Schikaneder would not have recognized his work, rewritten in four acts, and including such characters as Isménor, Myrrène and Bochoris, whom the reader may be pardoned for not immediately identifying as Tamino, the Queen of Night and Papageno.

With this French perversion we are close to the world of intentional parody. Travestied versions began to appear in Vienna early in the new century. The earliest attempt to mock the opera was made by Schikaneder himself, lampooning the Court Opera production in the first weeks of 1801. The librettist was not credited on the playbills at the Kärntnertor-Theater. Schikaneder's reaction was to mock the insufficiencies of his rivals, as is made clear by the report in the *Allgemeine musikalische Zeitung* of 8 April:

Because some transformations were carried out with unpardonable negligence in the Kärntnertortheater, Schikaneder soon afterwards parodied these representations in his own theatre. The disenchanted Papagena had to be freed from her costume [as Old Woman] with the help of some tailors' apprentices; the Goddess of Night, instead of sinking beneath the earth, was called off into the wings.   (column 484)

The first full-scale parody version is *Die Zauberflöte travestiert in Knittelversen* ('... travestied in doggerel verse'), 'with most of the Mozartian music kept'. It was passed by the censor in 1803, but was not performed; it remained unpublished until the 1930s.[50] The author was probably Perinet, and internal evidence suggests it was written for Schikaneder's new Theater an der Wien.[51] The plot and characters are amusingly trivialized − Tamino clambers up a tree to escape from the bear (replacing the serpent) that is pursuing him; the Queen's maids kill it with their broom, roasting-spit and poker, and then quarrel over the skin. Papageno, known as 'Wastel', has to help Tamino support the vast and ornately framed portrait of Pamina that the Queen gives him ('Dies Bildnis ist verzweifelt schwer!' − 'This portrait is damnably heavy!'). Sarastro keeps alive the old tradition of songs in praise of food by singing the second strophe of Monostatos' aria to words extolling 'Blue trout freshly grilled in butter, / Juicy pullets in ragout ...'

A later travesty that enjoyed some popularity on the stage was Karl Meisl's *Die falsche Zauberflöte* (later revised with the adjective 'false' replaced by 'travestied'); the music was arranged by Wenzel Müller, and it was given nineteen times in the Theater in der Leopoldstadt in 1818−19. References to Viennese fashions and foibles abound − Tamino sees Pamina in Monostatos' clutches through a kaleidoscope; Sarastro and his friends disport themselves on *Draisinen*, a forerunner of the bicycle; Pamina cannot easily forgive Tamino for taking coffee with the Queen's maids, and giving them a shawl each − bought on h.p. The final tableau shows the Queen, Pamina and Tamino having a ride on the carrousel in the Prater amusement park.

Parodies and travesties were by no means the only by-product of the craze for *Die Zauberflöte*; it also left a rich and varied legacy in

European literature. Goethe's interest in the opera left its mark not only on his unfinished sequel but also on works as varied as the verse epic *Hermann und Dorothea, Faust* and the *Märchen*; Grillparzer left two dramatic sketches derived from *Die Zauberflöte*; Tieck in two of his Romantic dramas satirized the inappropriate ubiquitousness of borrowings from, and references to, the opera. Hegel, Marx and Kierkegaard are among nineteenth-century philosophers and political thinkers who quote from and refer admiringly to the opera. The Prussian radical journalist Adolf Glassbrenner (1810–76) makes delightfully witty use of motifs and quotations from it in his satirical writings; another chronicler of the Prussian scene, the novelist Fontane, names three of the characters in *Stine* after those of *Die Zauberflöte*.

In the twentieth century, too, Schikaneder's and Mozart's opera has continued to fascinate writers. G. Lowes Dickinson's *The Magic Flute. A Fantasia* (1920) is a strange, haunting evocation and reinterpretation of the story, a parable of civilization after the First World War. During that war the Prague Expressionist Paul Adler published a novel which he named after the opera; Werfel's poem 'Zarastro' and Annette Kolb's diary, *Zarastro. Westliche Tage* (1921), invoke Mozart's High Priest; Hermann Hesse's poem 'Mit der Eintrittskarte zur *Zauberflöte*' ('With the ticket for *Die Zauberflöte*') muses on the enduring hold of the opera. Johannes Urzidil's *Prager Triptychon* (1960) concludes with a story named after the opera; reminiscent of Hoffmann's *Don Juan*, it takes the narrator to an extraordinary performance of the work that ends with a riot and theatre fire. Feminist mockery of the cult of *Die Zauberflöte* is contained in the final chapter of Christa Reinig's novel *Entmannung* ('Castration'; 1976); in Milan Kundera's *The Book of Laughter and Forgetting* (1978) the heroine, Tamina, is involved in un-Pamina-like activities with considerably more than Three Boys; Botho Strauss's *Kalldewey Farce* (1981) includes near-quotations from the duet for Papageno and Papagena, and more centrally the flute-accompanied march from the tests of fire and water. Most striking of all these recent tributes to and confrontations with *Die Zauberflöte* is Thomas Bernhard's *Der Ignorant und der Wahnsinnige* ('The ignoramus and the madman'; 1972). It takes place before, during and after a performance of the opera in an unidentified but contemporary German house, and concerns the prima donna's decision to make this, the occasion of her 222nd assumption of the rôle of Queen of Night, also her last performance of it.

Later performance history

Tradition has it that *Die Zauberflöte* continued to enjoy great popularity in German lands during the nineteenth century, but was largely ignored elsewhere in Europe. As so often, the true situation is very different. Certainly the opera had to wait until well into the twentieth century for a regular place in the repertory in Britain, but it is quite misguided to claim that it was virtually unknown here or in other European lands in the nineteenth century. That it was no stranger to London audiences is clear from the fact that it figured in no fewer than fourteen Covent Garden seasons between 1833 and 1888 — even if it was usually performed in Italian guise, and in most of its seaons enjoyed rather few repetitions. The contrast between London and Vienna in this respect is strongly marked — the work was given more than 600 performances in its native city in the nineteenth century, around 450 in the Court Opera and 150 in the Theater an der Wien (not forgetting the 220-odd that it had received in the Theater auf der Wieden from the *Uraufführung* in 1791 until the theatre's closure in 1801).

One example must suffice to convey the impact that this opera could make on Victorian London. *Il Flauto Magico*, as it was billed, was revived at the Royal Italian Opera (i.e. Covent Garden) at a Royal Command Performance on 10 July 1851. *The Times* devoted an immensely long notice (almost two full columns) to the event, discussing background, plot and music in great detail, despite the observation that 'the music, thanks to its beauty and variety, is familiar "as household words"'. This was no ordinary night — the Royal party was accommodated in 'a lofty tent, surmounted by a crown ... for the construction of which fourteen of the ordinary boxes ... were sacrificed'. The performance received high praise, as well it might — Grisi was Pamina, Mario sang Tamino, Ronconi, Formes and Anna Zerr from Vienna were the Papageno, Sarastro and Queen of Night; Viardot took the tiny part of Papagena. The house was packed and the audience enthusiastic, as indeed was the case on the same night at Her Majesty's Theatre for *Le nozze di Figaro* with Henriette Sontag and Lablache.

The serious reservations in *The Times*'s critique of *Die Zauberflöte* were directed against Schikaneder's contribution, which was also blamed for the shortcomings of Mozart's score which, though superior to that of *La clemenza di Tito*, was pronounced inferior to *Figaro, Don Giovanni* and even *Idomeneo* ('The Thunderer' did not deign to mention *Così fan tutte* in this context, though *The Athenaeum* did in its notice of 19 July).

That the score is crowded with beauties – that the melodies are abundant and fresh, and genuine – that the fact of having a tale of enchantment to set to music conducted Mozart into a new world, where the inexhaustible fertility of his invention was triumphantly demonstrated, cannot be denied

– as *The Times* conceded. However,

... as a counterbalance, there are many passages in *Zauberflöte* which discover neither the beauty of melody, nor the prodigious science, nor the lofty and passionate expression for which the dramatic music of Mozart is generally remarkable. The march, with flute solo, when Pamina and Tamino are passing through the ordeals of fire and water [later in the review referred to as the 'stupid scene'], with another flute solo near the opening of the first *finale* are absolutely trivial, and are evident proofs of Mozart's contempt for the excessive absurdity of the situation ... What is feeble or trivial, however, we readily lay to the stupidity of Schikaneder and the *libretto*; while that which is great and beautiful springs exclusively from the immortal genius of the composer.[52]

The warmest praise was for the Papageno – 'Ronconi was the life and soul of the opera ... restless as a squirrel, making everybody laugh', though at times guilty of attempting 'to exert his power over Mr. Costa and the members of the orchestra'. *The Times* was present again five days later – as were the Queen, Prince Albert and the royal children – when an indisposed Anna Zerr was replaced by the English singer Miss Louisa Pyne. 'It was her first appearance on the boards of a London Italian Opera, and her success was decided.' For Henry Chorley, Mademoiselle Zerr had sounded 'shrill and harsh'; and 'in her *bravuras*, the hearer was irresistibly reminded of a pea-hen masquerading as a lark'.[53]

The Times was positively lyrical in the short notice that followed the performance of 15 July, admiring 'the complete and gorgeous character of the *mise en scène*', and concluding:

The house was crowded to inconvenience and there is every reason now to count upon the *Flauto Magico* as a permanent and lucrative addition to the already extensive *repertoire* of the Royal Italian Opera.[54]

However, after a total of seven performances in two seasons, the work disappeared from Covent Garden for sixteen years, and though it was frequently revived in the 1870s, and Henry Wood mounted it at the Olympic Theatre in 1892, the popularity the opera continued to enjoy in Austria and Germany, and that had been forecast for it so confidently in London at the time of the 1851 production, lay many decades in the future.

Full appreciation of the opera in Britain, and the start of its popularity, may be precisely dated to the production at Cambridge in December 1911, in the English version that opened Edward J. Dent's long series of translations of libretti; the performances were preceded by Dent's brochure that introduced the work and its complex background to the British musical public.[55] The three performances at the New Theatre on 1 and 2 December drew large audiences from all over the country, and were hailed as a triumph of collaboration between amateur and young professional musicians. The conductor was Dr Cyril Rootham, and the production was by Clive Carey (who also won praise for his singing and acting as Papageno). *The Times* briefly reviewed the first performance – very favourably – on 2 December, and discussed the production at much greater length (one-and-a-half columns) on 4 December. In 'very simple' scenery and costumes designed by Mrs Sydney Cockerell 'an immense variety of effect' was obtained by the 'use of curtains and lighting'. 'This interesting and remarkable revival' was distinguished by the Tamino of 'Mr [later Sir] Steuart Wilson', the Pamina of Mrs Fletcher, and the Queen of Night of Miss Victoria Hopper. Dent's 'very vivid, readable, singable' translation was held up as 'a model of what operatic translation should be', and the panegyric included the perceptive phrase that Mozart's 'whole attitude ... binds the story into a coherent psychological whole.'[56]

The critic of *The Musical Times* succinctly confirms the great merits of the Cambridge venture:

We have learned several things from the production of the 'Magic Flute'. First, that it is an effective opera, granted intelligent management; secondly, that an elaborate work like this can be admirably given by amateurs; and thirdly, that good English is an excellent language for opera. Perhaps in time our first and third deductions will be appreciated by those dignitaries who control opera in England.[57]

Mr Thomas Beecham included *Die Zauberflöte* in his season at Drury Lane in the spring of 1914, having in the previous year given it in the course of a provincial tour. However, as the critic of *The Times* makes clear, there was a serious stylistic deficiency to be offset against the blow he had struck for the popularity of the opera.

Above all, Mr Beecham must have the credit for having begun and ended his season of German opera with a work which has always been called an immortal masterpiece – mostly by those who have never heard it or had the courage to test its immortality.

Operatic managers of late have fought shy of it as being tedious and obscure, and therefore unprofitable; it has been left to Mr Beecham to prove that *The Magic Flute* is good enough to lead off with, to draw full houses several times over, and to necessitate an extra performance. Next year we hope that he will not merely revive it but will go one better and give it to us as Mozart wrote it. It is ridiculous at this time of day to suppose that people will not listen to an opera because it has spoken dialogue in it and to convert the dialogue into musical recitative.[58]

The recitatives were the work of Beecham's chorus-master, Emil Kreuz. In other respects *The Times* was full of praise for the performance, which was notable for 'the beautiful voice of Herr Kirchner' as Tamino, 'the exquisite singing of Mme Claire Dux as Pamina', and Mme Frieda Hempel's masterly assumption of the Queen of Night: 'She not only sings the notes with complete assurance and absence of effort, but she makes the coloratura a means of expression instead of treating it merely as so much meaningless ornamentation stuck on to the surface of the music.'

The Magic Flute entered the repertory of the British National Opera Company in 1922, and a further stage in the opera's conquest came early in the following year:

8 January 1923 'what was probably the WORLD'S FIRST OPERATIC BROADCAST took place (*The Magic Flute*, from Covent Garden)'[59]

Between the wars it grew in popularity and estimation, a process that reached a peak in the late 1930s, with performances at Glyndebourne in 1935, 1936 and 1937, a revival at Covent Garden in May 1938 under Beecham, and above all with Sir Thomas's recording for HMV, made in Berlin in November 1937 – the first recording of the work, and for many connoisseurs still, even without the spoken dialogue, the greatest of all versions. The Covent Garden performances were notable for the singing of Richard Tauber and Tiana Lemnitz, but also for the use of scenery that was 'a copy [loaned by the Charlottenburg Opera] of what was designed by Karl Friedrich Schinkel for a production of *Die Zauberflöte* in 1816' – the most influential and famous of all sets designed for the work.[60]

There are plenty of examples from the early years of the twentieth century of the ignorance and prejudice to which *Die Zauberflöte* was exposed. If one looks the work up in the little book *Opera at Home*, published by The Gramophone Company, there is no entry under its German or English title.[61] If one thumbs through the contents, the eye will in time light on *Il Flauto Magico* (pp. 66–8) and take in the availability of a recording of the overture (by the Mayfair Orchestra, no conductor is named), one of 'Là dove prende amor ricetto' (i.e. 'Bei Männern'), three couplings of 'Qui sdegno non s'accende' ('In diesen heilgen Hallen') and 'Grand'Isi! Grand'Osiri!', sung by Plançon, Journet and Radford, and there are two versions listed of 'Ah! lo so' (Pamina's aria). Robert Radford is also credited with a recording of 'I'll have vengeance' ('*Sarastro* announces that he will take his revenge upon the *Queen of Night* by aiding *Tamino* to marry her daughter *Pamina*'); the aria in question turns out, perhaps not surprisingly, to be Bartolo's 'La vendetta' from *Le nozze di Figaro*! Since we also read in the notes that Mozart died in 1792, and that the opera was 'first produced in Vienna, September 20, 1801', we can readily see just what obstacles have had to be overcome ('It is with no confidence' − writes the mercifully anonymous commentator − 'that one sets out to describe the action, but the work of this great master is full of delightful music').

Writing at a time when there have already been more than twenty complete recordings of the opera, one is tempted to call the battle already won. However, the vagaries − at times even the solipsistic platitudes − of opera directors mean that ignorance and prejudice have not been totally vanquished. At the opening of his essay (chapter 8) Anthony Besch mentions some of the settings chosen by directors of *Die Zauberflöte* in recent years. Nicholas Hytner's 1988 production for English National Opera, which succeeded Besch's own, sets the work in a landscape inhabited by Pilgrim Fathers (with Papagena in curlers and head-scarf as a cockney tea-lady, fag hanging from her lips). Opera-goers in Scotland have had ample opportunities to enrich their experience − Tamino falls asleep in a library during the overture of Jonathan Miller's 1983 production for Scottish Opera; by odd coincidence the Prince wakes up as if from a dream towards the end of the production by Achim Freyer that the Hamburg State Opera brought to the Edinburgh Festival in the same year (this production has Papageno as a carrot-nosed circus clown swinging in on a rope, and twin Taminos and Paminas briefly on stage together during a particularly turbulent finale). Then in 1987 the Swedish Folkopera offered Edinburgh Festival visitors a science fiction *Magic Flute* (in Claes Fellborn's staging), with Sarastro a scheming baddie in a space laboratory, in due course blown up when Papageno tinkers with the controls. John Dew's production at Wuppertal in the same year showed Tamino falling in love with a portable TV image of Pamina against a set consisting of three step-ladders and some stage pillars in extension of the ones in the auditorium; Papageno's glockenspiel was a bright yellow walkman and his meal came from a ubiquitous fast-food carry-out.[62]

Die Zauberflöte is robust enough to take these and many other excesses in its stride; and there probably has not been a production that did not have some valid contribution to make to the work's performance history. However much of a reactionary one may feel oneself to be in preferring a traditional performance that respects the normally quite precise instructions of librettist and composer, only a bigot would refuse to admire the resourcefulness and enthusiasm that inform even the oddest of interpretations. To call a work indestructible may be to court trouble, but the fact is that over two centuries *Die Zauberflöte* has proved itself able to win and hold the admiration and love of performers and every level of the opera-going public.

Die Zauberflöte may have taken a long time to become totally accepted in English-speaking countries, but there is no doubt that since the Second World War it has enjoyed prolonged popularity, with numerous productions and almost annual revivals in both of London's opera houses and, since their foundation, frequent performances from Kent Opera, Opera North, Scottish Opera and Welsh National Opera, not to mention Glyndebourne, and also the many smaller companies, music colleges and universities that have staged it.

If one thumbs through the back-numbers of that invaluable monthly, *Opera*, one cannot fail to notice the vast number of new productions and, of course, revivals world-wide. With increasing gloom one also notes that of very few of these stagings did the reviewer report more than at best a partial success. Audiences, however, have seldom been put off by the critics' strictures, and have continued to flock to performances, to delight in the music and its interpreters, to laugh at the comic scenes, and to admire the sets, costumes and scenic effects.

From earliest times this last aspect of *Die Zauberflöte* has been one of its drawing-points – despite, or perhaps sometimes because of, the increased prices charged for admission to an opera that has almost always been very expensive to mount. Scene-designers, technical experts and directors have relished the challenge of realizing its spectacular demands. In Vienna, Schikaneder's own designers, Gayl and Nesslthaler, were succeeded by famous names like Anton de Pian (1818), the influential Josef Hoffmann (1869), Alfred Roller (1906, and again in 1933), and Georges Wakhevitch (1958). Vienna also has the cycle of murals depicting scenes from the opera that

Mortiz von Schwind created for the salons of the State Opera, and Max Slevogt's free interpretations drawn in the margins of facsimile pages from Mozart's autograph are preserved in the Albertina. In Munich two members of a noted theatre family designed productions, Joseph Quaglio in 1793 and Simon Quaglio in 1818. Berlin saw the most familiar of all décors for the opera, created by Karl Friedrich Schinkel in 1816, followed a few years later by those of his disciple Karl Friedrich Thiele, and in 1911 by Hans Kautsky's evocative designs. The Salzburg Festival lists a series of famous names among designers of *Die Zauberflöte*: Oskar Strnad (1928), Hans Wildermann (1937), Caspar Neher (1949), Oskar Kokoschka (1955), Oskar Laske (1956), Ita Maximowna (1959), Theo Otto (1967), and Jean-Pierre Ponnelle (1978); Kokoschka's designs were later used in Geneva (1965) and in Chicago (1966). Italy, seldom considered a Mozartian haven, has seen notable productions of *Il flauto magico*, with La Scala mounting it in 1950 in designs by Ludwig Sievert and supervised by Nicola Benois, in 1955 by Emil Praetorius, and in 1985 in David Hockney's designs created seven years earlier for the Glyndebourne Festival. Other designers of *Die Zauberflöte* for Glyndebourne have been Hamish Wilson (1935), Oliver Messel (1956) and Emanuele Luzzati (1963). New York had sets designed by Hans Kautsky in 1912, and more recently those by Marc Chagall (1967) have remained in use for many years. The illustrator Maurice Sendak designed a production for Houston Grand Opera in November 1981 which was later mounted in Montreal and Seattle.

The growth in popularity of the work in the United States has been a feature of post-1945 operatic history. By the mid-1960s it was becoming so widely performed there that as early as 11 December 1966 the fourth new production that season, the one at Houston, could be recorded.[63] It was by no means the last new staging of the season – in February, Kokoschka's designs were used for a production in Chicago. The most hotly debated, but also the most durable, American production of the work was the one mounted at the Met during the same prodigious season 1966–7. Andrew Porter summed up its merits during a revival five years later in a wide-ranging, quietly enthusiastic review-article in *The New Yorker* on 4 November 1972:

Günther Rennert has produced *Die Zauberflöte* many times. His New York version, first done in 1967 ... still has the essential quality of the others by him that I have seen: directness, naturalness. There was no overemphasis on pomp at the expense of the pleasantries, or the other way round, but a supple response to all the diverse elements – a theater man's understanding of the

kind of piece it is coupled with a poet's feeling for its sense. Mozart
brings out the best in Mr. Rennert ... Chagall's decor is pretty, as *Zauberflöte*
decor should be, but also aptly solemn in the ritual scenes. There is fancy
in it, and we sense a happy, enthusiastic response to Schikaneder's detailed
specifications.[64]

The production was still in use in 1981, when Nicholas Kenyon
reviewed it in the same periodical; by then, though, the *mise-en-scène*
(credited to Bodo Igesz as stage-director, as already in 1972) and the
sets were showing their age:

At the end of Act I, the chorus drifts on through the wings, through the temple
doors, and apparently through the temple walls; the impressive darkened entry
of the priests with lamps in Act II is ruined by their scrambled exit; the great
climax – Schikaneder's stage directions call for a 'brilliantly-lit temple ...
the most consummate splendor – at the end of the trial is confined to a
desultory group of elders miming behind a gauze. Chagall's sets begin by
charming the eye with their varied colors and profusion of detail and end
by satiating the senses.[65]

Since many directors nowadays feel that they can do almost
anything with a classic, it is not surprising that at the other extreme
someone should have decided to base a staging of *Die Zauberflöte*
as closely as possible upon what is known about the original realization of 1791. This feat was essayed by the Holland Festival in 1982,
as a co-production with the Teatro Communale, Bologna (where the
production was mounted on 27 May); Erato made a recording during
the performance in the Theatre Royal at The Hague in the following
month. Criticism was directed mainly against vocal and mimetic
inadequacies.[66] But more damaging to the whole enterprise seems to
have been the assumption that the six coloured engravings by the
brothers Schaffer (two of them are reproduced as Plates 7 and 8 on
pp. 185 and 188), which served as models for the sets and costumes
reconstituted by Tom Kleyn-Gijs Stuyling and Rudolf Corens,
depicted Schikaneder's staging in autumn 1791; they are much more
likely to be depictions of a provincial staging, perhaps the one
mounted at Brünn, where they were published in the *Allgemeines
Europäisches Journal* in 1795.

   A different kind of attempt to refashion *Die Zauberflöte* was that
undertaken for an American television production in 1956 by W. H.
Auden and Chester Kallman. The most ingenious addition is the
'Metalogue', to be spoken by the singer of Sarastro between the acts.
This splendid occasional poem, 132 lines long, was published in *The
Listener* the day before Mozart's 200th birthday and later included in

Homage to Clio (London, 1960, pp. 70–3) as well as in the translation of the complete opera (London, 1957). This witty deflation is written in stirring Augustan rhymed couplets and provides a wry, elegant commentary on the characters as brought up to date:

> In Nineteen Fifty-six we find the *Queen*
> A highly paid and most efficient Dean
> (Who, as we all know, really runs the College),
> *Sarastro*, tolerated for his knowledge,
> Teaching the History of Ancient Myth
> At *Bryn Mawr, Vassar, Bennington* or *Smith*;
> *Pamina* may a *Time* researcher be
> To let *Tamino* take his Ph.D. ...[67]

The thought that Papageno, 'one is sad to feel, / Prefers the juke-box to the glockenspiel', may well be the starting-point for the jolly updatings of the bird-catcher and his world that have occurred so often in modern productions.

Impossible as it is to dismiss any product of Auden's lightly, his version of *The Magic Flute* has much to answer for. The solution to the problem of the dialogue works well: he and Kallman cut it quite heavily, and they put the prose into rhyming couplets, mainly iambic pentameters. The reordering of Act II is where they most obviously lay themselves open to criticism. They start from the viewpoint stated in their preface that the 'libretto seems peculiarly silly', thus taking for granted weaknesses and inconsistencies, some at least of which are readily justified within the context of a complete reading of the original spoken text. Auden and Kallman alter the sequence of events and musical numbers extensively after the opening sequence of Act II (scenes 1–5, including nos. 9–12). Scenes 16–18 follow (including nos. 16 and 17), then comes scene 21 (no. 19) and a concocted scene in which Papageno tries to cheer up Pamina, before scenes 7–12 (with nos. 13–15). Another insertion follows, in which Sarastro bids the First and Second Priests prepare the tests of fire and water, and let Papageno after a merely nominal trial have his Papagena. The Priests' chorus (no. 18) is then succeeded by a free adaptation of scenes 23–5 (including no. 20). The Act II finale follows.

Auden and Kallman have removed some of the inconsistencies in the original (for instance, how Pamina comes to have the dagger for the opening scene of the second finale). But they create as many difficulties as they remove, showing that an over-ambitious adaptation is only too likely to emphasize the superiority of the original, even when that is in points of detail demonstrably flawed (nineteenth-century versions of *Così fan tutte* could have provided them with a cautionary example). There are wonderful touches in the translation, just as there are wise and challenging words in what is, nevertheless, a dangerously misleading preface. Their final touch is brilliantly ironic: a postscript addressed by Astrafiammante (as they call her, following Italian practice) to the translators, cheerily dactylic tercets from one who can mock them, confident in her immortality and the right that gives her to have the last word.

From an adaptation and translation that defiantly outlives the event for which it was conceived we turn to another that seems to me crucially limited in artistic value by the damage it inflicts on the opera. *Trollflöjten*, Ingmar Bergman's famous 1974 filmed version for Swedish television, the sound-track of which was issued by the BBC in 1976, seriously distorts Mozart's intentions. However memorable some visual images from the film are (others are of extraordinary banality), the musical listener is appalled by the liberties taken. Not only are nos. 11, 16 and 19 (the Priests' duet, the trio for the Three Boys and the trio for Pamina, Sarastro and Tamino) omitted, the carefully structured Act II finale is treated in cavalier fashion: the first section with Pamina's attempted suicide (bars 1–189) is followed by Papageno's attempted suicide and the ensuing duet with Papagena (bars 413–743); the threefold chords are then heard for the first and last time, followed by dialogue, no. 18 (the Priests' chorus, here taken flippantly fast), more dialogue; then back to Mozart's finale for the trials (bars 190–412); and finally the concluding section (from the Queen's last appearance until the end, bars 744–920). Such idiosyncratic mishandling of the original usefully points us forward to the next chapter.

8 *A director's approach*

ANTHONY BESCH

Egypt under the rule of the Pharaohs, Mexico at the time of the Aztecs, Zoroaster's Persia, Maria Theresia's Vienna, a library in an eighteenth-century country house, a white box, a black box – these are only a few of the settings with which productions of *Die Zauber-flöte* have been invested in recent years, while Marx, Freud, Jung, Wittgenstein, Hans Andersen, the Brothers Grimm and many another have been drawn upon for philosophical, psychological and literary inspiration. And just as every conductor will create a different musical interpretation of the opera, so will the theatrical concept and visual realization vary in the hands of each different director and designer. Further, each particular director will alter his or her concept in relation to the time, place and occasion of each successive production and adjust it to the different conductors, designers and performers with whom he or she may be working. There can be no such thing as a definitive production of *Die Zauberflöte*: in attempting to define one director's approach to the opera over a number of years, what follows in this essay can at best hope to provoke positive reactions or conflicting points of view.

The creation of an opera production for the theatre depends on a close collaboration between the conductor, director and designer, collectively referred to as the production team. The team will make their own researches into the background and content of the work and contribute their own specialized knowledge to the musical, theatrical and visual interpretation of the opera. The conductor will define his approach to the music and put forward his ideas on dramatic and visual expression. The director and designer will advance their own points of view on the significance of the music drama, and from these discussions the team will evolve a concept of how they will represent the work in this particular production. Director and designer will then collaborate in searching for a visual expression of the agreed intellectual concept. If the designs are to be executed in time for the

178

beginning of rehearsals, they will have to be submitted many months before the starting-date, and the director must ensure in the planning stage that he does not later have to ask for costly alterations. Sometimes it may take many months to come to a solution, while director and designer propose and consider, accept or reject alternative ideas: sometimes a solution may emerge immediately – some teams work best under pressure while others benefit from protracted opportunity for discussion. Time spent in the planning and preparatory stages can avoid the waste of time and money during the rehearsal and production weeks, and the director will need to formulate his own ideas with great precision so that the designer can give concrete physical expression to the ultimate design concept.

When the production team are all satisfied with this concept, the models of the sets and the drawings for the costumes will be presented to the opera management who, if they approve them, will then have them costed. If these costs exceed the production budget, the management may ask for modifications, and the designs will have to go back to the drawing-board for reconsideration by the production team. The construction and painting of sets and the making of costumes can take several months, so agreement on their final form must be reached well before rehearsals with the cast begin.

Research into the background of *Die Zauberflöte* can have several alternative points of departure – biographies of Mozart as man and composer, studies of the opera itself, source-works contributing to the creation of the libretto, designs for productions over nearly 200 years, photographic, cinematic and televisual material, together with further explorations in history, sociology, psychology, economics, aesthetics and architecture – the range of possibilities is extensive. Some production teams may decide to delve as deeply as time allows into background research, some may take a more pragmatic view, working directly from the music and text and relying upon their personal and intuitive reactions. Others may construct a middle way between these two extremes. But for all directors and designers a close study of Emanuel Schikaneder's libretto will be an essential prerequisite, and his stage-directions and descriptions will be studied both for their original significance and symbolism and for their relevance to a present-day production. It used often to be assumed that his stage-directions were merely a self-indulgent exercise in showmanship, evolved to take advantage of the existing sets and properties which his company happened to have available and which were worked into the production like the village pump and two washing-tubs in the play commissioned by Vincent Crummles from Nicholas Nickleby. But even the most cursory study of the Masonic content of the opera reveals that almost every detail in the stage-directions relates directly to Masonic theory and that their specifications of substances, metals, fabrics, colours and forms are all relevant to the personal and general symbolism of the action. The Masonic content and origins of the libretto were never in any doubt to Mozart's contemporaries, who were aware of his own membership of the lodge 'Zur Wohltätigkeit' and of Schikaneder's previous membership of the Regensburg lodge 'Zu den drei Schlüsseln'. But since Freemasonry is by nature a secret society, the precise nature of the finer details of the content has never been known – except presumably by Masons – until the publication of the revealing and fascinating book *The Magic Flute: Masonic Opera*, by Jacques Chailley (in France in 1968, and in an English edition, translated by Herbert Weinstock, in 1972). Merely by giving due observance to the details of the stage-directions, it could be possible for a production team knowing nothing of Freemasonry to evolve a production which was Masonic in its effect. But if they choose to investigate the parallel, then Chailley's book is essential reading.

In the twentieth century, most designers and directors have eschewed an overtly Masonic approach, partly because only a small proportion of any audience can be alive to the full Masonic significance of the work, and partly because the implications of contemporary Masonry cannot be the same as they were in 1790. Goethe himself gives us a justification, as M. Chailley reminds us: 'It is enough that the crowd should find pleasure in seeing the spectacle: at the same time, its high significance will not escape the initiates.' The little girl seen sitting in the audience in Ingmar Bergman's film of *Die Zauberflöte*, both wrapt and enraptured by what she sees, needs no knowledge of Masonry in order to respond to the compulsion of the performance. Her elders, equally untutored, can react as positively, though on different levels of sophistication. The strength of the opera can thus lie in its universal appeal to spectators who have no knowledge of Freemasonry, even though it exerts a special appeal for the Mason. M. Chailley's book describes the complex Masonic influence upon the construction of the libretto and upon its imagery and symbolism in the dialogue, key-relationships and progressions, and in scenic and dramatic detail. He points out that much of the specifically Masonic detail itself derives from symbols drawn from previous philosophies and religions – Jungians would say also from the collective subconscious, and in particular from

Plate 6. 'At the entrance to the temple' – watercolour by P.-J. de Loutherbourg (*c.* 1787). A guardian enjoins silence on a woman neophyte

the Renaissance theory of the elements and humours and the pictorial and physical images associated with them. That the *Zeitgeist* of the period caused independent artists to work along parallel lines is indicated in the series of drawings made by the Anglicized Strasbourg painter – himself a successful stage designer – Philippe-Jacques de Loutherbourg. He drew these at the request of Count Cagliostro who campaigned to reform European Freemasonry through conversion to the Egyptian Rite and undertook to illustrate Cagliostro's instructions for the precise type of picture to be hung in the Preparation Rooms of a new lodge in the Swiss town of Riehen near Basle. The drawings, dating from 1787, embrace a number of eclectic Masonic compounds and symbols, and to our eyes look extraordinarily like designs for a production of *Die Zauberflöte*, which, however, they predate.

We do not, of course, know who exactly was responsible for the Masonic elements in *Die Zauberflöte* – whether Schikaneder himself evolved the complex structure, whether Mozart influenced the course and content of the work or whether a 'ghost' writer provided the scenario upon which Schikaneder based his final text. It seems extremely unlikely that a busy actor-manager would have had time for all the necessary research into the source-books of which *Sethos*, by the Abbé Terrasson, provided the majority of the ritualistic content. But it was Schikaneder who imposed his actor-manager's imprint on the final work even if it was perhaps Mozart who insisted on retaining the Masonic element. Chailley shows that while Schikaneder always had the theatrical importance of the action in mind, Masonic symbolism was never absent from the parallel philosophy. When, for example, Papageno vanishes into the bowels of the earth in scene 25 of Act II ('Eh' ich mich zurückziehe, soll die Erde mich verschlingen' – 'Before I go away, the earth will have to swallow me up') his disappearance invariably evokes laughter and often applause as the audience reacts to the well-prepared surprise of the theatrical effect. In Masonic terms, he is undergoing his statutory trial by earth (he has already been submitted to the trials of water and fire). Schikaneder, the astute actor-manager, took ready advantage of Masonic implications because he knew that laughter at this point provided exactly the right audience reaction to achieve their relaxation and prepare them for the sublime beginning of the finale which immediately follows. Papageno's encounter with Sarastro's lions in II, 19 provides for a similar scene of humorous relaxation between the end of Pamina's sublime G minor aria and the Priests' chorus which follows. This scene with the lions (male symbol of supremacy) is often mistakenly cut as being destructive to the atmosphere of the two numbers, but the contrast it makes is precisely what Schikaneder intends. If the importance of the lions in II, 19 is accepted, the director must previously have considered their appearance in I, 18, when the rubric demands that Sarastro's triumphal chariot be drawn by six lions. Their Masonic significance is clear but stage lions are not easy to achieve. Shall he represent them? Cut them out? Or find an equivalent? A twentieth-century producer may very often need to find valid equivalents for Schikaneder's machinery and stage-effects, but their original significance should always be evaluated before they are rejected out of hand. What, for example, is the serpent at the beginning of the opera? A comical Jabberwock? The guardian of the Queen's realm? A reflection of Tamino's subconscious emotional turmoil? The feminine principle externalized? A production which reduces it to an interplay of laser-beams will ignore more questions than it answers.

When the director and designer have completed their research into the philosophic and psychological background of the opera, they will go on to consider its visual representation on the stage. Crucial to any effective interpretation of the opera is rapidity of movement from scene to scene. *Die Zauberflöte* is written to be performed with only one interval, which falls between the two acts, as is the case with the other operas of Mozart's maturity: *Don Giovanni, Così fan tutte* and *La clemenza di Tito* (one can also make a very strong case that *Le nozze di Figaro*, too, should be played with only one interval, placed between Acts II and III.) There are thirteen different scene-changes in *Die Zauberflöte*, three in Act I and ten in Act II. Unbroken continuity and fluidity of movement from one scene to the next is essential in order to fulfil the authors' musical and dramatic progression and preserve the concentration of the audience, except where it may feel impelled to applaud. But whereas the theatres of Schikaneder's day could achieve transformations with the turn of a handle, so that wings, borders and backcloths all changed magically and simultaneously, the modern theatre must often resort to infinitely more complicated methods. It is one of the anomalies in the development of theatre design since the eighteenth century that though technology has made enormous advances, especially since the introduction of electronics, many scenic effects are often much harder to achieve now than they were 200 years ago. We know from the baroque theatres at Drottningholm in Sweden and Český Krumlov in Czechoslovakia that elaborate transformations could be achieved with very few people in control of the baroque mechanisms. In spite of the electronic facilities available today, equivalent effects can often only be produced by the use of much more complicated machinery and a large technical staff. And in many theatres it can often be impossible to achieve the scenic effects which Schikaneder would have taken for granted.

Flying machines — such as that required by the libretto for the entrance of the Three Boys in II, 16, and later for their arrival with Papagena in II, 29, symbolizing in Masonic terms their identification with the element of air — had existed in most theatres since they had been invented for the baroque theatre on the continent and for the masques of Inigo Jones at the Stuart court in England. To instal a flying-machine today can be a costly and problematic business, and in touring theatres, since opera companies must frequently travel on tour, often impossible. Similarly, every theatre used to be equipped with trap-doors or star-traps — essential for the appearance of demons and fairies in pantomimes, Erda in *Das Rheingold* and *Siegfried*, Mephistopheles in *Faust*, and in *Die Zauberflöte* for the arrivals and departures of the Queen of Night, Monostatos, the Three Ladies and Papageno. As the use of trap-doors is often now considered old-fashioned, they have been removed from most old theatres and are rarely installed in new ones. So if a director feels it is important to fulfil Schikaneder's intentions, he and his designer will have to hit upon alternative means to create effects which were comparatively easy in the eighteenth and nineteenth centuries, but are much more costly and problematic today.

A particular challenge which confronts the stage-designer is the appearance of the Queen of Night in I, 6. Ever since the Berlin production in 1816, when Karl Schinkel designed this scene so brilliantly, every production has sought to find a striking and beautiful *coup de théâtre* for this moment. Schikaneder's stage-directions read: 'The mountains part and the stage is transformed into a magnificent chamber. The Queen is seated on a throne which glitters with sparkling stars.' The first stage-direction in the act has described 'a rocky landscape with a few trees, and mountains rising up on either side of a round temple'. This scene is represented in the engraving by Joseph and Peter Schaffer, first published in 1795. We do not know how the Queen's appearance was achieved on that occasion: if the central temple was painted on a backcloth, the backcloth would have been raised to reveal the Queen on her throne seen against another backcloth representing her palace. At the same time, the wings showing the rocks and trees would have slid away as their place was taken by another set of wings representing walls or columns in the palace. Then, at the end of the Queen's aria, the same machinery

PAPAGENO. Hier meine Schönen, übergeb ich meine Vögel.
Dritter Auftritt 1 Act.

Plate 7. Act I, scene 3: Papageno hands over his birds to the Three Ladies

would effect the change in reverse. If, which is less likely, the central temple had been three-dimensionally built, it could have revolved to show the Queen's throne inside it. At any rate it must have been intended that the dramatic and scenic effect was as exciting for the audience as it was awe-inspiring for Tamino. The designer's challenge today is to achieve an effect so original that on the one hand it has never been seen before and on the other no one can imagine how it has been created. Scene-changes and transformations such as these will obviously have to take advantage of the technical possibilities of the twentieth century when the equivalent baroque effects are no longer available. If the production team is to find an equivalent for Schikaneder's intentions it must call on a different form of magic – the magic of modern technology and electronics. The challenge, however, remains the same as in earlier centuries – to achieve a seamless and unbroken flow through the three scenes of the first act and the ten scenes of the second.

For a scene-change to take place effectively at the appropriate moment, it has to be prepared in advance. Just as da Ponte provides the stage-director with built-in opportunities in the Italian operas of Mozart, so Schikaneder creates specific moments for preparation during the action of *Die Zauberflöte*. It is axiomatic in all these operas that a delicately scored aria or ensemble must not be disturbed by noisy preparations. The librettists therefore took care to ensure that the stage-hands could do their work, either during recitative scenes in the Italian operas, or in the case of *Die Zauberflöte*, in dialogue scenes. The scene between the three slaves in Act I, scene 9, for example, is important for several reasons: to make an aural break between the end of the quintet (no. 5) and the trio (no. 6), to provide us with essential information about Pamina, but also to provide time for the preparation of the next scene-change into Act I, scene 15 (finale, no. 8), since the noise of a scene-change cannot be permitted to obtrude into the very subtle dialogue or the delicate duet between Pamina and Papageno. The many other scene-changes are likewise provided with built-in opportunities for preparation by leap-frog progression: for example, the scene-change from Act II, scene 1, in preparation for scene 7, will be dealt with during the dialogue and convenient claps of thunder during scene 2, and the change from scene 12 in preparation for scene 20 can be effected during the dialogue in scene 15. Schikaneder, as experienced man of the theatre, also gives us alternative moments in the action, so that we are not bound too rigorously. Of course, if the whole production is performed on an unchanging permanent set, none of these problems arise, but where scene-changes and stage-machinery are adopted, an unbroken and silent progression is essential.

As another example of the design and production problems, we may take the finale of the second act (no. 21) which itself falls into five scenes. The music of each scene follows on from its predecessor with only a pause written into the last bar of the scene, enabling the audience to intervene with applause: they can rarely resist applauding the ravishing quartet sung by Pamina and the Three Boys; they applaud the end of the fire and water scene because of its triumphal solemnity, but also because they often think this is the end of the opera which with its ceremonial trumpets and chorus it can well seem to be; the duet between Papageno and Papagena with its provocative bassoons and horns in cheerful G major is likewise irresistible, so in all the designer can hope to have some useful and by no means negligible seconds added to the time needed for his transformations.

The first scene of the finale makes fairly simple demands: a little garden. No more space is necessary on the stage than is needed for the four participants, though the Boys need to be able to watch Pamina unobserved when she first appears. In my productions, the flying-machine which had already been provided for the appropriate entry of the Boys in scene 16 again transported them in this scene, enabling them to hover in the air, their natural element, until they descended to prevent Pamina's suicide. But even as this scene is in progress, the preparations for the next scene have to be made. This scene, namely scene 28, makes the most elaborate demands of all the scenes in the opera: 'Two high mountains. From one mountain the rushing and roaring of a waterfall may be heard: the other spits out fire. Through a grille in each mountain, the fire and water can be seen … there are rocks all over the stage, which is divided into two separate parts, each enclosed by an iron gate … the inscription, illuminated from within, on a pyramid high up in the centre, above the grilles.' In the interpretation of this rubric, we are helped by the details of another of the Schaffers' engravings, which may well derive from the stage-plan of the original production in Vienna of 1791. The contribution of the lighting designer to the work of the production team is particularly important in this scene, as it will probably fall to him to achieve the major effects of fire and water, even if they are to be approached symbolically or impressionistically. The sound-engineer also has an important function in the scene; when Tamino and Pamina enter the flames, the rubric states: 'The spitting of fire and howling

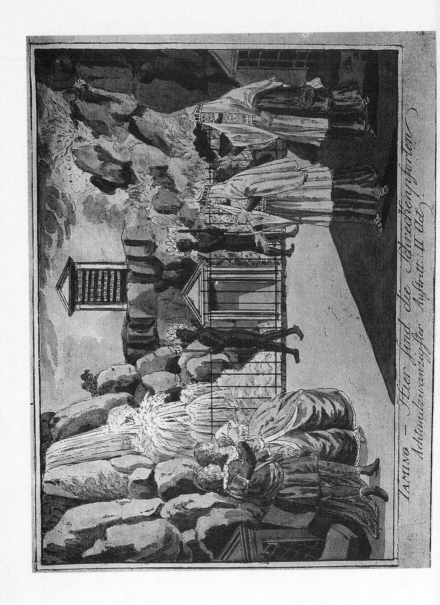

TAMINO – Hier sind die Schreckenspforten
Achtundzwanzigster Auftritt II Act.

of wind can be heard: at times also, the muffled sound of thunder and the rushing of water.' Many conductors have refused to permit these sound-effects during the march played on the flute and drums. But conductors such as Sir Charles Mackerras have recognized how greatly the effect of the march is actually augmented when the appropriate sounds have been included. Schikaneder's rubric for the end of this scene must also be taken into account: 'A door opens, through which may be seen a brilliantly lit temple. The vision must be of the utmost splendour. The choir, accompanied by trumpets and drums, begin to sing.' E. T. A. Hoffmann commented pertinently on the difficulties of both staging and singing this scene in the Berlin production of 1816, and refers to 'the practically unsurmountable difficulty of having the chorus perform off-stage'. He makes some ingenious suggestions about how the chorus could be placed in front boxes and galleries. Before the introduction of closed-circuit television into opera theatres, liaison between singers off-stage or back-stage always presented its problems, and in the past, assistant off-stage conductors were compelled to glue their eyes to small holes in the scenery and were usually perched precariously on the top of ladders in order to make sure of an unimpeded view of the conductor in the pit. Hoffmann's taste for magic in every form would surely have been delighted with the electronic solution to practical problems of communication.

Scene 28 has made imaginative demands on director, designer, lighting-designer and sound-engineer, and because of the scenic complexity will almost certainly have exploited the full depth of the stage. For scene 29, 'the scene changes again to the garden'. Papageno reluctantly prepares to hang himself from a tree − naturalistic or abstract, real or suggested? The Boys intervene − from above, says the rubric, the flying chariot also carrying Papagena. Then without a break, except for applause, the scene changes again, presumably to a subterranean gallery, along which the conspirators are burrowing, with the Priests assembled in conference above them, like James I and his Parliament over the cellars harbouring Guy Fawkes and the gunpowder. During scenes 29 and 30, the scene will be prepared for the final transformation: 'With a violent chord, thunder and lightning, the scene changes so that the whole stage represents a sun. Sarastro stands on high.' Using exactly the methods that would have been used in the eighteenth century we can materialize Sarastro through a gauze at the moment when he must cast out the conspirators. And if there is no stage equipment by which they can sink into the ground when he appears, they must run off into the wings, an exit so much less exciting than the baroque theatre would have achieved. The five scenes of the finale are so ordered that whereas the first, third and fourth take up little space on stage, the second and fifth need the full stage so that the action and cast can be fully deployed. Schikaneder knew his stage-craft well enough to smooth the path for the designers and directors who follow him, if they care to give due attention to what he has prescribed. But as the opera itself has so many facets they can experiment within an infinite variety of styles which may result in satisfactory solutions in permanent sets, composite sets or structures of steel, perspex or timber.

During my own career as an opera director, I have been responsible for two productions of *Die Zauberflöte*, both of which took place in 1975. The first, in January, was produced for the English National Opera at the London Coliseum and was frequently revived and repeated during subsequent seasons over a period of ten years. I also directed a smaller-scale version of the production which was toured by the company to many smaller theatres in the country and was subsequently presented twice by Opera North in Leeds. The second major production, in June, was created for the National Arts Centre in Ottawa, Canada, in a version which was also toured to Toronto and other Canadian cities.

The production for the London Coliseum was specifically designed for that theatre but also had to be performed in conjunction with other operas in the repertory, so though conceived on a large scale, its scope was inevitably limited by the need for daily change-overs of scenery within the theatre. As a festival production, the Ottawa version was the only opera occupying the theatre, so the scenic effects could be conceived on an even larger and more ambitious scale. The two designers were John Stoddart for the London production and Peter Rice for Ottawa. Since these two productions took place within so short a time, I naturally wanted them to be as different as possible; my discussions with the designers therefore covered much identical ground, but each pursued different objectives. For the London version John Stoddart and I decided to adopt a specifically Egyptian approach — taking our lead from the fact that the gods Isis and Osiris, so often invoked in the text, were Egyptian deities and that the libretto has so strong an Egyptian flavour, in itself derived partly from *Sethos* and partly from the Egyptian symbolism so pervasive in Masonic theory. The costumes, and the properties, furniture and architectural features, were based by John Stoddart on Egyptian sources, including many decorative features inspired by birds. The ancient Egyptians believed that the spirits of their enemies took physical form in the bodies of birds, which gives particular significance to Papageno's occupation as bird-catcher to the Queen and her Ladies. The Queen of Night made her first appearance riding on the back of a great black and silver night-bird whose gigantic feathered tail spread to fill the whole of the stage. The Boys' flying-machine was a jewelled phoenix; Pamina's bed was a gold and silver swan and Sarastro appeared beneath a golden falcon which spread its wings in protection over him. The stage of the London Coliseum, though reasonably well-equipped, possessed only two trap-doors, created for other operas and not conveniently situated for our needs in *Die Zauberflöte*. In order to achieve a supernatural appearance for the Queen of Night in Act II, scene 8, and to suggest that she had burrowed her way through subterranean galleries, John Stoddart caused her to emerge dramatically from the maw of a great Sphinx, between the paws of which Pamina had been lying asleep, like Cleopatra at the beginning of Shaw's *Caesar and Cleopatra*. For Papageno's disappearance into the earth in Act II, scene 25, he created a trap-door in a stair-unit up which Papageno had run in pursuit of Papagena. But the theatre did already possess a mechanism previously created for the flying sequences in a production of *Peter Pan* and with this it was possible to activate the flying-machine for Papagena and the Three Boys.

When the Coliseum version of this production was first commissioned, the management of the English National Opera informed us that it would never be sent on tour so that we should take full advantage of the full size and scope of the theatre. But a few months after the production had opened, and possibly because of its success with the public, the management changed its mind and asked us if we could adapt the existing production for touring to smaller theatres. However, the budget available to pay for the adaptation was extremely small and could not possibly cover the construction of entirely new sets. The designer and I therefore had to find ways to retain as much as possible of the existing scenery and effects, even though in many cases they had to be simplified. Some of the more massive elements had to be discarded – the flying-machine, the great Sphinx and the Falcon among others. But Papageno's trap-door could be retained in its self-contained unit, and so could the Queen of Night's chariot. I therefore had to create alternative action and business in order to compensate for the omitted effects. At the Queen's second appearance, lighting effects enabled her to materialize suddenly behind a gauze, while the Three Boys were provided with choreographic movement instead of flying in by mechanical means. Some of the scenery was redesigned to be lighter in weight and on a smaller architectural scale, and a 'touring serpent', which was operated on the principle of the Chinese paper dragon, could be activated by fewer people than its larger London equivalent.

The well-equipped Festival Theatre in Ottawa made it possible for us to achieve all our major effects, and in addition the stage floor was so constructed that it could accommodate three separate trap-doors. Thus the Queen could appear and disappear through a trap-door in Act II, scene 8, Papageno could vanish by another in Act II, scene 25, and for their final disappearance in the last scene of the opera, the Queen, Monostatos and the Three Ladies could all sink into the bowels of the earth. For Ottawa, Peter Rice and I decided to take our lead from the fact that Sarastro's name is derived from the Persian Zoroaster who was the founder of the religion bearing his name, which lays stress on the dualism between light and darkness, Ahura Mazdā and Ahriman, and which is visually represented in so many of the buildings and bas-reliefs of Persepolis and on the tombs of Pasargadae. In endowing the opera with a Persian setting, we made the pragmatic assumption that the worship of Isis and Osiris could have spread from Egypt further to the East, which could probably not be substantiated in fact, though it could be accepted in fantasy. In place of the bird symbols of Egypt, we substituted the animal and reptile symbols of Persia – winged bulls and serpents, lions and horses. Two different productions therefore provided the opportunity to create two different but equally relevant iconographies, each reflecting the detail and symbolism prescribed by Schikaneder.

The director of a new production of *Die Zauberflöte*, whether the performance is to be in German or in translation, will have to decide what version or adaptation of the dialogue is to be adopted. In the full published version of Schikaneder's dialogue there is a considerable disproportion between the spoken words and the musical numbers, which is why it is invariably shortened even in festival performances before a German-speaking public. We have no means of knowing whether it was performed uncut even in the first production under Mozart and Schikaneder. At that period, audiences were used to much longer evenings in the theatre than we are now, especially as it was the accepted custom to go in and out of the auditorium during the course of the performance, depending on the social preoccupations of the individual. But cuts have been made in performing versions of

Plate 9.   Act I, scene 15: Peter Rice's design for the first finale in Anthony Besch's production at the National Arts Centre, Ottawa, 1975

the libretto from an early stage, and every year there is increasing managerial pressure to reduce the overall length of performances in a period when musicians' unions have fixed a total length of three hours (including intervals) as the pragmatic duration after which overtime payments must be made.

During the rehearsals for one revival of my production for the English National Opera at the London Coliseum, the British Musicians' Union had imposed a work-to-rule by which they refused to play any overtime until an industrial dispute had been settled. My production used to run overall for about three hours and ten minutes, depending on the tempi of each particular conductor. When I was asked if I could make cuts in the dialogue to bring the playing-time within three hours, I pointed out that the total length of my version of the dialogue itself lasted only ten minutes, and that a performance deprived of all dialogue would make no sense.* To enable the performances to take place at all the only solution would be to cut out the overture – unthinkable under normal circumstances but at least permitting the rest of the opera to be performed. (It was suggested that recordings of the overture might be made available on sale to the public in the foyers.) In the event, the industrial dispute was settled just in time for the overture to be included for the opening and successive nights.

Nowadays, most directors prefer to make their own translation of the dialogue of *Die Zauberflöte* or to prepare their own adaptation if the production is to be given in the original German. Each director will include as much of the dialogue as he feels is relevant to the characterization in his particular concept. My own instinct has been to include the maximum amount of dialogue proportionate to an effective balance between drama and music.

The dialogue adopted for the production will be sent to the members of the cast well before they arrive for the rehearsal period and the director will have asked them to read and study it without as yet committing it to memory. They will have been required to learn the music of their rôles before rehearsals begin, but as with a play, the interpretation, inflections and timing of the dialogue will develop as the rehearsals progress. The first days of the rehearsal period will be allocated to the conductor and his music staff so that they can acquaint the singers with the appropriate vocal and musical style. The cast will then pass to the director, though ideally the conductor will continue to be present at all staging and production rehearsals. The first production session will be devoted to discussion of the opera:

the director and designer, with a model of the set to hand, will explain their concept and exchange ideas with the singers on the interpretation of their rôles. The artists will be working primarily from the words and music of their own rôles, and the director will contribute his overall view of the opera and its libretto.

The spectator's understanding of an actor's performance is built up through the words he speaks, the actions he performs, or what may be said about him by other members of the cast. The actor himself, however, must already have created in his own imagination a concept of what he had been doing and thinking before he walked through an entrance from the wings – or on to the screen – whether one minute, a day, a year, or indeed his own life-time before he becomes involved in the course of the story. It is not sufficient for the performing artist merely to be aware that Tamino enters pursued by a serpent, or that Pamina will be dragged on stage by Monostatos – the three artists in question must previously construct for themselves the events and motives which have led them up to the situation. Some playwrights – Shaw and Ibsen for example – will present their characters *in medias res*, already involved in a complicated history which then, as in an ingenious detective story, is gradually elucidated and unravelled for the audience. But in most cases, the interpreters and their director will need to create a picture of the preceding events by piecing together the evidence and indications which the author has embedded in the text. It can be a fruitful and constructive experiment when each member of the cast is invited to contribute his or her own theories about the background to *Die Zauberflöte*. If rehearsal conditions do not provide time enough for this, it can be helpful if the director presents his own reconstruction, if only as a talking-point for discussion.

In my own case, I like to provide my cast with a reconstruction of the events leading up to the beginning of the opera from the time of the birth of Tamino and Pamina. Any such survey will be conjectural and idiosyncratic, and every director will evolve differing theories, even though they may be based on the same textual evidence. But there are certain questions which cannot be avoided and must, if possible, be explained: how did Pamina's father know Sarastro and what was his precise involvement in the priesthood of the sun? Had there been dynastic negotiations between the fathers of Tamino and Pamina, possibly also involving the Queen of Night, preparing for a later union between the children? How else did Tamino's father – probably the Emperor of Japan – know of the existence of the Queen of Night, and why else did father and son discuss her? What are Papageno's origins? Can the text be interpreted to read that he was, in fact, the bastard son of the Queen, put out to a foster-father in the forest, and therefore Pamina's half-brother? These and many other points will arise when the text is closely analysed, and will lead in turn to a discussion of the characters as they are revealed in the dialogue and music.

It had been an established convention of baroque opera, both in tragedy and comedy, that the private thoughts and emotions of the individual were communicated through the aria of soliloquy, whereas development of the plot and action were advanced during the intervening recitatives. In his other works for the stage before *Die Zauberflöte*, Mozart made continuous use of the baroque soliloquy, though as his style matured he found the means of carrying the dramatic action through from the recitatives into ever more ingenious ensembles. Even his earlier experiment with Singspiel, *Die Entführung aus dem Serail*, to a libretto by Stephanie the Younger, relied mainly on a sequence of introspective soliloquies, though the brilliant finale to Act II already pointed the way to the corruscating ensembles of the later Italian operas. In *Die Zauberflöte*, Schikaneder's innovation was to tell his story through naturalistic ensemble situations and hardly at all through formalized individual soliloquy. Where solo arias do occur, as in the Queen of Night's two arias, they are dramatically really duets in which the listener's reactions are as significant as the singer's statement. As Tamino listens to her first aria, and Pamina to her second, their contribution to the scene is vital to the performance of the singer. To listen on the stage is an important facet of every performer's art, and careful rehearsal ensures that his reactions on stage contribute to the tension of the scene without distracting from it. The only two actual soliloquies in the opera are both Tamino's – the first when he falls in love with Pamina's portrait (no. 3) and the second, during the Act I finale, when he invokes the aid of the magic flute, though even this is sung to the silent audience of wild beasts which the orphic flute has tamed – and if the animals in the production are controlled by human animation, they, too, must be rehearsed to listen without distraction. It is true that Papageno has three solo arias, appropriate both to Schikaneder's actor-managerial status and to Papageno's extrovert panache, but these songs are conceived as direct addresses to the audience, whose sympathies they enlist in the manner of the *commedia dell'arte*, rather than as introspective soliloquies. It is mainly to the girls in the audience that he sings, especially in his third song when he has lost Papagena. Schikaneder's originality, of which Mozart took full advantage, was to establish his characters and develop his story through action rather than reflection.

The soloist studying the aspects of his own character will at first work from his own music and dialogue, but as he becomes progressively more involved with the other characters he will explore his relationship with them and investigate not only what he thinks about them, but what they, both individually and collectively, may think about him. The Queen of Night's assessment of Tamino, for example, will be quite different from Sarastro's — the one seeing him as a convenient but gullible agent for her conspiracies, and the other as a future ruler, impressionable but honourable. Tamino's attitude to Pamina will in no way be that of Monostatos — the first sees her as an object of love and respect, the second as a provocation to lust: to Tamino she seems sympathetic and affectionate, to Monostatos wayward and elusive. There will, therefore, be as many different viewpoints of one character as the multiple of the other members of the cast. In collaboration with the director, the cast weave a web of interlocking threads into a fabric in which the individual strands are still clearly distinguishable, each strand being significant in proportion to the rôle it represents.

The Two Men in Armour, for example, through appearing on the stage for so short a time, will need to analyse their significance in the plot and their functions in the hierarchy of the temple. To sing a unison duet in octaves might seem purely a vocal matter, but in order to achieve a total unity of thought and intention, the two singers must previously have agreed on the significance of the inscription which they read to Tamino. The Three Boys must be clearly aware of their functional and philosophic relevance to the action. The qualities which they require from Tamino — constancy, patience and discretion — are perhaps a clue to their individual characteristics, though musically they always perform in trio. They also invoke the same qualities in Papageno and Pamina, reminding Papageno that his bells can restore his sense of humour and divert him from self-slaughter, and expressing the promptings of Pamina's subconscious in their comments on her attempted suicide. The two mentor Priests in the second act have strongly differentiated personalities: Tamino's mentor is serious and formal, catechizing him and preparing him for the trials which are to come. Papageno's mentor has a distinct sense of humour and displays a knowledge of the common touch. He deals with Papageno as he would with a recalcitrant child and enjoys the repartee which they exchange. But he probably realizes from the start that his candidate will not graduate in the school of enlightenment and will have to be accepted as an honourable failure. The guardian Priest who greets Tamino outside the Temple of Wisdom is sometimes for casting convenience doubled with Tamino's mentor in Act II. In Act I, he is Sarastro's representative and spokesman and is possibly his successor-elect (as Sarastro may have been to Pamina's father). He has the maturity of experience to deal expertly with Tamino's puzzled questions and preconditioned reactions. He, too, has a sense of humour and is able in their short but seminal dialogue to transform Tamino's impetuosity and impatience into interested involvement.

Monostatos is a subtly conceived portrait of a man coerced by circumstances, colour and creed into resentful isolation and neurotic repression. No one else can exceed his efficiency as overseer to the work-force of the temple, but in order to take up this position he has had to leave his own country. If there had been women of his own race in the temple he might never have felt the urge to rape Pamina, though his predicament also reflects the fascination felt by black for white, and *vice versa*. He is no mere blackavized villain, but a man of human emotions and desires, as his intense and fastidious aria suggests. His closest parallel in Mozart's operas is Osmin in *Die Entführung aus dem Serail*: one may wonder why men of sensibility like the Bassa Selim in one opera and Sarastro in the other should employ and trust servants so potentially dangerous – the answer perhaps in both cases being that the servant represents and is indulged by the subconscious urges of the master.

The Three Ladies of the Queen of Night are witty, elegant and hyper-industrious, and by virtue of their vestal isolation, implicitly nymphomaniac. They reflect the surface brilliance of their mistress, and, when they cannot get what they want, her spite and malevolence. The Third Lady is differentiated both musically and dramatically from the other two – she is probably an amateur painter ('Ja, ja, gewiss, zum Malen schön' – 'Yes, yes, indeed, handsome enough to paint!'), may therefore have made the portrait study of Pamina which she brings on the Queen's behalf to Tamino, and often sings a line counterpointing the primmer thirds and fifths of the other two Ladies, always with a sensual, and often with a comic, effect. Their trio and their two quintets are masterpieces of witty writing and provide kaleidoscopic opportunities as the director develops their musical and dramatic content.

The five rôles of Tamino, Pamina, Papageno, Sarastro and the Queen of Night will probably take up most time in rehearsal and be subject to the closest scrutiny. Within this group, the Queen is the only character who undergoes no change of personality during the course of the story. In his book *Shakespearian Comedy*, Professor George Gordon pointed out that major dramatic works usually contain one pivotal character whose idiosyncrasies remain unaltered even though all may be flux and change around him – the *punctum indifferens*: Bottom in *A Midsummer Night's Dream*, Dogberry in *Much Ado About Nothing*, Touchstone in *As You Like it*, Malvolio in *Twelfth Night*. The Mozart operas contain comparable characters around whom the rest of the cast revolve and with whom they are seen in contrast: Leporello in *Don Giovanni*, Don Alfonso in *Così fan tutte*, Osmin in *Die Entführung aus dem Serail*, and in *Die Zauberflöte*, the Queen of Night. It is true that to different people she displays alternative aspects of her personality – with Tamino she is persuasive, cajoling and disarming, and with Pamina she is dogmatic, unyielding and vindictive – but these are all aspects of an unwavering megalomaniac personality. At the end of *Twelfth Night*, Malvolio rushes from the stage, crying: 'I'll be revenged on the whole pack of you', and we may feel sure that he intends to keep his promise. When the Queen is cast like Lucifer into subterranean darkness, she will preserve her vindictive integrity in the bottomless pit – until summoned by Schikaneder and Goethe (in their sequels) back to the world she despises.

Discussion of the Queen's rôle in the opera will probably lead to mention of the old red herring which claims that the plot of *Die Zauberflöte* underwent revision and alteration by Mozart and Schikaneder during the early stages of composition. Most modern commentators agree that this theory has no basis in fact: Rodney Milnes, in his article 'Singspiel and symbolism' (English National Opera Guide III) considers and effectively dismisses the theory. The first time that I saw the opera, it never crossed my mind that the plot held any inconsistencies, and I am convinced that 99.9 per cent of any audience will be similarly untroubled. Of course, the Queen misleads Tamino about the facts of Pamina's abduction, it is in her interest to do so, though she is ingenious enough to resort to half-truths rather than to actual lies. And, of course, she and her ladies blacken Sarastro's reputation in their desire to fire Tamino to rescue Pamina – his readiness to believe them accords with his guileless credulity on which they are relying and from which he must in due

Plate 10.   Act I, scene 14: Valerie Masterson and Alan Opie as Pamina and Papageno in Anthony Besch's production (designs by John Stoddart) at the English National Opera.

course be weaned by the guardian Priest and his colleagues in the temple. The Queen's appeal to Tamino is ingenious in its deviousness and prevarication; Mozart sets the slow section in the same key of G minor which he later gives to Pamina for her lament in Act II: the family key, as it were. But whereas Pamina's aria is deeply moving in its sincerity and grief, the Queen's aria is self-pitying and over-contrived – beautifully expressed but hypocritically conceived. But even if, like Tamino, we are wooed into acquiescence by her honeyed insincerities, the glittering brilliance and hysterical elaborations of her cabaletta swiftly convince us of her superficiality. She convinces Tamino because of his eagerness to be confirmed as Pamina's *preux chevalier*. But even if we so far identify with Tamino as to be taken in by her protestations, an echo of disbelief will be aroused when Sarastro and his Priests expose her motives to Tamino.

The soprano studying the rôle of Pamina will consider her mother's influence and what characteristics she may have inherited from her. When she studies the conversation between mother and daughter in Act II, scene 8, she will also be led to conjecture the nature of her father's personality. We may assume that she takes more after her father than her mother, but presumably Sarastro was anxious to prevent her from developing her mother's megalomania. It must have been partly to reassure her that the Queen sent as Tamino's companion Papageno, whom Pamina had often heard of but never seen. Pamina is at once reassured by Papageno's arrival, and an immediate empathy is established between them in the charming exchange of confidences leading to their E flat major duet (no. 7). If my own interpretation of Papageno's account of his upbringing is correct, the empathy between the princess and the bird-catcher is explained by their sibling relationship of which they are unaware (see p. 196).

Analysis of Sarastro's character will raise questions for the artist and the director: how old is he? Has he taken vows of celibacy? Is he, even if only subconsciously, in love with Pamina? If Sarastro had been the same age as Pamina's father, or, as his successor, possibly younger, at the time of the action he need be no more than forty or forty-five, at the height of his physical and intellectual powers – like Nimrod, a mighty hunter. There is no necessity for assuming that the priesthood of the sun was celibate: Pamina's father had been its initiate and the choruses in the finales of both acts include women as well as men. From Chailley we know that Lodges of Adoption had been founded in France in the mid-eighteenth century in order to provide women with their own order of Freemasonry. On the other hand, the duet (no. 11) sung by the mentor Priests is firmly anti-feminine, as is the chorus with which the Priests banish the Three Ladies in no. 12. The Priests who confer with Sarastro in scenes 1 and 21 of Act II are men, and we may therefore assume that though the temple was open to female initiates, the inner circle was restricted to men, who were not however bound by vows of celibacy. David Cairns, in his article 'A vision of reconciliation' (in the English National Opera Guide) suggests that it was Sarastro's innovation to introduce women into the innermost ranks of the priesthood. Before the arrival of Tamino, Pamina and Sarastro had probably met daily as he instructed her in philosophy and the sciences which had previously been withheld from her. During these meetings, Sarastro may subconsciously have begun to feel more than a platonic affection for her, which she herself sensed and respected. It is these deeper feelings which Sarastro rejects, along with Monostatos, the agent of Pamina's fears, when he tells her that he will not compel her to love ('Zur Liebe will ich dich nicht zwingen') because she has now fallen in love with another man. Thenceforward he will act as guide and protector to the two neophytes who have come within his charge.

Another theory which has been raised by scholars and commentators, though once again it never seems to provide any problem for the audience in performance, is that the trio between Tamino, Pamina and Sarastro in Act II, scene 21, occurs in the wrong place: it is argued that since Sarastro reassures both lovers that all three of them will meet again, in spite of the present need for separation, it is illogical that the next time we see Pamina she is on the verge of suicide. To assume that the trio should therefore be moved to a place earlier in the act is to assume, either that Mozart and Schikaneder did not intend what they had written, or that there has been a corruption of the original order. No textual evidence for an adjustment of the original score has so far been discovered, and when the trio takes place in its traditional context, there is actually no theatrical or psychological problem for the audience. For Pamina and Tamino, both musically and dramatically, the trio is almost a duet, as they are so much involved in one another that they pay almost no attention to Sarastro's interjections or to his promise: 'Wir seh'n uns wieder' ('We shall meet again'). Tamino is agonized that, though on this occasion he is allowed to speak to Pamina, he must still banish her from his presence. Pamina, unable to comprehend his rejection of her for the second time, is driven almost to the verge of insanity. She has undergone a long series of traumatic experiences: abduction from her mother and childhood home, three attempts of rape, temporary loss of faith in Sarastro, the demands and accusations of her mother, separation from Tamino and a twofold rejection. She is unaware that through Sarastro's organization she is undergoing a parallel series of ordeals to those imposed on Tamino. Indeed, of the two, her trials are the more arduous. Her reason begins to falter and she leaves the assembly of Priests, convinced that she has been deserted by the only three people she loves and respects – her mother, Tamino and Sarastro. The knife which her mother gave her shall be the bridegroom to bring her peace through oblivion. But through the medium of the Three Boys she is persuaded to listen to reason and to the voice of her rational subconscious: constancy, patience and discretion prevail and lead her to search once more for Tamino.

In his novel, *Rasselas*, Dr Samuel Johnson sends his hero-prince on a voyage of exploration and self-discovery. Tamino likewise explores the world and his own nature, and we observe the phases in the development of this character. Adventurous and enterprising by instinct, he progresses from inherent impetuosity and credulity towards circumspection, tolerance and balance of judgment. Through the trials imposed on him by Sarastro, he learns that he must reject instinctual solutions for wider philosophic satisfaction. The inscription read to him by the Two Men in Armour informs him that he must be prepared to face death before he can graduate from earth to heaven. When Pamina arrives to accompany him through the trials of fire and water, they have travelled by different but converging paths. It is now Pamina who takes the lead and invokes the power of the magic flute whose music will protect them. They prove themselves worthy to accompany each other, not only through the ordeals but through life, together in private and in the public responsibilities which will confront them as prince and princess. Already in *Idomeneo*, Mozart had shown us a monarch redeemed not only by his son, but by his daughter-in-law. In *Die Zauberflöte*, he celebrates with Schikaneder the dual equality of woman and man.

In 1792, the co-director of the Berlin National-Theater wrote to King Frederick William II of Prussia: 'It seems to have been the author's intention to crowd together every conceivable difficulty for the stage-designer and technicians, and a work has thus been created whose sole merit is visual splendour ' (Deutsch, *Documents*, p. 444). Even though he totally underestimated the quality of the work, the director was quite right in his assessment of the technical problems of what is one of the most complicated operas to stage in the whole classical repertory. A production must in all its aspects satisfy the most sophisticated member of the audience, but it has failed if it does not also satisfy a child of eight. A production of *Die Zauberflöte* which the audience will see and judge in a single performance may have taken anything between six months and two years to stage. The spectator who rejoices to think he has witnessed a definitive production may find it superseded the following month. The richness of content, of thought and sublimity of aspiration will constantly evoke new approaches and solutions, and the highest hope of the spectator, whether in London, Berlin, New York or San Francisco, Vienna, Tokyo, Sydney or Buenos Aires, will be to find facets of the work explored which he has never hitherto considered, and a production of the opera which is exciting, original and takes him completely by surprise.

* Since this chapter was written, Peter Sellars's production of the opera at Glyndebourne in May 1990 did in fact cut out all the spoken dialogue.

9 Problems

The intention in this final chapter is to tie in some of the loose ends left in the opera by Schikaneder and Mozart, and to consider some of the many problems not addressed earlier in this book with which both scholars and the ordinary opera-lover experience difficulty.

The theory of the change of plan

A recurrent problem that cannot have failed to strike both the casual opera-goer and the person who is well read in the secondary literature is the apparent change of plan that affects the structure and motivation of *Die Zauberflöte*. This matter, referred to by German commentators as the *Bruchtheorie* (theory of a break in the storyline), is often given undue prominence. It is, however, more an apparent problem than a real one. Certainly there are inconsistencies in the text, as indeed there are in some of Wagner's music dramas – undeniable but relatively unimportant lapses, with which a director and his cast have to cope as best they can: how is one to equate the Sarastro who sings that vengeance is unknown within the temple precincts with the Sarastro who a short while before had sentenced Monostatos to seventy-seven strokes with the bastinado? Or how is one to account for Pamina's attempted suicide so soon after she has been told by Sarastro during the trio 'Soll ich dich, Teurer, nicht mehr sehn?' that they would meet again in gladness? To problems of this kind we shall be returning.

The reason usually adduced to justify the belief that the opera suffers from a change of plan inadequately carried out when the authors had reached the finale of Act I is that Mozart and Schikaneder were disturbed by the success of their rival Marinelli's production of *Kaspar der Fagottist* in the early summer of 1791 (see chapter 1, pp. 29–34), and wished to avoid direct confrontation with the Perinet/Müller Singspiel. The fact that Mozart in his letter of 12 June

205

1791 was so dismissive about *Der Fagottist* (see pp. 31–2) does not automatically rule out the possibility that this work did influence *Die Zauberflöte*; but all the evidence – internal, documentary and chronological – is against its having done so. Not least because in the Viennese theatre of the late eighteenth century no one – author or audience – was in the least bothered by similarities in the story-line, or even by obvious 'borrowings'. Further, it would be totally out of character for Mozart, who took such a careful hand in the shaping of every stage work about which we have information, to embark on the composition of an opera before its libretto was firmly settled, at least in outline, let alone agree at a late stage to accept a far-reaching revision of the plot.

The earliest formulation of the theory of the change of plan seems to occur in the letter written to Treitschke by Seyfried *c.* 1840 – a letter we have already examined critically for its information about the identity of the librettist of the opera (pp. 70–1). Among numerous readily disproved claims – for instance, that the libretto was complete only as far as the Act I finale when the Perinet/Müller Singspiel was first performed, whereas Mozart quoted the last line of II, 3 (no. 11) to his wife on 11 June, the day before he attended the fourth night of *Der Fagottist* – stands the statement of Ignaz von Seyfried that, faced with the rival work, 'our Emanuel ... soon knew what to do, and turned the whole plan round; to the salvation and good fortune of the whole ...'[1] This laconic observation was greatly extended by Otto Jahn,[2] and still enjoys considerable currency to this day. Interestingly, this view dates from a period two generations after Mozart's day, by when the lingering remnants of the baroque tradition were largely forgotten. As indeed were the principles of Austrian Freemasonry, though these had from an early date been perceived in *Die Zauberflöte*.

In the late eighteenth century the baroque was still a living force; Schikaneder made full use of the spectacular elements of the old theatrical tradition, constructing his plays with an eye to the effectiveness of powerful contrasts, and able to rely on his audience's perception of the dramatic conventions. One such is the certainty that the sin of pride – *superbia* – will surely be punished. To cite just one example (without suggesting that it was known to Schikaneder), the Breslau poet Daniel Casper von Lohenstein in 1666 wrote a five-act tragedy, *Sophonisbe*, which among other things is an allegorical celebration of the marriage of Emperor Leopold I to the Infanta Margarita of Spain. Sophonisbe, the passionate Queen of Numidia, opposed to Roman steadfastness, exemplified by Scipio Africanus, has several characteristics that we find in the Queen of Night, notably the ability to bewitch men into doing her bidding, a fine sense of the justice of her (unjust) cause, and an overweening pride that leads to her downfall (and, in the case of the African queen, to her ultimate self-destruction).

Balanced judgment requires the audience to await the full exposition of the opposing principles. We should thus not be too swift to accept our first impressions of the Queen as a woman wronged (she is after all Queen of Night). Along with Tamino we sense the majesty and righteousness of the world of the temple from the moment the curtain rises on I, 15 (having been puzzled, perhaps, by the middle ground in the presentation of the 'splendid Egyptian room' of I, 9–14 that seems to be Monostatos' apartment); apart from the beauty of the grove that is prescribed in the stage-direction (in marked contrast to the rocky region of the Queen's domain), the solemnity of the temple leads Tamino to ask 'Is this place the seat of the gods?' This is not a break in the story-line, but a revelation of a state of affairs different from our expectations that requires us to rethink our first impressions. In this task we are helped by heeding the advice given to Tamino by the Three Boys: 'Be steadfast, tolerant and discreet.'

The 'new' numbers performed in 1802

Mozart did not live long enough after the première of *Die Zauberflöte* to be faced with the problems attendant on a new production of the work such as he had experienced with *Idomeneo*, *Le nozze di Figaro* and *Don Giovanni*. Which is not to say that there are no textual problems at all with *Die Zauberflöte* – one concerns the instrumentation and barring of the duet 'Bei Männern, welche Liebe fühlen' (see pp. 122–3, 209); another is raised by Schikaneder's claim, made on the playbill for the first performance of the work at the new Theater an der Wien on 5 January 1802, that two additional numbers by Mozart would be included. The wording, translated in full, reads:

As I was so fortunate as to enjoy Mozart's friendship, and he – out of true brotherly love towards me – set his master-tones to my original work, I shall perhaps pleasantly surprise the respected public today with two pieces of music of Mozart's composition which he bequeathed to me alone. As, furthermore, the good child is appearing once again for the first time today, not only in the new house but also in new clothes, I as father allowed myself the liberty of here and there putting some new words into his mouth; whether they please,

I leave to the judgment of a gracious and estimable public, as whose most obedient servant I sign myself   Emanuel Schikaneder
I & R priv. Theatre Manager[3]

The 'good child' is, of course, Mozart's and Schikaneder's ten-year-old opera; the 'new clothes' refer to 'the entirely new decorations ... partly the work of Herr Vinzenz Sachetti, partly of Herr Gail the younger', advertised in larger type on the playbill; and the reference to the 'new words' points to Schikaneder's propensity for writing replacement lyrics for Papageno's first aria on special occasions.[4]

What were these 'two pieces of Mozart's composition' with which Schikaneder hoped to surprise the audience? One of them was almost certainly the B flat duet for Tamino and Papageno, 'Pamina, wo bist du?' (see pp. 57–8). This piece, discovered by George Richard Kruse in a manuscript copy, and published in Peters Edition vocal scores and in the Belwin-Mills (formerly Kalmus) miniature score, claims descent from the period following Mozart's death. Its musical quality is not such as to permit an undeniable claim to authenticity, but it is certainly good enough to enjoy the occasional airing, as in Wolfgang Sawallisch's 1972 recording of the opera (reissued on CD). If it is actually by Mozart, there is no documentary evidence to support the claim – the words are not included in the first edition of the libretto, nor in any early edition known to me. One factor that may be held to count against its right to a regular place in performances is that it comes in untypically close proximity to two other musical numbers – assuming that the indication of its place between the duet 'Bewahret euch vor Weibertücken' (no. 11) and the quintet 'Wie? Wie? Wie' (no. 12) is correct. It is here that it is sung in the Sawallisch recording. But, despite this ordering of numbers in the source found by Kruse, one might be tempted to propose a later place for it, not only to break up a lengthy spoken scene, but also because Papageno's words ('O little woman [wife], where art thou? / To be separated from thee is the greatest anguish for me') make better sense after he has seen Papagena for the first time. However, by the time he first sees her in her youthful charm (at the end of II, 24), his path has separated from that of Tamino, and there is no scene in this later stage of the action in which he and Tamino could sing a duet. Doubtless, none of these considerations would have worried the audience in the Theater an der Wien in 1802.

The most likely other candidate for the second 'new' item in the 1802 production is also a duet. Nissen states that Schikaneder constantly interfered with the work of his composers, and that Mozart was not spared this annoyance: 'The duet: *Bey Männern welche* etc. he even had to compose five times, before it was good enough for Schikaneder.'[5] Jahn, who takes this anecdote from its original source, Rochlitz's series of reminiscences of the composer derived from his widow, adds the gloss that the exigent impresario found Mozart's attempts at the duet beautiful but too learned in style; only at the third (or fifth) attempt did Mozart find 'the simple tone of warm emotion' that Schikaneder was looking for.[6] The fact that there are other variants of this story – including the forged letter of 5 September 1790 from Schikaneder to Mozart that purports to indicate the librettist's grudging acceptance of the setting of the duet for Papageno and Papagena[7] – makes it no more inherently compelling; certainly no other versions of, or sketches for, 'Bei Männern' survive. Nor is there any evidence to support the claim of the oboist Joseph Trübensee (Triebensee) that, as a member of the Freihaus orchestra at the time of the première, he recalled from later performances the announcement on the playbill that the evening's performance would be 'with the old duet' or 'with the new duet': none of the surviving bills includes this wording. Certainly the possibility that in the early years of the opera's existence there was a discarded setting of 'Bei Männern', 'written wholly in the grand manner' – words attributed to Trübensee[8] is more plausible than the alternative suggestion that Schikaneder was referring merely to the earlier form of the familiar duet found in Mozart's autograph score. This version, which lacks the clarinet and horn chords in bars 1 and 2, and is differently accentuated, would certainly not live up to Schikaneder's claim of 5 January 1802 that he was offering his public two unknown pieces by Mozart. The earlier version is, nevertheless, of considerable interest; Erik Smith discusses it on pp. 122–3, and it may be heard in the recording under Ton Koopman.[9]

A further possibility is that one of the new numbers was another aria for Pamina; the statement is made by Gernot Gruber in the preface to the edition of the opera in the *Neue Mozart-Ausgabe*, without explanation. It will presumably be discussed in detail in the still-awaited 'Kritischer Bericht'.

The order of the numbers in Act II

It has long been recognized that a major dramatic and psychological problem seems to be presented by the position of the Act II terzetto, 'Soll ich dich, Teurer, nicht mehr sehn?' (no. 19). There can be no doubt that its present position − after the chorus 'O Isis und Osiris, welche Wonne!' (no. 18), and before Papageno's aria 'Ein Mädchen oder Weibchen' − corresponds to the wishes of librettist and composer in the period leading up to the first night of the opera. For this is the position it occupies in the first edition of the libretto (as indeed in all the authentic early editions, and in the sales-lists of items from the score advertised by the various Viennese publishers in the *Wiener Zeitung*), as well as in Mozart's autograph ('score' would at this period have been a misnomer for the loose assemblage of individual numbers; more important is the fact that the terzetto is clearly numbered '20' in Mozart's hand, in his unusual sequence which, beginning with the overture as no. 1, makes the Priests' chorus no. 19 and Papageno's aria no. 21).

The problem presented by the terzetto in its traditional place in II, 21 can be simply put: Tamino addresses Pamina, though the imposition of silence is not lifted until Tamino expressly asks the Men in Armour in II, 28 whether he may speak to Pamina, and is told he may. Further, Tamino and Sarastro assure Pamina in the sung text that Tamino loves her, and will be true to her. Admittedly, Sarastro's words before the terzetto, when Pamina is led in, blindfolded ('He [Tamino] awaits thee, in order to say his final farewell to thee') can be taken to imply that the young lovers will never see each other again, whereas his real meaning is that they will hereafter not be separated, as his opening words in the terzetto confirm: 'Ye will meet again in joy!' Pamina draws no comfort from these words − her grief and despair, kindled by her apparent rejection at Tamino's hands in II, 18, will reach their nadir with her attempted suicide in II, 26−7.

Before considering a possible alternative position for this group of scenes set in the vaults of the pyramids we should briefly examine the predicament of Pamina as it is presented in the traditional order of events. Why does she reject the message of hope that is conveyed by Sarastro's first and last words in the terzetto, and of love expressed by Tamino ('Believe me, I feel the same desire [as thou dost], will always be faithful to thee!')? Pamina is initially isolated in the trio, what duettings there are being for Tamino and Sarastro (to bar 33); later she and Tamino do sing together, with Sarastro providing an undercurrent that emphasizes their coming separation. A simple practical solution is to produce scene 21 in such a way that Pamina already reveals here, following Tamino's unresponsiveness to her pleas in II, 18, the early signs of the derangement on which the Three Boys comment in the opening section of the finale ('The poor girl is

close to madness ... Madness rages in her mind'). This reading
is borne out by her otherwise incomprehensible exclamation when
the Three Boys tell her that Tamino loves her: 'Pamina (recovers)
"What? He returned my love, / And hid his feelings from me, /
Turned his face from me? / Why did he not speak to me?"' – She
simply does not remember their last meeting. One could argue
that the obsessive three-note rising quaver figure in bassoons,
violas and cellos which dominates the accompaniment for the
first thirty-two bars, and recurs with and without variation later
in the number, is a kind of *idée fixe*, particularly relevant to Pamina's
predicament. That this scene need not necessarily create major
difficulties for a director is argued by Anthony Besch on pp. 202–3,
and by Erik Smith in note 3 to chapter 6.

There have been several attempts to alter the order of scenes and
musical numbers in Act II. W. H. Auden and Chester Kallman bring
forward the scene showing Pamina's grief at Tamino's apparent
rejection, placing it before, rather than after, her exposure to the
threats of Monostatos and her mother, claiming thereby to strengthen
the motivation for her attempt on her own life. They argue that by
the time we see Pamina in Schikaneder's ordering of Act II she has
apparently forgotten Tamino's existence.

Secondly, the effect of Monostatos and her mother upon her would be a much
greater temptation to suicidal despair if she had to endure them after she
imagines her lover has deserted her rather than before, when she could console
herself with the thought of him and even call on him for help and guidance.[10]

Thirdly, this ordering makes Pamina's 'appearance in the finale with
a dagger more plausible and more dramatic'. Ingmar Bergman evades
this problem, as we saw in chapter 7, in that he removes the terzetto
no. 19 entirely in his filmed version. As Auden and Kallman recognized, any reordering must involve 'a change in key-relationships',
but as they point out: 'Were the music continuous, this would
probably be a fatal objection, but it is not.'[11] Mozart himself takes
the unusual step at the start of Act II of having the march followed
by Sarastro's aria with chorus in the same key of F (separated, it is
true, by the lengthy dialogue of II, 1, and the threefold triple blasts
– in the subdominant – of the wind instruments). In this act in
particular the key-sequence is less tightly organized than in the da
Ponte operas (see p. 129): F, F, C, G, C, D minor, E, A, G minor, D,
B flat, F, E flat. The lengthy stretches of dialogue between most of the
numbers further diminish the potential damage of changes in order.

What problems are solved, and what new ones are created, by repositioning the terzetto no. 19 and the group of scenes (II, 20–5; the scenes involving Papageno, 22–5, could remain in their traditional place) of which it forms part? Brian Trowell has put forward the hypothesis[12] that the authors' original intention may have been to open Act II with the march in D minor that survives as a sketch (it is published in the *NMA* score, p. 376), followed by the Priests' chorus (no. 18), the dialogue of II, 1 and II, 21, and the trio no. 19. Attractive as the idea may be (Professor Trowell emphasized that we must perform the opera as Mozart left it), the traditional order alone makes sense of important stretches of dialogue: Sarastro's praise of Tamino's 'manly and composed' bearing thus far in his ordeals, and his need to tread 'two further dangerous paths' (II, 21) keeps this scene late in the sequence of trials; further, Tamino and Pamina could hardly say their 'final farewell' to each other if they have met but once, and briefly, in the Act I finale. We must conclude that the familiar order, codified in the printed libretto that was on sale in the theatre at the first performance, represents neither an early revision (for the sketched D-minor march is written on paper that Mozart used only after he returned from Prague in mid-September, see p. 84) nor a last-minute change (since the libretto must have gone to the printer well before the première).

Minor inconsistencies

There are numerous superficial inconsistencies in the libretto, both real and apparent. But far from being a source of weakness in the work, they add to its depth and attractiveness: between the stark contrast of darkness and light there are many shadings. The Queen of Night, though the Allegro moderato section of her first aria conveys her arrogant and imperious nature ('Thou shalt go to free her ...'), seems to us, as to Tamino, to be above all a mother wronged. Even when we have learnt that Sarastro kidnapped the Queen's daughter for good reason (see II, 8) we are justified until late in the story in having equivocal feelings about him – for a high priest he may strike us as over-fond of hunting (as Pamina tells Papageno and us in I, 14); and he hints that he may not have removed Pamina from her mother's care solely for altruistic reasons ('I will not compel thee to love, yet I shall not give thee thy freedom', he tells her in I, 18). We would be unwise to accept the wholly negative depiction of Sarastro furnished by the Swedish Folkopera production (see p. 172) or the

highly critical view of him put forward by Attila Csampai.[13] Yet he
is far from being dully, predictably benevolent. Similar points could
be made about virtually all the characters: like most human beings
they are not perfectly consistent in their thinking and their deeds; and
though the opera is basically a fairy-story, the problems that they face
do not permit stereotyped solutions.

Let us now consider some of the puzzling details. Why does
Sarastro have in his entourage a lustful Moor who specializes in
oppression and blackmail? There is no single answer. He is perhaps
a former aspirant for initiation who failed the tests (see pp. 14–15).
Certainly he is useful in the temple compound as overseer of the slaves.
He seems also to have been given responsibility for keeping an eye
on Pamina. A deeper reason, similar to that found in Goethe's *Faust*,
may be that, as God (in Goethe's 'Prologue in Heaven') tolerates
Mephistopheles as sardonic tempter, allowing him *carte blanche* to
try and bring Faust down, but confident that Faust's restlessly striving
nature will in the end save him, so Sarastro can see a positive force
for good not so much in Monostatos himself as in the challenging
effect his solipsistic nature may exert on the education of Pamina.
This is not to minimize the danger of rape in which she three times
finds herself – first as described by the slaves in I, 9, before we first
see her, then in the terzetto no. 6, in which Monostatos hopes to have
his revenge for her attempted escape, and finally in II, 7, when he
finds her sleeping in the moonlit garden and thereupon tries to
blackmail her. But powerful forces are at work on her side: respectively her uttering of Sarastro's name, the arrival of that cheerful son
of nature, Papageno, and the entry first of the Queen of Night, and
later (II, 11) of Sarastro.

Why should the Three Boys – revealed as goodly spirits – be in
the employ of the Queen? The short answer is, despite what the Three
Ladies maintain, that the Boys are no longer subject to the Queen's
will. In the quintetto (no. 5) the Three Ladies tell Tamino and
Papageno that they will be guided on their way to Sarastro's castle
by 'Three little boys, young, beautiful, good and wise', and the music
(though not the stage-direction) might be thought to justify the effect
often adopted in performance whereby the Boys appear at this
juncture. Mozart's music (bar 214, change of tempo from Allegro
to Andante; modulation from the dominant back to the tonic, B flat;
aethereal scoring with pairs of clarinets and bassoons accompanying
hushed pizzicato quaver figuration on first and second violins; and
sotto voce singing from the Three Ladies) perfectly conveys the tone

of disembodied serenity that will be associated with the Boys on their three appearances. It is clear, however, that they do not appear here — we see them for the first time at the opening of the Act I finale; at their next appearance, in the terzetto no. 16 (II, 16), they sing 'We greet you for the second time'. Papageno confirms in his dialogue with Pamina in the middle of I, 14 that he and Tamino had seen no sign of their promised guides. The Boys lead Tamino to the entrance of the temple at the start of the first finale; but they do not do so at the command of the Queen, who (we may suppose) no longer has any power over them since the death of her husband, though she may not hitherto have needed to call on their aid, and thus has not realized the loss of them. They serve the cause of good, in II, 16 returning to Tamino and Papageno their magic instruments, and bringing them food and drink, and in II, 27 and 29 saving first Pamina and then Papageno from their attempts to commit suicide. The Three Boys are the apotheosis of the *dienstbare Geister* — obedient spirits — of the traditional Viennese magic plays and operas (a famous example is Pizichi in *Kaspar der Fagottist*).

Smaller points can also cause confusion. Of what material is Tamino's flute made? — The stage-direction in the quintetto no. 5 reads: 'First Lady (*gives him a golden flute*)'. After its virtues have been extolled — its power to give protection and succour in adversity, and to transform men's passions — all five unite to proclaim that such an instrument is 'worth more than gold and crowns'. Before the tests of fire and water in II, 28 Pamina tells Tamino the story of the flute's manufacture: 'In a magic hour my father carved it from the deepest core of the thousand-year-old oak in lightning and thunder, storm and din.' There is no reason why we should not think of the flute as a wooden instrument, with its keys (perhaps four or six in number, in Mozart's day) of gold (for the Ladies, with their superficial scale of values, the precious metal would be paramount, for Pamina the solid and ancient wood from which her father fashioned it).

It was in part as an attempt to solve the problem of Pamina's dagger that Auden and Kallman altered the order of events in Act II of their translation. How does Pamina come to have the weapon for her suicide attempt at the start of the second finale? It was given to her by her mother at the end of II, 8 ('Dost thou see this steel [dagger]? — It has been sharpened for Sarastro. — Thou shalt kill him, and deliver unto me the mighty circle of the sun.'). Monostatos takes it from her in scene 10, and at the beginning of the following scene Sarastro intercepts the fatal blow that the Moor aims at her.

He presumably disarms Monostatos and keeps the dagger. For it to be in Pamina's hand in II, 27 we must assume that Sarastro returned to her in scene 12, as a mark of his trust in her, the weapon with which she had been commanded to kill him.

The parting of the ways for prince and bird-catcher comes at the end of II, 19, when Tamino returns with his flute to save Papageno from Sarastro's lions, after the latter has been keener to finish his meal in peace than to obey the summons of the threefold chord. Scenes 20–1, set in the vaults of the pyramids, contain the Priests' chorus, the dialogue during which Pamina is led in to hear Tamino's last farewell, and the terzetto 'Soll ich dich, Teurer, nicht mehr sehn?' – the stage then empties. Scene 22, in the same setting, begins with Papageno groping his way in, calling in vain for Tamino. The stage-direction '(*He comes to the door through which Tamino was led off*)' probably refers to the exit of Tamino after the terzetto at the end of the previous scene – though it could refer to a deleted scene in which the two companions were separated by their mentors. At all events it is at this moment that Papageno is exposed to the comic repetition of Tamino's experience when knocking to gain entry to the temples in the first finale; and from this time forth his path does not again cross Tamino's.

An interesting and generally unremarked alteration in Mozart's score in II, 27, the first section of the second finale, deserves attention. In the autograph Mozart originally wrote a five-bar passage in short score (i.e. he deleted it before reaching the stage of adding the instrumentation) beginning at bar 81, Pamina's 'Durch dich leide] ich, und dein Fluch verfolget mich! – Sieh! Pamina stirbt durch dich! Dieses [...]'. Since the next leaf in the autograph is an insertion on a different paper-type (Type VII, p. 83) it is likely that the deleted passage was longer than the surviving five bars. Two explanations suggest themselves: either Mozart's concentration flagged, causing him to skip three lines of text, or – and this second possibility seems more likely – he felt the need for additional lines (supplied in time for the printing of the libretto) and an extended musical setting. The familiar vocal line rises to g'' on the word 'Fluch'; the tessitura of this phrase was originally lower, though the setting of 'Sieh! Pamina ...' is similar in both versions. The reason why I favour the hypothesis that Mozart asked Schikaneder for three additional lines of text (or supplied them himself – but in that case would they have been printed in the libretto?) is that the line for the Three Boys, 'Mädchen! Willst du mit uns gehn?' is unique in the entire second finale as having no rhyming partner.[14]

Another group of inconsistencies embraces the mainly minor changes in wording and layout that occur between the printed libretto and the autograph score.[15] There are around fifty of these. The evidence suggests strongly that the first edition of the text was not correlated with the composer's score. Thus the three brief passages of verse that Mozart omitted in his setting are nevertheless printed in the libretto. Conversely, important lines that occur in Mozart's setting were presumably omitted in error by the printer (most obviously, 'Stirb, Ungeheu'r, durch unsre Macht!' in no. 1). A third category includes passages where Mozart departed from the distribution of rôles specified by Schikaneder – notably, no. 10, Sarastro's aria with chorus, is headed plain 'Chorus' in the book; other examples occur at Monostatos' entry when he captures Pamina and Papageno in the first finale, and in the trials in the second finale. The last category for consideration here is around thirty examples of minor changes to words or phrases – verbal repetitions, alterations to articulation, and changes that make lines more singable. My favourite instance concerns Papageno's despairing cries for his new-found girl-friend just before his suicide attempt. He sings 'Papagena! HerzensWeibchen! / Papagena liebes Täubchen' ('... little wife of my heart! ... dear little dove'). The libretto here reads 'Papagena! Herzenstäubchen! / Papagena! liebes Weibchen!' Why the change? (That Mozart was consciously reshaping the words is made clear by the crossing-out of his first thought, which was to place first the phrase 'Papagena! liebes Täubchen!') The reason, I suggest, is that Mozart wanted to encode a favourite form of address in his letters to Constanze, whom (from 1789 on) he sometimes called his 'HerzensWeibchen' – for instance in the letters of 16 and 19 May 1789, and 3 July 1791, the last date being perhaps exactly when he was composing this part of the Act II finale (most of his letters from this summer begin with variations on 'Liebstes, bestes Weibchen' or 'Ma trés chere Epouse').

Two features of Sarastro's government cause some discomfort to a modern audience: he keeps slaves; and women are disadvantaged and looked down upon. Two points should be made: the general one, that it is unhelpful to judge these matters from the perspective of our own times; and the more specific one, that Sarastro's community of priests and their entourage represents not paradise on earth but a still-developing society. The Slaves are not maltreated, except by Monostatos (see I, 9); that there are slaves in this otherwise enlightened land is not surprising, even if this is hardly the ancient Egypt in which the temples and pyramids are actually being built by slave labour. For Schikaneder's contemporaries, abolition of serfdom in the Habsburg lands was a recent memory (1781), and though torture had officially been abolished five years before that, very severe and public punishments were still common. The sentencing of Monostatos to a flogging on the soles of his feet (though as we have seen, it was commuted – pp. 55 and 58) can thus be placed against a background of harsh punishment of offenders. In fact an early enactment of Leopold II's brief reign did away with the sentencing of offenders to forced labour towing Danube barges upstream, but some harsh, demeaning penalties remained.

What of the low opinion in which women are held? To this there are two answers: women were looked upon by Freemasons as unworthy to participate in their activities (for Ignaz von Born's view on women in a Masonic context, see pp. 23 and 40) because they were held to be indiscreet; but in Pamina, Sarastro and the brotherhood identify for the first time a woman with exceptional qualities that command more than mere admiration ('A woman who does not fear night and death / Is worthy, and will be initiated', II, 28). Without the advantage accorded to Tamino and Papageno of knowing about the trials to be undergone, she survives her own trials, and even leads Tamino through the fire and water. She is honoured as no woman has been honoured before – the final stage-direction specifies 'Tamino, Pamina, both in priestly raiment'.

Conclusion

A modicum of the time expended in searching for the meaning of the story of 'Die Zauberflöte', if devoted to considering its history, would, we think, have been well bestowed. But it is easy and delightful to dive for meanings, – whereas to rest content in facts, when the same are not picturesque, requires some courage and calmness of mind.

(*The Athenaeum*, 19 July 1851, p. 775)

This closing section does not seek to impose any one interpretation on this most cornucopian, indeed in the hands of its interpreters Procrustean, of operas. We shall (perhaps fortunately) never know what deeper intentions may have been in the minds of its creators in the summer of 1791. Which is not to deny scholars and directors the right to search in libretto and score for hidden meanings – provided they respect what author and composer have actually given us in the text as evidence of their intention. Goethe – himself a Freemason – gave good advice when on 29 January 1827 he commented to Eckermann on the recently completed Helena act of *Faust II*:

If it is only the case that the general run of spectators takes pleasure in what they see, at the same time the higher meaning will not escape the initiate, as is the case with the Zauberflöte and other things.[1]

This 'higher meaning' is a clear reference to the Masonic qualities that are brought out particularly in Act II of the opera. As we have seen, there is a firm Masonic background in Mozart's case, and a more equivocal one in Schikaneder's. What we cannot say, in the present state of our knowledge, is precisely what relationship there was between Viennese lodge ritual in 1791 and the speeches and activities of Sarastro and his Priests. This uncertainty allows two contrasting approaches: that the authors were openly striking a blow for the beleaguered Craft[2] or – the more common interpretation – that they were concealing allusions to it behind an allegorical pantomime.

The emphasis that Goethe places on the visual impact is important. Though no iconographical material survives from the earliest performances of *Die Zauberflöte*,[3] and references to Egypt and things Egyptian are (apart from the invocations to Isis and Osiris) infrequent in the text, it is to be assumed that, despite the classical rotunda

218

depicted in several early illustrations, the sets and costumes were intended to evoke that civilization. Though we may tend to imagine that Western European interest in things Egyptian dates from after Napoleon's expedition of 1798, which has its lasting monument in the series of ten volumes entitled *Description de l'Egypte* and published in Paris between 1809 and 1822, the fact is that there was already a lengthy history of Egyptianization in European arts and literature. We have already seen that three of the sources of the opera – those by Terrasson and Born, in addition to Mozart's own music to *Thamos, König in Egypten* – are specifically Egyptian. Rameau's *Les Fêtes de l'Hymen et de l'Amour ou Les Dieux d'Egypte* was performed for a court wedding at Versailles in March 1747, with entrées entitled 'Osiris', 'Canope' and 'Arueris ou Les Isies'. The title of another opera by Rameau, *Zoroastre* (1749) deserves mention. And a court wedding at Dresden in October 1781 was celebrated by J.G. Naumann's opera *Osiride* (with libretto by Mazzolà, who revised Metastasio's *La clemenza di Tito* for Mozart ten years later).

The Egyptian influence on the visual arts is well attested from the seventeenth century, when Versailles was laid out with its Egyptian-izing sculptures; Poussin included Egyptian motifs in a number of his paintings. In Austria, J.B. Fischer von Erlach (1656–1723) included many details from the same culture in his *Entwurff einer Historischen Architektur* (1721), and he as well as his rival Lukas von Hildebrandt created sphinxes, canopic vases, obelisks and pyramids for the embellishment of some of the grandest Viennese palaces and their gardens – several of the parks and gardens were open to the public by the middle of the eighteenth century, which helped spread an awareness of ancient cultures. This influence also invaded the sacred sphere with Egyptian motifs being included in church architecture and paintings (there are clear links between Marian symbolism and that of the Mysteries of Isis). Renewed impetus came from Comte de Caylus's *Recueil d'Antiquités Egyptiennes, Etrusques, Grecques et Romaines*, which appeared in seven large volumes between 1752 and 1767.[4]

More complex than the visual aspects of the opera are the allegorical interpretations to which it has been exposed. These begin at the latest in 1794, in which year an anonymous Viennese pamphlet, *Dialogues of the Gods against the Jacobins* (identified as the work of the jurist Joseph Valentin Eybel), was published. In the *Dialogues* Pamina is the republic, born of night, and intended for a Jacobin marriage; however, she is brought to a sanctuary where she will be protected by the priests of nature and reason until she can be married to a prince who proves himself to be a son of the true light. Papageno is the 'Jacobin bird-catcher who entices the people into the Jacobin clubs, locks them in the national cage, and so delivers them to the night'.[5] In 1795 a book appeared with the fictive place of publication of London that includes a socio-political interpretation of the opera. *Geheime Geschichte des Verschwörungs-Systems der Jakobiner in den österreichischen Staaten. Für Wahrheitsfreunde* ('Secret history of the conspiratorial system of the Jacobins in the Austrian states. For friends of truth') includes an interpretation of the opera with the Queen representing Louis XVI's despotic regime, Pamina the cause of Liberty, and Tamino the people.[6]

Apart from numerous political readings (which include Franz Grillparzer's satirical depiction in his fragment *Der Zauberflöte zweiter Teil* of the police state of Monostatos/Metternich, plenipotentiary of Franz II/Queen of Night[7]) we find others that more understandably emphasize the moral and social aspects. Less controversially, Constanze Mozart's second husband, Georg Nikolaus von Nissen, asks and answers a question in the appendix to his biography of Mozart: 'What then was the intention of the poet? "A parody, an apotheosis of the Order of Freemasons." Symbolically: the battle of wisdom with foolishness − of virtue with vice − of light with darkness.'[8]

There is no doubt that *Die Zauberflöte*, especially its second act, has a strong Masonic content. However, in the absence of precise information about the rituals, beliefs and attitudes of Viennese Masons in 1791, we should be very unwise to try and interpret its constituent elements with any precision. The 'knocking' rhythmic figures of the opening of the overture and in several numbers from the first finale on are Masonic.[9] And certainly the numbers three and five have particular significance. But whether one thinks in terms of the number of appearances of a character on stage, or the number of accidentals in a key-signature, let alone the number of notes in a particular passage or piece,[10] one may well be more puzzled than convinced by the theorizings of scholars. Nevertheless, there are several studies that can be recommended to the open-minded reader who is anxious to explore in depth the Masonic associations that have been discerned in the opera. These are − in chronological order (details may be pursued in the bibliography) − the monographs by O.E. Deutsch, Paul Nettl, Alfons Rosenberg, Jacques Chailley, Katharine Thomson, Robbins Landon, and Hans-Josef Irmen.

And anyone who requires a compact outline of theories about the hidden meanings that have been discerned in *Die Zauberflöte* may be referred to an elderly but still very useful survey, E. K. Blümml's 'Ausdeutungen der "Zauberflöte"', in the first issue of the *Mozart-Jahrbuch* (1923), pp. 109–46.

Faced with so many and varied interpretations of Schikaneder's and Mozart's opera, the reader may feel like throwing up his or her hands in despair. This may be an understandable reaction, but it is born of impatience. Even if one agrees with the present writer that the most faithful, least obtrusive reading gives the greatest pleasure, the fact remains that the range of interpretations to which the opera has been subjected provides the clearest evidence of its hold on the imagination alike of directors, performers and the opera-loving public.

Notes

Introduction

1. O. E. Deutsch, *Mozart. Die Dokumente seines Lebens. Addenda und Corrigenda* (Kassel etc., 1978), p. 79 (and p. 80); English edition, *Mozart. A Documentary Biography* (London, 2nd edn, 1966), p. 467 (and p. 470).
2. R. Wagner, *Gesammelte Schriften und Dichtungen* (Leipzig, 2nd edn, 1888), vol. x, p. 98. For a less tortuous expression of Wagner's admiration for the opera, see the early essay, 'Über deutsches Musikwesen' of 1840–1 in *Gesammelte Schriften und Dichtungen*, vol. i (1887), pp. 162–3.
3. *The Works of John Ruskin*, ed. E. T. Cook and A. Wedderburn, vol. xvii (London, 1905), pp. 335–6. G. B. Shaw referred mockingly to this comment of Ruskin's in a contemporary review; see *Music in London 1890–94*, vol. iii (London, 1932), pp. 201–2.

1. Sources

1. Wer diesen Weg allein geht, und ohne hinter sich zu sehen, der wird gereinigt werden durch das Feuer, das Wasser und durch die Luft; und wenn er das Schrecken des Todes überwinden kann, wird er aus dem Schooss der Erde wieder herausgehen, und das Licht wieder sehen, und er wird das Recht haben, seine Seele zu der Offenbarung der Geheimnisse der grossen Göttin Isis gefasst zu machen!
2. Der, welcher wandert diese Strasse voll Beschwerden, / Wird rein durch Feuer, Wasser, Luft und Erden; / Wenn er des Todes Schrecken überwinden kann, / Schwingt er sich aus der Erde Himmel an. – / Erleuchtet wird er dann im Stande seyn, / Sich den Mysterien der Isis ganz zu weih'n.
3. Horus, Gott der durch die Weisheit erworbenen Verschwiegenheit, / Der du die unschuldige schwache Kindheit / Jedes Dinges auf dem Wege zu seiner Reise gängelst; / Erhalte einem Prinzen, der noch Kind, dein Blut, dein Ebenbild ist, / Einen Beystand, den dir selbst in seinem Alter / Deine Mutter Isis geleistet hat.
4. O Isis, grosse Göttin der Egypter, gieb deinen Geist dem neuen Diener, der so viel Gefahren und Beschwerlichkeit überstanden hat, um vor dir zu erscheinen. Mache ihn auch sieghaft in den Proben seiner Seele, und lehre sein Herz deine Gesetze, damit er würdig werde, zu deinen Geheimnissen zugelassen zu werden.

222

5. The injunction to be silent is found in II, 3–5, 13–19, and 29 of the opera.
6. We learn from *Sethos* that there are two kinds of initiation, the greater and the lesser; foreigners are only allowed to undergo the second kind.

2. The intellectual background: Freemasonry

1. One could see in Sarastro's response to Monostatos' threat to Pamina's virginity in II, 11 an example of Leopold II's desire 'to lead criminals back to their duty by a more lenient treatment, rather than to harden them against all decent inclinations by excessively severe penalties'. See Ernst Wangermann, *From Joseph II to the Jacobin Trials* (London, 2nd edn, 1969), p. 91, citing F. Hegrad, *Versuch einer kurzen Lebensgeschichte Kaiser Leopolds II* ... (Prague, 1792), p. 170.
2. Published as an appendix to H. C. Robbins Landon's study, *Mozart and the Masons: New Light on the Lodge 'Crowned Hope'* (London, 1982), pp. 65–72.
3. Philippe A. Autexier, *Mozart & Liszt sub Rosa* (Poitiers, 1984) and 'Mozart a-t-il écrit un opéra maçonnique?', *Chroniques d'histoire Maçonnique*, vol. 34, no. 1 (1985), pp. 11–17.
4. Born was married; his daughter Maria was spoken of as 'beautiful and stimulating', and as 'an excellent pianist' (Joachim Hurwitz, 'Haydn and the Freemasons', *Haydn Year Book*, vol. xvi, p. 34).
5. Paul Nettl, *Mozart und die königliche Kunst. Die freimaurerische Grundlage der 'Zauberflöte'* (Berlin, 1932), pp. 87–91, and *Mozart and Masonry* (New York, 1957; reprint 1970), pp. 61–2.
6. See the appendix to Robbins Landon's study (cf. note 2, above).

3. Synopsis

1. Or Javanese? Early editions are undecided.
2. When it is first played in the Act I finale it is designated 'istromento d'acciajo' ('steel instrument'). The keyed glockenspiel was played in the wings; Mozart's letter to his wife of [8 and 9] October 1791 relates that he had the urge to play the glockenspiel himself (in 'Ein Mädchen oder Weibchen'), and teased Schikaneder by supplying an unexpected arpeggio, and then declining to play it next time round. This impromptu by-play was for many of the audience the first indication that Papageno did not play the bells himself, says Mozart.
3. In IV, 2 of Schiller's *Die Verschwörung des Fiesco zu Genua*, which entered Schikaneder's repertory in 1784, Zenturione attempts to gain entry first at the right-hand gate, then at the left, and is each time turned back by the command 'Zurück'.
4. Mozart wisely omitted four moralizing lines in the libretto to the effect that truth is not always good because it hurts the great; but if truth were always hated, life would not be worth living. Mozart kept the point about the great, turning Schikaneder's 'the great (broad?) path' in the concluding chorus into 'the path of the great'.

4. The writing of *Die Zauberflöte*

1. There is no reason to think that Mozart departed from the then normal practice of conducting the first two or three performances of a new opera himself.
2. Cf. the memoir of Ignaz von Seyfried: Deutsch, *Dokumente*, p. 472 (English edition p. 556).
3. A variant of this rumour is recorded by I. F. Castelli (vol. ii, p. 236), where the duet that Schikaneder was dissatisfied with is identified as that between Papageno and Papagena (cf. p. 157); see also J. C. Schikaneder's reminiscence, Deutsch, *Dokumente: Addenda*, p. 100.
4. Treitschke names the prompter as Haselböck (in Seyfried's letter the spelling is Haselbeck). In fact, as Deutsch points out (*Dokumente*, p. 472; English edition p. 556), Joseph Anton Haselbeck was one of Schikaneder's theatre poets; Christoph Helmböck (whom Cornet names as the prompter – see below) was the property man (*Dokumente*, p. 475; English edition p. 560). Many of the numerous minor discrepancies in identification and fact are elucidated in Deutsch's notes.
5. Deutsch, *Dokumente*, p. 475; English edition p. 560.
6. Furthermore, Cornet had the reputation of being a thoroughly unreliable, boorish, even malevolent character; see Ferdinand, Ritter von Seyfried, *Rückschau in das Theaterleben Wiens seit den letzten fünfzig Jahren* (Vienna, 1864), p. 41.
7. For the notion that the opera was already well advanced by September 1790, see Peter Branscombe, '*Die Zauberflöte*: some textual and interpretative problems', in *Proceedings of the Royal Musical Association*, 92nd session (1966), pp. 45–63 (here pp. 47–9).
8. Quotations are translated from the revised second edition (Leipzig, 1867), vol. ii, p. 465.
9. Alan Tyson's study of paper-types warns us, for instance, against inferring from the date '5. Januar 1791' that the B-flat Piano Concerto, K 595, was actually composed, rather than completed, at about this date. Alan Tyson, *Mozart. Studies of the Autograph Scores* (Cambridge, Mass., and London, 1987), pp. 33, 135 and 156. This volume, and several personal communications from Dr Tyson, have provided the basis for the evidence of dating put forward in this chapter.
10. *Verzeichnüß aller meiner Werke Vom Monath Febrario 1784 bis Monath ...*, facsimile edition by Otto Erich Deutsch (New York, n.d.)
11. These divergencies are examined in P. Branscombe, '*Die Zauberflöte*' (1966).
12. Gernot Gruber, 'Das Autograph der "Zauberflöte". Eine stilkritische Interpretation des philologischen Befundes', *Mozart–Jahrbuch 1967*, pp. 127–49, and *Mozart–Jahrbuch 1968–70*, pp. 99–110.
13. Karl-Heinz Köhler, 'Zu den Methoden und einigen Ergebnissen der philologischen Analyse am Autograph der "Zauberflöte"', *Mozart–Jahrbuch 1980–83*, pp. 283–7.
14. I should like to express my particular thanks to Alan Tyson for his generosity in making available to me his as-yet unpublished analysis of the paper-types that make up the autograph score.
15. Personal communication from Alan Tyson.

5. The libretto

1. If this was so, it must have been before the summer of 1790, as Schikaneder's *Der Stein der Weisen*, first performed on 11 September that year, is in part derived from the story of that name in the first volume of *Dschinnistan*.

2. According to the 'Biographical sketch of Sir Charles Lewis Metzler von Giesecke', which was published in *The Dublin University Magazine*, 3 (1834), pp. 161–75 and 296–306, Gieseke left Vienna in February 1819 (p. 299); however, E. J. Dent provides plausible evidence, derived from his album, that Gieseke was in Vienna from late 1818 until May 1819, and concludes that the incident reported by Cornet must have taken place shortly before Gieseke's final departure from Vienna (*Mozart's Operas*, London, 2nd edn, 1947, p. 239).

3. The portrait is reproduced in E. K. Blümml, *Aus Mozarts Freundes- und Familienkreis* (Vienna, Prague and Leipzig, 1923), facing p. 72 and, with less clarity, in Dent's *Mozart's Operas* (London, 2nd edn, 1947), facing p. 236.

4. 'Stammbuch des Otto Hattwig Fagottisten am Theater an der Wien 1797–1818', Stadt- und Landesbibliothek, Vienna, shelf-mark 45935 Ja. Other members of Schikaneder's company who made entries in the album (many pages of which are lost) include 'Frid. Seb. Meier' (who created the rôle of Pizarro in *Fidelio*), his wife 'Josepha Meier gewesene Hofer, geborene Weber' ('… formerly Hofer, née Weber' – the first Queen of Night), both of whom made their entries on 12 February 1800, and Joachim Perinet (10 March 1800). Hat[t]wig (1766–1834) gave up the bassoon and became a prominent violinist, well known to Schubertians.

5. I. F. Castelli, *Memoiren meines Lebens*, vol. i, ed. J. Bindtner (Munich, [1913]), pp. 236–7.

6. Austrian National Library, Musiksammlung, shelf-mark 685928–A.

7. La Roche as 'Casper der Hausknecht' in *Die Schwestern von Prag* (1794) in an engraving signed 'Watteau, inv. / Renard. sc.', reproduced in Franz Hadamowsky, *Das Theater in der Wiener Leopoldstadt 1781–1860* (Vienna, 1934), facing p. 160.

8. Described and illustrated in *The Times* of 18 December 1987, p. 10.

9. In R. S. Loomis, ed., *Arthurian Literature in the Middle Ages* (Oxford, 1959), pp. 439–40. I am indebted to Professor D. D. R. Owen for this lead.

10. *Festschrift Otto Erich Deutsch zum 80. Geburtstag*, ed. W. Gerstenberg, J. LaRue and W. Rehm (Kassel etc., 1963), pp. 183–6.

11. F. Nicolai, *Beschreibung einer Reise durch Deutschland und die Schweiz*, vol. iv (Berlin and Stettin, 1784), p. 610 n. 2.

12. Original-Feenkomödie *Die Reiche der Schwannen und Pfauen oder: Die Königin Blandine*; see E. K. Blümml and G. Gugitz, *Alt-Wiener Thespiskarren* (Vienna, 1925), pp. 155–6. See also Claire D. Crosby, 'The fairy tale on the old Viennese stage', PhD thesis (University of St Andrews, 1986), p. 111.

13. *Theatralische Werke von Carlo Gozzi*, translated into German by F. A. C. W. Werthes, 5 vols. (Berne, 1777–9).

14. J. P. Eckermann, *Gespräche mit Goethe*, 23 April 1823.
15. P. Branscombe, '*Die Zauberflöte*: some textual and interpretative problems', *Proceedings of the Royal Musical Association*, 92nd session (1966), pp. 45–63.
16. Bonn: Simrock, 1814; see M. Freyhan, 'Toward the Original Text of Mozart's *Die Zauberflöte*', *Journal of the American Musicological Society* 39 (1986), pp. 355–80.
17. This point is discussed by Erik Smith on pp. 122–3; readers requiring a more extensive study may be referred to Arnold Feil's article 'Mozarts Duett "Bei Männern, welche Liebe fühlen". Periodisch-metrische Fragen', in *Festschrift Walter Gerstenberg zum 60. Geburtstag* (Wolfenbüttel and Zurich, 1964), pp. 45–54.
18. See P. Branscombe (1966), pp. 54–5 and 58.
19. For examples, see P. Branscombe, '*Die Zauberflöte*. A lofty sequel and some lowly parodies', *Publications of The English Goethe Society* 48 (1978), pp. 1–21, here pp. 3–5. It is of interest that many of Nissen's quotations from the libretto in his *Biographie W. A. Mozarts* are taken from the Vulpius translation.
20. See Bernhard Paumgartner, 'Eine Text-Bearbeitung der "Zauberflöte" von 1795', in *Festschrift Otto Erich Deutsch* (see note 10 above), pp. 128–34.
21. See Willi Schuh, 'Die "Zauberflöte" im Mannheimer Nationaltheater 1794', and 'Die "verdeutschte" Zauberflöte im Kärntnertortheater', in *Umgang mit Musik* (Zurich, 1970), pp. 37–49 and 14–21.

6. The music

1. Apart from the last two quartets for the King of Prussia and the D major Quintet, which are the equal, or nearly so, of his finest works in these forms, there are no major works, for the E flat Quintet is certainly not the peer of the other quintets and the last piano concerto, K 595, though completed in 1791, was mostly composed three years earlier (as suggested by Dr Alan Tyson on the evidence of the watermarks of the autograph, in his article 'The Mozart fragments in the Mozarteum, Salzburg: A preliminary study of their chronology and their significance', *Journal of the American Musicological Society* 34, no. 3 (1981), pp. 471–510, here p. 502). Reprinted in Alan Tyson, *Mozart. Studies of the Autograph Scores* (Cambridge, Mass. and London, 1987), pp. 125–61, here p. 156.
2. 'Spart' was Mozart's normal word for a score or vocal score. In composing his operas, Mozart always began by writing out a simple vocal score consisting of all the vocal parts with their texts and the bass. There were only a few indications of the instrumental accompaniments. We know this both from the fragments that never got beyond this stage and from a study of the ink of the autographs. This practice had the advantage of enabling him to set down the entire piece at great speed, leaving the scoring to be filled in later on at leisure (sometimes while he was being read to or even conversing). Moreover, the 'Spart' could be copied (in this case by his pupil Süssmayr) for the singers to learn their rôles even before the completion of the scoring.

3. Ernst Lert in *Mozart auf dem Theater* (Berlin, 1918), p. 465, proposed a change in the sequence of Act II, feeling that his order represented Mozart's original concept. The main problem seemed to him to be Pamina's illogical behaviour. As the opera stands, she sings of her sorrow at Tamino's silence in her aria (no. 17). In the terzetto (no. 19) Tamino and Sarastro promise her a happy ending once the trials are over, yet at her next appearance, in no. 21, she is again on the point of suicide. To overcome this 'illogicality' Lert rearranges the opera roughly as follows:

No. 21 part 1: Pamina's suicide bid
No. 21 part 3: Papageno's suicide bid
No. 19: Terzetto, immediately followed by
No. 21 part 2: the trials of fire and water
No. 21 part 4

August Everding's 1983 production at Covent Garden solved the problem by placing the terzetto near the beginning of Act II, soon after the march.

Ingmar Bergman's film also introduced a new sequence for Act II. In fact, Mozart's intentions are quite clear and have worked perfectly well for two hundred years. Besides, Pamina's behaviour is perhaps less illogical than most protagonists' in operas! In the terzetto she continues to express her misgivings: what reason had she to put her faith in Sarastro? However, the point to be made here is about the looseness of the construction which allows the possibility of carving up a finale, unthinkable in any other opera.

4. One might, however, agree with Edward Dent (*Mozart's Operas*, 2nd edn (London, 1947), p. 244) that Mozart let his musical ideas run away with him (relatively) at the *beginning* of an opera, for the terzetto of the Three Ladies around the swooning Tamino is longer than its relevance to the opera as a whole would warrant. This is doubtless one reason for Mozart's later deletion of the cadenza of the Three Ladies; cf. pp. 132–3.

5. An article by Michael Freyhan, 'Toward the original text of Mozart's *Die Zauberflöte*' (*Journal of the American Musicological Society* 39/2 (1986), pp. 355–80) makes out a case that the text of the 1814 Simrock full score was the original libretto to which Mozart composed the opera. It frequently has a more satisfactory (or conventional) setting of the words than the autograph of the score, as in the places cited in this article and, most strikingly, where Pamina relates in the Act II finale how her father made the flute. Gottfried Weber's 1814 review of this edition claimed that 'in any event the whole thing is in accordance with Mozart's own wishes, because Herr Simrock's edition, by his assurance, is taken from an original manuscript score that the former Elector of Cologne, Max Franz of Austria, had obtained from Mozart himself'.

But, apart from an unconvincing suggestion that the changes had to be made to the libretto in order to conceal dangerous Masonic references, Freyhan fails to explain convincingly how, when and why the libretto was revised. All the changes are of the kind which might have been made by an intelligent editor wishing to improve Mozart's unconventional word-setting. Indeed, there are other nineteenth-century editions in which the text differs from the autograph and from the Simrock edition. For the present the theory must be dismissed.

6. See Richard Engländer, 'The sketches for "The Magic Flute" at Upsala', *The Musical Quarterly* 27 (1941), pp. 343–55, here p. 346.

7. When he had composed the duet as far as the penultimate bar, Mozart decided to move his bar-line half a bar and had to make this correction throughout (the first page (Plate 2) is reproduced on p. 123). He had gone through exactly the same procedure with the Allegretto of the Piano Concerto K 459. A slowish $\frac{6}{8}$ often shows this ambiguity. To change it to $\frac{3}{8}$ was not the right solution (though it was adopted by several early vocal scores, not including the first edition), because that would lead to too many accents. 'Ach, ich fühl's' (no. 17) might have been another candidate for a change of bar line, for it seems to go for the greater part against the shape of the melody. But this is perhaps our clue to Mozart's purpose: in order to keep an even flow with only the slight accents demanded by the words, he deliberately made the bar lines contradict the strong notes of the melody, thus avoiding the excessive stresses that a coincidence of the important notes of the melody and the bar-line would be inclined to bring.

The other point of special interest on the page illustrated is in the omission of the chords, B flat resolving on to E flat, of the clarinets and horns in bars 2–3. There is no known explanation: they do appear in the first vocal score (Artaria, November 1791) and were presumably played at the first performance, since the gap left by the absence of the chords seems to make no sense.

8. This article expresses the view that Mozart used particular phrases, harmonies and instrumentations to express particular emotions or movements, but did so in a more or less instinctive way. According to Gunthard Born's *Mozarts Musiksprache* (Munich, 1985), Mozart consistently used a specific language of musical symbols, not only for abstracts like fear, triumph, defeat, fate or freedom, and for movements like running, falling, riding or departing, but even for more concise concepts like darkness, approach, hiding, wide and narrow.

9. An article by Christopher Raeburn in the *Österreichische Musikzeitschrift* for September 1957 (year 12, number 9, p. 329) quotes an important correspondence in the *Allgemeine Musikalische Zeitung* for 1815 (Vol. 17, p. 247) also referred to in Abert's *Mozart* (7th edn (Leipzig, 1956), note on p. 669). In it Gottfried Weber, a composer and teacher, suggested that Pamina's 'Ach, ich fühl's' was normally taken far too slowly: he believed that it should express passion rather than resigned sorrow and that its tempo should be at the swing of a pendulum on a cord 6 *Rhineland Zoll* in length (which equals a quaver of 138–52 on the metronome). His article was accompanied by a reply from an anonymous musician, who claimed to remember Mozart's own tempo and to have discussed the matter with musicians who had played under Mozart. He entirely agreed with Weber's tempo for Pamina's aria and added that no. 19 'Soll ich dich, Teurer, nicht mehr sehn?' was taken nearly twice as fast by Mozart as was the custom in 1815.

Even if one finds today's tempi generally too turgid, it is hard to imagine 'Ach ich fühl's' at Weber's tempo, for the expressive semiquavers would seem to turn into mere brilliant roulades. But how it would change our view of Pamina's entire character!

10. A very thorough review of Mozart's use of woodwind is given by Uri Toeplitz in *Die Holzbläser in der Musik Mozarts und ihr Verhältnis zur Tonartwahl* (Baden-Baden, 1978).

11. C minor is associated with death elsewhere, too, for example in Mozart's *Maurerische Trauermusik* and in the funeral march of Beethoven's 'Eroica' symphony.

12. Charles Rosen in *The Classical Style* (London, 1971), p. 321, writes: 'This is Mozart's late style developed as far as he carried it: the purity and the baredness are almost exotic, so extreme have they become, and this almost wilful leanness is only emphasized by the exquisite orchestration.' He is right to call this leanness 'almost wilful', for we have seen that there was a dramatic and emotional purpose in it. Apart from the Horn Concerto K 417, all Mozart's forty-odd concertos have cadenzas, until the final two, of 1791: the Horn Concerto K 412 (386b) + 514, and the Clarinet Concerto K 622.

13. Another possible reason for this revision may be found in a textual change in the autograph: 'die listige Schlange' ('the cunning serpent') was originally 'der grimmige Löwe' ('the fierce lion'). Mozart and Schikaneder must have eliminated the lion in case people thought that it had escaped from Sarastro's stable, since he later enters drawn by six lions. The braying of the trumpets had perhaps suggested the roaring of the lion and became out of place when the serpent took over. Or again, the serpent may have been intended as a Masonic symbol of evil, when the Masonic elements became increasingly important during the composition of the libretto and music.

14. The Singspiel always used spoken dialogue in place of the *recitativo semplice* (which we now call *secco* recitative) of Italian opera. Greatly impressed by Jiři Benda's melodramas (Mozart heard them in 1778), in which the *spoken* word was accompanied by the orchestra, Mozart used this form in *Thamos* and *Zaide*, but for *Die Entführung* he returned to the sung *recitativo accompagnato* of *opera seria*.

15. In the most innocent way they announce the end of superstition and look forward to men finding heaven on earth, nothing less than the dream of eighteenth-cetury Enlightenment! It is one of the many incongruous charms of the opera that it is those supernatural beings that announce an end to the belief in supernatural beings.

16. Abert, *Mozart*, p. 642. He adds that the intervening oboe phrase seems to mock the pathos of the Three Ladies.

7. Performance and reception

1. Else Spiesberger, *Das Freihaus*, Wiener Geschichtsbücher, vol. xxv, (Vienna and Hamburg, 1980). Her chapter 'Das Theater im Freihaus', pp. 39–60, contains much valuable information, but the principal source for details of performances and repertory remains Otto Erich Deutsch, 'Das Freihaustheater auf der Wieden. Zur Feier seiner Eröffnung vor 150 Jahren (14. Oktober 1787)', in *Mitteilungen des Vereines für*

Geschichte der Stadt Wien, vol. xvi (1937), 30–73; revised edition *Das Freihaustheater auf der Wieden 1787–1801* (Vienna, 1937).

2. H.-J. Irmen, *Mozart. Mitglied geheimer Gesellschaften*, Prisca-Verlag [Mechernich], 1988, pp. 278–9; the announcement was repeated in the two following issues, on 5 and 9 February.

3. *Ibid.*, p. 280.

4. *Ibid.*, p. 279. That Mozart found a buyer for his organ is indicated by the absence of the instrument from the list of his possessions at the time of his death; see Deutsch, *Dokumente*, pp. 495–6 (English edition pp. 585–7).

5. L. von Sonnleithner, 'Materialien zur Geschichte der Oper und des Balletts in Wien' (MS), Archiv der Gesellschaft der Musikfreunde: vol. ii, 'Das Theater an der Wien, früher auf der Wieden'.

6. For a useful summary of these printed *Vorschriften und Gesetze*, see Egon Komorzynski, *Emanuel Schikaneder. Ein Beitrag zur Geschichte des deutschen Theaters*, 2nd edn (Vienna and Wiesbaden, 1951), pp. 162–4.

7. Cited from the edition by R. M. Werner, *Schriften der Gesellschaft für Theatergeschichte*, vol. xiii (Berlin, 1910), p. 125.

8. F. L. W. Meyer, *Friedrich Ludwig Schröder. Beitrag zur Kunde des Menschen und des Künstlers*, vol. ii (Hamburg, 1819), p. 86.

9. *Ibid.*, vol. ii, p. 85.

10. *A Mozart Pilgrimage. Being The Travel Diaries of Vincent & Mary Novello in the year 1829*, transcribed and compiled by Nerina Medici di Marignano, edited by Rosemary Hughes (London, 1975), pp. 59 and 61–2.

11. On this point see Gernot Gruber's introduction to the score (*NMA* II/5/19), p. xvi.

12. It is not clear whether this Herr Moll is identical with the 'H. Moll' who was a member of Schikaneder's company in Nuremberg in 1779: 'H. [Franz] Moll, fathers, kings, officers; sings ...' (E. K. Blümml, *Aus Mozarts Freundes- und Familienkreis* (Vienna, Prague and Leipzig, 1923), p. 99, citing *Theater-Kalender auf das Jahr 1780*, Gotha, pp. 259–60).

13. See Seyfried's letter to Treitschke, Deutsch, *Dokumente*, p. 471–2 (English edition, pp. 555–6).

14. Meyer, *Schröder* (see n. 8 above), vol. ii, pp. 85–6.

15. *Ibid.*, vol. ii, p. 86.

16. *Gallerie von Teutschen Schauspielern und Schauspielerinnen nebst Johann Friedrich Schinks Zusätzen und Berichtigungen*, ed. R. M. Werner (see n. 7 above), pp. 106 and 221.

17. I. F. Castelli, *Memoiren meines Lebens. Gefundenes und Empfundenes, Erlebtes und Erstrebtes*, ed. J. Bindtner, 2 vols. (Munich, [1914]), vol. i, pp. 243–4. Pater Anselm Handelgruber (or Hanlgruber, see Castelli, vol. ii, p. 540) was presumably the last surviving member of the original cast when he died (at Stift Göttweig) on 10 February 1862, aged eighty-eight, though Anna (Nanny) Schikaneder also died in 1862.

18. The testimony of Urban Schikaneder's son Joseph Carl, published in 1834 (see Deutsch, *Dokumente. Addenda und Corrigenda*, ed. J. H. Eibl, Kassel etc., 1978, pp. 99–100), likewise needs to be treated circumspectly (he names Jakob Haibel as Monostatos, and also misidentifies the

Ladies); there is, however, no call to doubt his statement that his sister sang First Boy, and like Castelli he names Maurer as one of the Boys. When he says that his father sang the 'Sprecher' he is presumably referring to the part of the Old Priest in the Act I finale.

19. A. Tyson, 'Two Mozart puzzles', *The Musical Times*, March 1988, pp. 126–7.
20. Deutsch, *Dokumente*, p. 358 (English edition, p. 409, modified).
21. *Ibid.*, *Addenda*, p. 72 (English edition, p. 412).
22. All the references to early editions in this and the following paragraph are taken from Deutsch, *Dokumente*, pp. 360–85, *passim* (English edition, pp. 412–39).
23. Deutsch, *Dokumente*, p. 414 (English edition, pp. 472–3).
24. A. H. King, *Mozart in Retrospect* (London, 1955), p. 11.
25. In his article 'Toward the original text of Mozart's *Die Zauberflöte*', *JAMS* 39/2 (Summer 1986), pp. 355–80; cf. chapter 6, n. 5.
26. I. F. Castelli, *Memoiren meines Lebens*, vol. i, ed. J. Bindtner (Munich, 1913), p. 236.
27. *Kleine Wiener Memoiren und Wiener Dosenstücke*, 2 vols., ed. A. Schlossar and G. Gugitz (Munich, 1918).
28. *Vertraute Briefe zur Charakteristik von Wien*, 2 vols. (Görlitz, bei Hermsdorf und Anton, 1793), vol. ii, pp. 50–3.
29. Deutsch, *Dokumente: Addenda*, pp. 99–100.
30. *Allgemeine musikalische Zeitung*, year xiv, 19 August 1812, cols. 558ff.
31. Joseph Schmidt-Görg, 'Wiener Opernaufführungen im Winter 1815/16', *Studien zur Musikwissenschaft*, vol. xxv (1962), pp. 453–62 (here p. 457).
32. *Ibid.*, pp. 454–5.
33. Deutsch, *Dokumente: Addenda*, pp. 81–4 (here p. 82).
34. He continued to exaggerate, calling the performance on 1 January 1798 the 300th; according to the figures assembled by Leopold von Sonnleithner (see n. 5 above) the total reached by the time the company moved to the Theater an der Wien in 1801 was 223.
35. O. Teuber, *Geschichte des Prager Theaters*, 3 vols., vol. ii (Prague, 1885), p. 305.
36. T. Volek, 'Die erste Aufführung der "Zauberflöte" in tschechischer Sprache in Prag 1794', *Mozart-Jahrbuch 1967* (Salzburg, 1968), pp. 387–91.
37. *Ibid.*, p. 390.
38. *Ibid.*, p. 390.
39. Details of first performances of *Die Zauberflöte* are derived from A. Loewenberg, *Annals of Opera*, 2nd edn (Geneva, 1955), cols. 494–8, augmented and modified in the light of specialist studies printed in the *Mozart-Jahrbuch*.
40. For entertaining comments on the more popular aspects of the Frankfurt production see the letters of Goethe's mother of 9 November 1793 and 6 February 1794 to her son, *Die Briefe der Frau Rath Goethe*, vol. i (Leipzig, 1923), pp. 240–1 and 252, also included in Deutsch, *Dokumente*, pp. 410–11 (English edition, pp. 468–9).
41. For the opposition of court officials to Frederick William II's desire to have the opera staged at Berlin two years earlier, see Deutsch, *Dokumente*, p. 389 (English edition, p. 444).

42. See Trevor Fawcett, 'The first undoubted "Magic Flute"?', *R.M.A. Research Chronicle* 12, pp. 106–14.
43. Willi Schuh, '"Il Flauto magico"', *Umgang mit Musik* (Zurich, 1970), pp. 22–36 (here p. 28).
44. See P. Branscombe, '*Die Zauberflöte*. A lofty sequel and some lowly parodies', *The Publications of the English Goethe Society*, 48 (1978), pp. 1–21 (here pp. 3–5). The wittiest comments on Vulpius's trivialization of the opera are probably those contained in E. T. A. Hoffmann's *Seltsame Leiden eines Theater-Direktors* (Berlin, 1818); 'der Graue' ('the Man in Grey') summarizes with faux-naïf admiration the absurdities in this version. See E. T. A. Hoffmann, *Fantasie- und Nachtstücke*, ed. W. Müller-Seidel (Darmstadt, 1961), pp. 668–9.
45. *Ibid.*, pp. 6–14.
46. According to Loewenberg (see n. 39 above); B. Paumgartner ('Eine Text-Bearbeitung der "Zauberflöte" von 1795', Deutsch *Festschrift* (see Ch. 5, n. 10), pp. 128–34) gives the date as 31 January 1794.
47. A probably coincidental link with the newly proposed knightly source for *Die Zauberflöte*, Chrétien's *Yvain*; see chapter 1, pp. 7–10).
48. For a detailed analysis see Rudolph Angermüller, '"Les Mystères d'Isis" (1801) und "Don Juan" (1805, 1834) auf der Bühne der Pariser Oper', *Mozart-Jahrbuch 1980–3*, pp. 32–97.
49. H. Berlioz, *Mémoires*, vol. i (Paris, 1969), p. 120.
50. F. Brukner, *Die Zauberflöte. Unbekannte Handschriften und seltene Drucke aus der Frühzeit von Mozarts Oper* (Vienna, [1934]), pp. 145–203.
51. See P. Branscombe, (1966), pp. 45–63 (here pp. 49–50).
52. *The Times*, London, Friday, 11 July 1851, p. 5.
53. H. F. Chorley, *Thirty Years' Musical Recollections* (London, 1862), p. 150.
54. *The Times*, London, Wednesday, 16 July 1851, p. 8.
55. E. J. Dent, *Mozart's Opera 'The Magic Flute'. Its history and interpretation* (Cambridge, 1911).
56. *The Times*, London, Saturday, 2 December 1911, p. 6, and Monday, 4 December 1911, p. 6.
57. *The Musical Times*, 1 January 1912, p. 46.
58. *The Times*, London, Monday, 8 June 1914, p. 56. It is surprising to learn from John L. Walsh's review of a performance of *Il flauto magico* in Mexico City in summer 1965 that Beecham had performed the opera there in 1944 with recitatives; the practice still pertained there twenty-one years later (*Opera*, October 1965, p. 755).
59. Percy A. Scholes, *The Mirror of Music 1844–1944*, vol. ii (London, 1947), p. 795.
60. *The Times*, London, Saturday, 7 May 1938, p. 10.
61. *Opera at Home*, 'Written and compiled by the staff of The Gramophone Co., Ltd. Hayes, Middlesex, with a Preface by Henry Coates'; no date, but *c.* 1920.
62. *Die Bühne* (Vienna), January 1988, pp. 37–8.
63. *Opera*, March 1967, p. 210.
64. Reprinted in A. Porter, *A Musical Season* (London, 1974), here pp. 39 and 41.

65. N. Kenyon in *The New Yorker*, 23 February 1981, pp. 113–14.
66. Piero Mioli on the Bologna performance, *Opera*, September 1982, pp. 958–9; Jowel Kasow on the Holland Festival performance, *Opera*, Autumn 1982, pp. 93–5.
67. W. H. Auden, 'Metalogue'; reprinted by permission of Faber and Faber Ltd. and Random House.

9. Problems

1. Deutsch, *Dokumente*, p. 472 (English edition pp. 555–6, modified).
2. O. Jahn, *W. A. Mozart*, vol. ii, 2nd edn, 1867, p. 465, and especially pp. 490–1.
3. A facsimile of the playbill is reproduced in F. Brukner, *Die Zauber-flöte* (Vienna, 1934), facing p. 160; and in E. Komorzynski, *Emanuel Schikaneder* (Vienna and Wiesbaden, 2nd edn, 1951), facing p. 289.
4. The new words for this occasion do not seem to have survived; those sung by Schikaneder on 12 March 1801 are printed by F. Brukner (see n. 3), pp. 111–12; for the text sung on 13 June 1802, see *ibid.*, pp. 143–4.
5. G. N. von Nissen, *Biographie W. A. Mozart's* (Leipzig, 1828), p. 551.
6. Jahn, *Mozart*, vol. ii, p. 525 and n. 62.
7. See P. Branscombe, *'Die Zauberflöte*: some textual and interpretative problems', *Proceedings of the Royal Musical Association*, 92nd session (1966), pp. 45–63 (here pp. 47–51).
8. Deutsch, *Dokumente: Addenda*, p. 108 (English edition, pp. 567–8, modified).
9. For a detailed study of this number see Arnold Feil, 'Mozarts Duett "Bei Männern, welche Liebe fühlen". Periodisch-metrische Fragen', in *Festschrift Walter Gerstenberg zum 60. Geburtstag*, ed. G. von Dadelsen and A. Holschneider (Wolfenbüttel, 1964), pp. 45–54.
10. W. H. Auden and Chester Kallman, *The Magic Flute* (London, 1957), preface, p. 12.
11. *Ibid.*, p. 13.
12. 'A musico-dramatic problem in Act II of Mozart's "The Magic Flute"'; a summary of Professor Trowell's lecture was printed in the 'Minutes of the Ordinary Meeting of Convocation [of London University] held at the Senate House on Tuesday 9 May 1978 at 6 p.m.', pp. 31–3.
13. Attila Csampai, ' "Böse" Königin, "guter" Sarastro, oder: Abschied vom alten Zauberreich. Wandlungen des Wertsystems in Mozarts "Zauberflöte" ', *Offizielles Programm der Salzburger Festspiele 1985*, pp. 71–4.
14. The injunction of the Three Boys to Papageno in II, 29 ('Nun, Papageno, sieh dich um!') is only apparently an unrhyming line – Mozart omitted five lines from the libretto here, including its partner, 'Sey dieses Mannes Eigenthum!', the content of which ('Be this man's property!') he perhaps found offensive to women.
15. See P. Branscombe, *'Die Zauberflöte'* (1966), pp. 52–63.

Conclusion

1. *Goethes Gespräche*, vol. ii, ed. F. von Biedermann, 2nd edn (Leipzig, 1909–11) p. 628.
2. The former viewpoint is taken by Jahn, *Mozart*, vol. ii, pp. 490–1 and H. C. Robbins Landon, *1791. Mozart's Last Year* (London, 1988), pp. 132–6, and the latter by, for instance, Audrey Williamson, 'Who was Sarastro?', *Opera* 21 (April 1970), pp. 297–305. She suggests that the authors of *Die Zauberflöte* were put on to the defensive by the death sentence (later commuted by the pope to life imprisonment) passed on Cagliostro by the inquisition in March 1791. It is possible that the initiation of Pamina owes something to Cagliostro's Egyptian Rite, which admitted female Masons, even perhaps that in the Three Ladies Mozart and Schikaneder were mocking the members of the 'Grand Copt's' Masonry of Adoption.
3. The two illustrations printed in the libretto are very interesting, but because they must have been engraved well before the première they cannot be considered authentic representations of the production.
4. James Stevens Curl, *The Egyptian Revival. An Introductory Study of a Recurring Theme in the History of Taste* (London, 1982). This book contains a wealth of information and interpretation.
5. Jay Macpherson, '*The Magic Flute* and Viennese opinion', *Man and Nature / L'Homme et la Nature* 6 (1987), pp. 161–72; here p. 162.
6. Deutsch, *Dokumente*, p. 415 (English edition, p. 477).
7. F. Grillparzer, *Sämtliche Werke*, ed. P. Frank and K. Pörnbacher, vol. iii (Munich, 1963), p. 25.
8. *Anhang zu Wolfgang Amadeus Mozart's Biographie* (Leipzig, 1828), p. 113.
9. Philippe A. Autexier, 'La Musique maçonnique', *Dix-huitième siècle* 19 (1987), pp. 97–104.
10. H.-J. Irmen, *Mozart. Mitglied geheimer Gesellschaften* ([Mechernich], 1988), pp. 281–351.

Select bibliography

Abert, Hermann, *W. A. Mozart*, 7th edn (Leipzig, 1955–6, index 1966)
Allgemeine musikalische Zeitung, ed. F. Rochlitz (Leipzig, *passim*, but especially years 1798, 1801, 1812 and 1815)
Auden, W. H. and Chester Kallman, *The Magic Flute*, English version (London, 1957)
Autexier, Philippe A., *Mozart & Liszt sub Rosa* (Poitiers, 1984)
Batley, E. M., *A Preface to The Magic Flute* (London, 1969)
Bauer, Wilhelm A. and Otto Erich Deutsch, with J. H. Eibl, *Mozart. Briefe und Aufzeichnungen*, 7 vols. (Kassel, 1962–75)
Blanning, T. C. W., *Joseph II and Enlightened Despotism* (London, 1970)
Blümml, E. K., *Aus Mozarts Freundes- und Familien Kreis* (Vienna, Prague and Leipzig, 1923)
  'Ausdeutungen der "Zauberflöte"', *Mozart-Jahrbuch*, vol. i (1923), pp. 109–46
Bodi, Leslie, *Tauwetter in Wien. Zur Prosa der österreichischen Aufklärung 1781–1795* (Frankfurt am Main, 1977)
Bortolotti, Nadine and Toni Ebner (eds.), *Intorno al Flauto Magico* (Milan, 1985)
Branscombe, Peter, '*Die Zauberflöte*: some textual and interpretative problems', *Proceedings of the Royal Musical Association*, 92nd session (1966), pp. 45–63
  '*Die Zauberflöte*. A Lofty Sequel and some Lowly Parodies', *Publications of the English Goethe Society*, 48 (1978), pp. 1–21
Brukner, F., *Die Zauberflöte. Unbekannte Handschriften und seltene Drucke aus der Frühzeit von Mozarts Oper* (Vienna, [1934])
Castelli, I. F., *Memoiren meines Lebens*, ed. J. Bindtner (Munich, [1913])
Chailley, Jacques, *The Magic Flute, Masonic Opera*, translated by Herbert Weinstock (London, 1972)
Crosby, Claire D., 'The fairy tale on the old Viennese stage', Ph.D. thesis (St Andrews, 1986)
Dent, E. J. *Mozart's Operas* (London, 1913; 2nd edn, 1947)
Deutsch, Otto Erich, *Mozart und die Wiener Logen* (Vienna, 1932)
  Das Freihaustheater auf der Wieden 1787–1801 (Vienna; 2nd edn, 1937)
  Mozart. Die Dokumente seines Lebens (Kassel etc., 1961)
  Mozart. Die Dokumente seines Lebens. Addenda und Corrigenda, ed. J. H. Eibl (Kassel etc., 1978)

Mozart. A Documentary Biography, translated by Eric Blom, Peter Branscombe and Jeremy Noble (London, 1965; 2nd edn, 1966)

Dschinnistan oder auserlesene Feen- und Geister-Mährchen, theils neu erfunden, theils neu übersezt und umgearbeitet, ed. C. M. Wieland, 3 vols. (Winterthur, 1786–9)

Eckelmeyer, Judith A., 'Structure as hermeneutic guide to *The Magic Flute*', *The Musical Quarterly* 72 (1986), pp. 51–73

Engländer, Richard, 'The sketches for "The Magic Flute" at Upsala', *The Musical Quarterly* 27 (1941), pp. 343–55

Feil, Arnold, 'Mozarts Duett "Bei Männern, welche Liebe fühlen". Periodisch-metrische Fragen', in *Festschrift Walter Gerstenberg zum 60. Geburtstag*, ed. G. von Dadelsen and A. Holschneider (Wolfenbüttel, 1964), pp. 45–54

Festschrift Otto Erich Deutsch zum 80. Geburtstag, ed. W. Gerstenberg, J. LaRue and W. Rehm (Kassel, 1963)

Freyhan, M., 'Toward the original text of Mozart's *Die Zauberflöte*', *Journal of the American Musicological Society* 39 (1986), pp. 355–80

Friedrich, Götz, *Die humanistische Idee der "Zauberflöte". Ein Beitrag zur Dramaturgie der Oper* (Dresden, 1954)

Gallerie von Teutschen Schauspielern und Schauspielerinnen der ältern und neuern Zeit, ed. R. M. Werner (Schriften der Gesellschaft für Theatergeschichte vol. xiii, Berlin, 1910)

Grossegger, Elisabeth, *Freimaurerei und Theater, 1770–1800* (Vienna, Cologne and Graz, 1981)

Gruber, Gernot, 'Das Autograph der "Zauberflöte". Eine stilkritische Interpretation des philologischen Befundes', *Mozart-Jahrbuch 1967*, pp. 127–49, and *1968–70*, pp. 99–110

Hadamowsky, F., *Das Theater in der Wiener Leopoldstadt 1781–1860* (Vienna, 1934)

Hurwitz, Joachim, 'Haydn and the Freemasons', *Haydn Year Book* 16 (1985), pp. 5–98

Irmen, H.-J., *Mozart. Mitglied geheimer Gesellschaften* (Prisca-Verlag [Mechernich], 1988)

Jahn, Otto, *W. A. Mozart* (Leipzig, 1856–9, cited in the revised 2nd edn of 1867)

John, Nicholas, ed., *The Magic Flute*, English National Opera Guides 3 (London, 1980)

'Monostatos: Pamina's incubus', *Opern und Opernfiguren. Festschrift für Joachim Herz*, ed. Ursula and Ulrich Müller (Salzburg, 1989), pp. 101–14

Journal für Freymaurer (Vienna, 1784–6)

King, A. Hyatt, *Mozart in Retrospect* (London, 1955; 3rd edn, 1970)

Köchel, Ludwig Ritter von, *Chronologisch-thematisches Verzeichnis sämtlicher Tonwerke Wolfgang Amadé Mozarts*, 7th edn (Wiesbaden, 1965)

Koenigsberger, Dorothy, 'A new metaphor for Mozart's *Magic Flute*', *European Studies Review* 5/3 (1975), pp. 229–75

Köhler, Karl-Heinz, 'Zu den Methoden und einigen Ergebnissen der philologischen Analyse am Autograph der "Zauberflöte"', *Mozart-Jahrbuch 1980–3*, pp. 283–7

Komorzynski, Egon, *Emanuel Schikaneder. Ein Beitrag zur Geschichte des deutschen Theaters*, revised 2nd edn (Vienna and Wiesbaden, 1951)

Kuéss, G. R. and B. Scheichelbauer, *200 Jahre Freimaurerei in Österreich* (Vienna, 1959)

Landon, H. C. Robbins, *Mozart and the Masons: New Light on the Lodge 'Crowned Hope'* (London, 1982)

1791: Mozart's Last Year (London, 1988)

Lennhoff, Eugen and Oskar Posner, *Internationales Freimaurerlexikon* (Vienna, 1932)

Lert, Ernst, *Mozart auf dem Theater* (Berlin, 1918)

Loewenberg, Alfred, *Annals of Opera*, 2nd edn (Geneva, 1955)

Metzger, Heinz-Klaus and Rainer Riehn (eds.), *Ist die Zauberflöte ein Machwerk?*, Musik-Konzepte, vol. iii (Munich, 1978)

Meyer, F. L. W., *Friedrich Ludwig Schröder. Beitrag zur Kunde des Menschen und des Künstlers* (Hamburg, 1819)

Mozart, W. A., *Briefe und Aufzeichnungen. Gesamtausgabe*, ed. W. A. Bauer, O. E. Deutsch and J. H. Eibl, 7 vols. (Kassel etc., 1962–75)

Verzeichnüß aller meiner Werke vom Monath Febrario 1784 bis Monath ..., ed. O. E. Deutsch (New York, n.d.)

Die Zauberflöte, ed. Gernot Gruber and Alfred Orel, *NMA* II/5/19 (Kassel etc., 1970)

Nettl, Paul, *Mozart und die königliche Kunst. Die freimaurerische Grundlage der 'Zauberflöte'* (Berlin, 1932)

Mozart and Masonry (New York, 1957)

Niemetschek (Němetschek), Franz Xaver, *Lebensbeschreibung des K.K. Kapellmeisters Wolfgang Amadeus Mozart*, 2nd edn (Prague, 1808, cited in the edition of P. Krause, Leipzig, 1978)

Nissen, G. K. von, *Biographie W. A. Mozart's* (Leipzig, 1828, cited in the edition of R. Angermüller, Hildesheim etc., 1984)

Novello, Vincent and Mary, *A Mozart Pilgrimage. Being the Travel Diaries of ... in the Year 1829*, transcribed and compiled by Nerina Medici di Marignano, edited by Rosemary Hughes (London, 1975)

Österreichisches Freimaurermuseum, Schloss Rosenau bei Zwettl: *Österreichische Freimaurerlogen. Humanität und Toleranz im 18. Jahrhundert* (3rd edn, 1978)

Freimaurerei um Joseph II. Die Loge zur Wahren Eintracht (1980)

Ideen und Ideale Deutscher Freimaurer. Aufklärung, Klassik, Romantik (1986)

Perinet, Joachim, *Der Fagottist oder Die Zauberzither ('Kaspar der Fagottist')*, cited in the edition of O. Rommel, Deutsche Literatur in Entwicklungsreihen, Reihe Barock: Barocktradition im österreichisch-bayrischen Volkstheater, vol. i (Stuttgart, 1935)

Plath, Wolfgang, 'Beiträge zur Mozart-Autographie II: Schriftchronologie 1770–1780', *Mozart-Jahrbuch 1976/7* (Kassel, 1978), pp. 131–73

Porter, Andrew (translator), *The Magic Flute* (London, 1980)

Rochlitz, F., 'Verbürgte Anekdoten aus Wolfgang Gottlieb Mozarts Leben, ein Beytrag zur richtigern Kenntnis dieses Mannes, als Mensch und Künstler', *Allgemeine musikalische Zeitung* (Leipzig, 1798)

Rommel, Otto, *Die Alt-Wiener Volkskomödie* (Vienna, 1952)

Rosenberg, Alfons, *Die Zauberflöte. Geschichte und Deutung von Mozarts Oper* (Munich, 1964)

Schikaneder, Emmanuel, *Die Zauberflöte.* Eine große Oper in zwey Aufzügen (Vienna, 1791; facsimile edition by M. M. Rabenlechner, Vienna, 1942)

Schlichtegroll, Friedrich, *Mozarts Leben* (Graz, 1794, cited in the edition of J. H. Eibl = Documenta Musicologica I:32, Kassel etc., 1974)

Schuh, Willi, 'Die "Zauberflöte" im Mannheimer Nationaltheater 1794', *Umgang mit Musik* (Zurich, 1970), pp. 37–49

'Die "verdeutschte" Zauberflöte im Kärntnertortheater', *Umgang mit Musik* (Zurich, 1970), pp. 14–21

Schwartz-Bostunitsch, Gregor, *Die Freimaurerei. Ihr Ursprung, ihre Geheimnisse, ihr Wirken* (Weimar, n.d.)

Smyth, Frederick, 'Brother Mozart of Vienna', *Ars Quatuor Coronatorum* 87 (1974), pp. 37–73

Stefan, Paul, *Die Zauberflöte. Herkunft, Bedeutung, Geheimnis* (Vienna, Leipzig and Zurich, 1937)

Terrasson, Abbé Jean, *Sethos, Histoire ou Vie Tirée des Monumens Anecdotes de l'ancienne Egypte. Traduite d'un Manuscrit Grec* (cited in the edition Amsterdam, 1732)

Thomson, Katharine, *The Masonic Thread in Mozart* (London, 1977)

Treitschke, Friedrich, 'Die Zauberflöte. – Der Dorfbarbier. – Fidelio. Beitrag zur musikalischen Kunstgeschichte', *Orpheus. Musikalisches Taschenbuch für das Jahr 1841*, ed. A. Schmidt (Vienna, [1841])

Tyson, Alan, *Mozart. Studies of the Autograph Scores* (Cambridge, Mass., and London, 1987)

Waltershausen, Hermann von, *Die Zauberflöte. Eine operndramaturgische Studie* (Munich, 1920)

Wangermann, Ernst, *From Joseph II to the Jacobin Trials*, 2nd edn (London, 1969)

Wiener Theater Almanach für das Jahr 1794 (and for 1795 and 1796)

Discography

S   = Sarastro
T   = Tamino
OP = Old Priest (Sprecher – Spokesman)
Q   = Queen of Night
Pam = Pamina
OW = Old Woman (Papagena)
Pap = Papageno
M   = Monostatos

Unless otherwise indicated, all recordings are three-disc stereo sets. CDs are identified as such; MC = Musicassette; ⓜ = mono; ⓔ = electronically reprocessed stereo. Dates are the year of recording.

1937   Toscanini / Vienna PO / Vienna State Opera Chorus (live recording, Salzburg Festival); Kipnis *S*; Rosvaenge *T*; Jerger *OP*; Osvath *Q*; Novotna *Pam*; Komarek *OW*; Domgraf-Fassbaender *Pap*; Wernigk *M*
Cetra LO 44/3 ⓜ (Rare Opera Editions EA 056); little dialogue included

1937–8 Beecham / Berlin PO / Favres Solisten Vereinigung; Strienz *S*; Rosvaenge *T*; Grossmann *OP*; Berger *Q*; Lemnitz *Pam*; Beilke *OW*; Hüsch *Pap*; Tessmer *M*
EMI RLS 1434653 ⓜ (MC TC – RLS 1434659); (2 CDs EMI: CHS 7 610342; Pearl GEMM CDS 9371); no dialogue included

1949   Furtwängler / Vienna PO / Vienna State Opera Chorus (live recording, Salzburg Festival); Greindl *S*; Ludwig *T*; Schöffler *OP*; Lipp *Q*; Seefried *Pam*; Oravez *OW*; Schmitt-Walter *Pap*; Klein *M*
IGI – 337 ⓜ

1950   Karajan / Vienna PO / Singverein der Gesellschaft der Musikfreunde; Weber *S*; Dermota *T*; London *OP*; Lipp *Q*; Seefried *Pam*; Loose *OW*; Kunz *Pap*; Klein *M*
HMV SLS 5052 ⓔ (2 CDs CHS7 69631–2); no dialogue included

1951   Furtwängler / Vienna PO / Vienna State Opera Chorus (live recording, Salzburg Festival); Greindl *S*; Dermota *T*; Schöffler *OP*; Lipp *Q*; Seefried *Pam*; Oravez *OW*; Kunz *Pap*; Klein *M*
Cetra LO 9/3 ⓜ

239

1955   Fricsay / Berlin Radio SO / RIAS Chamber Choir; Greindl *S*;
        Haefliger *T*; Borg *OP*; Streich *Q*; Stader *Pam*; Otto *OW*; Fischer-
        Dieskau *Pap*; Vantin *M*
        DG 2701 015 ⓜ
1955   Böhm / Vienna PO / Vienna State Opera Chorus; Böhme *S*;
        Simoneau *T*; Schöffler *OP*; Lipp *Q*; Gueden *Pam*; Loose *OW*;
        Berry *Pap*; Jaresch *M*
        Decca 414 362–1D03; (CD 414 362–2D03; MC 414 362–4D03);
        no dialogue included
1959   Szell / Vienna PO / Vienna State Opera Chorus (live recording,
        Salzburg Festival); Böhme *S*; Simoneau *T*; Hotter *OP*; Köth *Q*;
        Della Casa *Pam*; Sciutti *OW*; Berry *Pap*; Dönch *M*
        Melodram MEL 007 (3)
1964   Klemperer / Philharmonia Orchestra and Chorus; Frick *S*; Gedda *T*;
        Crass *OP*; Popp *Q*; Janowitz *Pam*; Pütz *OW*; Berry *Pap*; Unger *M*
        HMV SLS 912; (2 CDs CMS7 69971–2; MC 2C295 00031–3); no
        dialogue included
1965   Böhm / Berlin PO / RIAS Chamber Choir; Crass *S*; Wunderlich *T*;
        Hotter *OP*; Peters *Q*; Lear *Pam*; Otto *OW*; Fischer-Dieskau *Pap*;
        Lenz *M*
        DG 2709 017; (CD 419 566–2GH3; MC 3371 002)
1968   Suitner / Dresden State Orchestra / Leipzig Radio Chorus; Adam *S*;
        Schreier *T*; Vogel *OP*; Geszty *Q*; Donath *Pam*; Hoff *OW*; Leib *Pap*;
        Neukirch *M*
        Ariola Eurodisc XG 80584R; (CD RCA GD 86511; MC 500221)
1969   Solti / Vienna PO / Vienna State Opera Chorus; Talvela *S*;
        Burrows *T*; Fischer-Dieskau *OP*; Deutekom *Q*; Lorengar *Pam*;
        Holm *OW*; Prey *Pap*; Stolze *M*
        Decca SET 479–81; (CD 414 568-2DH3; MC K2A4)
1972   Sawallisch / Bavarian State Opera Orchestra and Chorus; Moll *S*;
        Schreier *T*; Adam *OP*; Moser *Q*; Rothenberger *Pam*; Miljakovic
        OW; Berry *Pap*; Brokmeier *M*
        EMI 1C 197 30154-6Q; (2 CDs CDS 7 47827 8)
        (This performance includes the duet for Tamino and Papageno,
        no. 11a, 'Pamina, wo bist du?')
1974   Ericson / Swedish Radio SO and Chorus; Cold *S*; Köstlinger *T*;
        Saedén *OP*; Nordin *Q*; Urrila *Pam*; Eriksson *OW*; Hagegård, *Pap*;
        Ulfung *M*
        BBC REK 223 (MC CS-4577)
        (Sung in Swedish (*Trollflöjten*); sound-track of television film,
        directed by Ingmar Bergman; nos. 11, 16 and 19 are omitted, and the
        order within the finale to Act II has been altered)
1978   Lombard / Strasbourg PO / Rhine Opera Chorus; Moll *S*;
        Hofmann *T*; van Dam *OP*; Gruberová *Q*; Te Kanawa *Pam*;
        Battle *OW*; Huttenlocher *Pap*; Orth *M*
        Barclay 960 012-4; (MC 4-960 012-4)
1980   Karajan / Berlin PO / Chorus of the German Opera, Berlin; van
        Dam *S*; Araiza *T*; Nicolai *OP*; Ott *Q*; Mathis *Pam*; Perry *OW*;
        Hornik *Pap*; Kruse *M*
        DG 2741 001 digital; (CD 410 967-2GH3; MC 3382 001)

1980   Levine / Vienna PO / Vienna State Opera Chorus; Talvela *S*;
        Tappy *T*; van Dam *OP*; Donat *Q*; Cotrubas *Pam*; Kales *OW*;
        Boesch *Pap*; Hiestermann *M*
        RCA RL 03728 digital (4 discs) (3 CDs GD 84586; MC CTC4 4124)

1981   Haitink / Bavarian Radio SO and Chorus; Bracht *S*; Jerusalem *T*;
        Bailey *OP*; Gruberová *Q*; Popp *Pam*; Lindner *OW*; Brendel *Pap*;
        Zedník *M*
        EMI SLS 5223 digital; (CDS7 47951–8; MC TCC-SLS 5223)

1982   Koopman / Amsterdam Baroque Orchestra / Utrecht Chamber
        Choir Viva la Musica; van der Kamp *S*; de Mey *T*; van Tassel *OP*;
        Poulenard *Q*; Kweksilber *Pam*; van der Putten *OW*; Verschaeve
        Pap; Fuhr Jørgensen *M*
        Erato NUM 750803 digital; (MCE 750803)
        (This performance, recorded live at the Théâtre Royal, The Hague,
        was made using period instruments; the original version of the duet
        'Bei Männern', no. 7, is used)

1984   Davis / Dresden State Orchestra / Leipzig Radio Chorus; Moll *S*;
        Schreier *T*; Adam *OP*; Serra *Q*; Price *Pam*; Venuti *OW*; Melbye
        Pap; Tear *M*
        Philips 411 459-1PH3 digital (CD 411 459-2PH3; MC 411 459-
        4PH3)

1987   Harnoncourt / Zurich Opera House Orchestra and Chorus;
        Salminen *S*; Blochwitz *T*; Hampson *OP*; Gruberová *Q*; Bonney
        Pam; Schmid *OW*; Scharinger *Pap*; Keller *M*
        Teldec 6 35766 EX digital; (2 LPs); (2 CDs 8 35766 ZA; 2 MCs
        4 35766 EX); dialogue mostly replaced by narration

1989   Jordan / Romand Chamber Choir and Lausanne Pro Arte Choir /
        Paris Orchestral Ensemble; Selig *S*; Winbergh *T*; Muff *OP*; Jo *Q*;
        Orgonasova *Pam*; Bovet *OW*; Hagegård *Pap*; Vogel M
        Erato/WEA 2292-45469-2; 2 CDs; digital

1989   Marriner / Academy of St Martin in the Fields / Ambrosian Opera
        Chorus; Ramey *S*; Araiza *T*; van Dam *OP*; Studer *Q*; Te Kanawa
        Pam; Lind *OW*; Bär *Pap*; Baldin *M*
        Philips 426 276–1 (2 discs) digital (2 CDs 426 276–2, 2 MCs 426
        276–4)

Index

Abert, Hermann 72, 130, 138, 139
Adamberger, Valentin 42
Adler, Paul 167
Alberti, Ignaz 79
allegory 219–20
Apuleius 20, 23
Aristophanes 98
Artaria & Co. (publishers) 155
Auden, W. H. 175–7, 211, 214
Autexier, Philippe 39
autograph score of *Die Zauberflöte*
  80–6

Bach, Johann Sebastian 139
Barbazan, Etienne 7
Bauernfeld, Joseph von 143, 144
Baumann, Friedrich 6
Beecham, Sir Thomas 170–1
Beer, Franz Anton, Court Councillor
  37
Benois, Nicola 174
Berg, Alban 120
Bergman, Ingmar 177, 180, 211, 227
  (n3)
Berlioz, Hector 165
Bernhard, Thomas 167
Besch, Anthony 172, 178–204, 211
bird-man figure 98–101
Blumauer, Alois 20
Blümml, Emil Karl 19, 221
Bodmer, Johann Jakob 7–8
Böhm, Johannes 19
Böhm, Karl 154
Born, Gunthard 228 (n8)
Born, Ignaz von 20–5, 39, 40–1, 44,
  217, 219
Breitkopf & Härtel (publishers) 68, 156
Britten, Benjamin 120
Bruchtheorie 205–7

Cagliostro, Alessandro di, Count 182

Cairns, David 202
Campi, Antonia and Gaetano 160
Canada 190, 192
Carey, Clive 170
cast
  first performance 145–52
  London première 162
  London, later performances 168–9
Castelli, Ignaz Franz 91–2, 151, 157
Cavalieri, Caterina 139, 153
Caylus, Comte A. C. P. de 219
Chagall, Marc 174
Chailley, Jacques 138, 180, 182, 202,
  220
Chantavoine, Jean 124
characterization 127–9, 194–203
Chédeville, E. Morel de 165
Chorley, Henry 169
Chrétien de Troyes (*Yvain*) 7–10
clarinet 135–6
Claudius, Matthias 11, 12
Colloredo, Hieronymus, Prince-
  Archbishop 13
Corens, Rudolf 175
Cornet, Julius 71, 72, 88
Csampai, Attila 213
Czechoslovakia 160–2

da Ponte, Lorenzo 113, 118, 124,
  140–1, 186, 211
Deiters, Hermann 72
Denmark 162
Dent. Edward J. 27, 87, 170, 227 (n4)
designers 173–4, 178–9
Deutsch, Otto Erich 203, 220
Dew, John 172
dialogue 192–4
Dickinson, G. Lowes 167
Diderot, Denis 100
Dietrichstein, Johann Baptist, Prince
  38, 39

242

Diodorus Siculus 20, 21–2
direction 178–204
  and design 178–9
  background research 179–83
  dialogue 192–4
  London Coliseum 190–2, 194
  Ottawa production 190, 192
  rôle characterization 194–203
  Schikaneder's libretto 179–80,
    186, 189, 196–7
Dittersdorf, Karl Ditters von 144
Dschinnistan 8, 25–7, 28, 72, 144

Eckermann, Johann Peter 218
Egypt 10–19, 20–5, 26–7, 218–19
Einstein, Alfred 42
Eschenbach, Wolfram von 7
Everding, August 227 (n3)
Eybel, Joseph Valentin 219

fairy-tales 25–7, 30
Fellborn, Claes 172
film 177
finales 118–20
Fischer, Ignaz 40
Fischer von Erlach, J. B. 219
Fontane, Theodor 167
Formes, Karl 168
Forti, Mme (Henriette Teimer) 160
Francis I, Holy Roman Emperor 37
Francis II, Holy Roman Emperor
  39
Frasel, Wilhelm 151
Frederick William II, King of Prussia
  203
Freemasonry 20, 22–5, 180–3
  and Mozart 41–3, 218
  and Schikaneder 43–4
  and symbolism in *Die Zauberflöte*
    137–8, 220–1
  and women 23, 40, 217
  in Vienna 20, 23, 37–41
Frey, Michael 160
Freyer, Achim 172
Freyhan, Michael 157, 227 (n5)
Friedel, Johann 143, 146
Fuhrmann, Barbara 100
Furtwängler, Wilhelm 154

Gamerra, Giovanni de 161
Gayl, Joseph 151, 173, 208
Gebler, Tobias Philipp, Baron
  (*Thamos, König in
  Egypten*) 18–20, 39

Gemmingen-Hornberg, Otto, Baron
  von 41, 100
Gerl, Barbara (*née* Reisinger) 73, 147
Gerl, Franz Xaver 5, 6, 74, 128, 143,
  147, 159
Germany, early performances in 162
Gieseke, Carl Ludwig 8, 28, 29, 44,
  71–3, 151
  and debate over authorship of
    libretto 28, 87–92
  copy of libretto 92–8
Glassbrenner, Adolf 167
Gluck, Christoph Willibald von 119
Goethe, Johann Wolfgang von 11, 71,
  101, 164, 167, 180, 213, 218
Gordon, George 199
Gottlieb, Anna 150, 158
Gozzi, Carlo 100
Gräffer, Franz 157–8
Grillparzer, Franz 167, 220
Grisi, Giulia 168
Grossmann, Gustav Friedrich
  Wilhelm 147
Gruber, Gernot 131, 209
Guardasoni, Domenico 163

Handel, George Frideric 139
Handelgruber, Anselm 151, 230 (n17)
harmonic scheme 129–31
Hartmann von Aue 8
Haselbeck, Joseph Anton 224 (n4)
Hatwig, Otto 89
Haydenreich, Joseph 155
Haydn, Joseph 42, 144
Hegel, Georg Wilhelm Friedrich 167
Helmböck, Christoph 72, 224 (n4)
Hempel, Frieda 171
Henneberg, Johann Baptist 6, 71, 78,
  151–2
Hensler, Karl Friedrich 29, 43, 100
Henze, Hans Werner 100
Herodotus 20
Hesse, Hermann 167
Hildebrandt, Lukas von 219
Hockney, David 174
Hofer, Franz de Paula 149, 153
Hofer, Josepha 6, 139, 149–50
Hoffmann, E. T. A. 167, 189
Hoffmann, Josef 173
Hoffmann, Leopold Alois 24
Hoffmeister, Franz Anton 100, 155
Hofmannsthal, Hugo von 107, 110
Holland 162
Hummel (publisher) 156

Hytner, Nicholas 172

Igesz, Bodo 175
Irmen, Hans-Josef 145, 220
Iwain 7–10

Jacquin, Gottfried von 73
Jahn, Otto 72–3, 206, 209
Johnson, Samuel 203
Joseph II, Holy Roman Emperor 5,
　35–7, 38, 142, 146

Kallman, Chester 175–7, 211, 214
*Kaspar der Fagottist, oder Die Zauber-
　zither* 26–7, 29–34, 76, 112,
　205–6
Kautsky, Hans 174
Kenyon, Nicholas 175
Kierkegaard, Søren 167
King, A. Hyatt 124, 156
Kistler, Johann Michael 149
Klöpfer, Mlle (singer) 150
Köhler, Karl-Heinz 81–2, 85
Kokoschka, Oskar 174
Kolb, Annette 167
Kolowrat-Krakowsky, Leopold, Count
　38
Komorzynski, Egon von 28, 29, 87
Koopman, Ton 209
Koželuch, Leopold (publisher) 155
Kreuz, Emil 171
Kruse, George Richard 208
Kucharž, Johann Baptist 161, 163
Kumpf, Hubert 146
Kundera, Milan 167

Lachnith, Ludwig Wenzel 165
La Curne de Sainte-Palaye, J.-B. 7
Landon, H. C. Robbins 220
La Roche, Johann ('Kasperl') 32, 94,
　143
Laske, Oskar 174
Lausch, Laurenz 155
Le Grand d'Aussy, P.-J.-B. 7
Leopold II, Holy Roman Emperor 29,
　36, 37, 69, 144, 217
Lert, Ernst 227 (n3)
Lessing, Gotthold Ephraim 100
Leutgeb, Joseph 75, 153
libretto 87–110
　bird-man figure 98–101
　first edition 79–80
　Gieseke's copy 92–8
　identity of author 87–110 *passim*

language and prosody 101–6
　motivation of the action 106–10
　Schikaneder's stage directions
　179–80, 186, 189, 196–7
Liebeskind, Jakob August 26, 30,
　32
Lohenstein, Daniel Casper von 206
London 168–70, 173
　Coliseum production 190–2,
　194
Loutherbourg, Philippe-Jacques de
　181, 182
Ludwig, Mathias (publisher) 26
'Lulu, Prince' 26, 27, 30–3
Luzzati, Emanuele 174

Mackerras, Sir Charles 189
Maria Theresia, Empress of Austria 4,
　37
Marinelli, Karl 5, 29, 32, 100, 205
Mario, Giovanni Matteo 168
Marx, Karl 167
Masterson, Valerie 200
Maurer, Franz Anton 151
Maximowna, Ita 174
Mayer, Friedrich Sebastian 150, 157
Mazzolà, Caterino 219
Meisl, Karl 166
melody 124–7
Messel, Oliver 174
Metastasio, Pietro 219
Michaeler, Karl Joseph 8
Middle Ages, poetry and legend of
　7–10
Migazzi, Christoph Anton, Cardinal-
　Archbishop 36
Milder-Hauptmann, Anna 159
Miller, Jonathan 172
Milnes, Rodney 199
Moll (singer) 149
Monteverdi, Claudio 119
Mozart, Carl 77
Mozart, Constanze 68, 77–8, 148,
　156, 220
　Mozart's letters to 75–7, 112,
　152–4, 216
Mozart, Leopold 20, 124, 147, 149
Mozart, Wolfgang Amadè
　and popular theatre 4–6, 112–13
　as Freemason 41–3, 218
　Catalogue of all my Works 6, 78–9,
　112
　Così fan tutte 82, 111, 113, 129,
　131, 140, 183

Die Entführung aus dem Serail 28, 33, 35, 80, 84, 101, 112, 120, 124, 131, 138, 139, 196, 198
Don Giovanni 82, 113, 140, 156, 183
Idomeneo 80, 101, 111, 124, 131, 203
  in 1791 73–5, 111–12
La clemenza di Tito 74, 75, 82, 84, 111, 131, 132, 137, 138, 152, 156, 183, 219
La finta giardiniera 113
Le nozze di Figaro 81, 82, 101, 113, 118, 124, 140, 156, 183
  letters 75–8, 112, 152–4, 216
L'oca del Cairo 101
  music and libretti 140–1
  'new' numbers claimed for *Die Zauberflöte* 207–9
Thamos, König in Egypten 18–20, 124, 219
  writing of *Die Zauberflöte* 67–75
Müller, Wenzel 26, 27, 29, 31, 76, 112, 166, 205–6
music 111–41
  and libretti 140–1
  and text 120–4
  characterization 127–9
  finales 118–20
  harmonic scheme 129–31
  innovations in form 113–18
  Masonic symbolism 137–8
  melody 124–7
  Mozart in 1791 73–5, 111–12
  orchestration 131–7
  style 138–41
  writing of *Die Zauberflöte* 67–75
Myller, Christoph Heinrich 8

Naumann, J. G. 219
Neher, Casper 174
Nesslthaler (designer) 151, 173
Nestroy, Johann 2
Nettl, Paul 220
Niemetschek, Franz Xaver 67–8, 161
Nissen, Georg Nikolaus von 68–9, 208, 220
Norrington, Roger 132, 154
Nouseul, (Johann) Joseph 150–1
Novello, Vincent 148

Oberon, König der Elfen 5, 8, 27–9, 69, 88, 139, 143
Opie, Alan 200

orchestration 131–7
order of numbers and scenes 209–12, 214
Ottawa 190, 192
Otto, Theo 174
Owen, D. D. R. 7–10

paper-types, in autograph score 82–5
Paris 165
parodies 164–7
Peiba, Abraham 146–7
performances 144–77
  first 145–52
  later 168–77
  outside Vienna 160–3
  sequels and parodies 164–7
Pergen, Johann Anton, Count 36–7
Perinet, Joachim (*Kaspar der Fagottist*) 26–7, 29–43, 76, 90–1, 166, 205–6
Petran, Franz 44
Pian, Anton de 173
Pischelberger, Friedrich 6, 74
Plath, Wolfgang 19
Plutarch 20, 21, 22, 24
Poland 162
Ponnelle, Jean-Pierre 174
Porter, Andrew 174–5
Poussin, Nocolas 219
Praetorius, Emil 174
Prague 78, 86, 161–2, 163
Prehauser, Gottfried 4
publications of music from *Die Zauberflöte* 155–7
Puchberg, Michael 76
Pyne, Louisa 169

Quaglio, Joseph and Simon 174

Radant, Else 39
Rademin, Heinrich 98–9
Radford, Robert 172
Radicchi, Giulio 160
Raeburn, Christopher 228 (n9)
Raeburn, Sir Henry 88
Raimund, Ferdinand 26
Rameau, Jean-Philippe 219
Rautenstrauch, Johann 36
reception of *Die Zauberflöte* 152–60
recordings 172, 239–44
Reichard, Heinrich August Ottokar 98
Reinig, Christa 167
Rellstab (publisher) 156
Rennert, Günther 174–5

Rice, Peter 190, 192–3
Rochlitz, Friedrich 68, 209
rôle characterization 194–203
Roller, Alfred 173
Rommel, Otto 87–8
Ronconi, Giorgio 168, 169
Rootham, Cyril 170
Rosen, Charles 229(n12)
Rosenbaum, Therese 159
Rosenberg, Alfons 220
Rossbach, Christian 5, 142–3
Rossini, Gioachino 118
Rushton, Julian 113
Ruskin, John 2
Russia 162

Sachetti, Vinzenz 151, 208
Salieri, Antonio 153
Sawallisch, Wolfgang 164, 208
scenery 24, 171, 173–4, 184
Schack, Benedikt 5, 74, 143, 144,
    147–8
Schack, Elisabeth (*née* Weinhold) 148,
    150
Schaffer, Joseph and Peter 97, 184,
    187
Schenk, Johann 144
Scherzer, Franz 5
Schikaneder, Anna 151
Schikaneder, Eleonore (*née* Arth) 143,
    145
Schikaneder, Emanuel 145–6
    and Freemasonry 37, 43–4, 180,
        182, 218
    and the Theater auf der Wieden 5,
        112, 143–6
    ?nd the Theater an der Wien 146,
        158–9
    as performer 146–7, 158
    authorship of libretto 28, 71–2,
        87–110 *passim*
    financial problems 69–70, 73
    influence on Mozart 124, 139–40
    language and prosody 101–6
    problems and inconsistencies in *Die
        Zauberflöte* 207–9, 215–16
    sources 19, 21–2, 28, 32–4
    stage directions 179–80, 186, 189,
        196–7
Schikaneder, Joseph Carl 159
Schikaneder, Urban 149
Schiller, Friedrich von 28, 144
Schinkel, Karl Friedrich 24, 171, 174,
    184

Schlichtegroll, Friedrich 67
Schmidt, August 70
Schönborn, M. von 100
Schönaich-Carolath, Heinrich von,
    Prince 148
Schott (publisher) 156
Schröder, Friedrich Ludwig 29, 100,
    147, 149, 150
Schubert, Franz 54, 164
Schwarzenberg, Joseph Johann
    Nepomuk, Prince 1
Schwind, Moritz von 174
score, autograph 80–6
Sendak, Maurice 174
sequels and parodies 164–7
Sethos 10–18, 22, 182, 219
settings 172–3
sexes, equality of 40, 203, 217
Seyfried, Ignaz von 70–1, 88, 206
Seyler, Friederike Sophie 28, 88
Shakespeare, William 141, 199
Sievert, Ludwig 174
Simrock (publisher) 49, 106, 156, 157,
    227(n5)
singers *see* cast
Singspiel 4–6, 112
Slevogt, Max 174
Smith, Erik 111–41, 159, 209, 211
soliloquy 196–7
Soliman, Angelo 40
Sonnenfels, Joseph von 35, 41
Sonnleithner, Leopold von 145
sources 4–34
    Born's essay 20–5
    Dschinnistan 25–7
    Kaspar der Fagottist 29–34
    Oberon, König der Elfen 27–9
    popular theatre and Mozart 4–7
    Sethos 10–18
    Thamos, König in Egypten 18–20
    Yvain 7–10
Sparnaay, Hendricus 98
Spengler, Franz 161
Stadler, Anton 135
Starhemberg family 142
Stephanie, Gottlieb 80, 120–1, 124,
    196
Stoddart, John 190–1, 200
Stoll, Anton 77
Stranitzky, Joseph Anton 4
Strauss, Botho 167
Strauss, Richard 107
Strnad, Oskar 174
Stuyling, Tom Kleyn-Gijs 175

style, musical 138–41
Süssmayr, Franz Xaver 75, 76, 77–8, 79, 89, 112
Sweden 162
Swieten, Gottfried van 36
synopsis 45–66

Terrasson, Abbé Jean (*Sethos*) 10–18, 22, 182, 219
text, and music 120–4
Teyber, Franz 146
Thamos, König in Egypten 18–20, 39
Thiele, Karl Friedrich 174
Thomson, Katharine 138, 220
Tieck, Johann Ludwig 167
Tippett, Michael 110, 112
Toscanini, Arturo 154
Traeg, Johann 155
Treitschke, Friedrich 70–1, 206
Trowell, Brian 211
Trübensee, Joseph 209
Tuček, Vincenc 161
Tyson, Alan 19, 75, 81, 82–5, 152

Umlauf, Ignaz 112
United Kingdom 168–70, 173
United States of America 174–7
Urzidil, Johannes 167

Varesco, Gianbattista 80, 101
Victoria, Queen 169
Vienna 35–7
  Burgtheater 100, 146, 150
  Freemasonry 20, 23, 37–41
  Kärntnertor-Theater 4, 146, 159, 166
  reception of *Die Zauberflöte* 152–60
  Theater in der Josefstadt 5
  Theater in der Leopoldstadt 5, 29, 76, 148, 150, 166
  Theater auf der Wieden 5, 27, 44, 69, 71, 142–4, 146, 158
  Theater an der Wien 5, 70, 146, 151, 158–9
Volánek, Antonín 161
Volek, Tomislav 161
Vulpius, Christian August 89–90, 106, 163

Wagner, Richard 2, 111–12, 120
Wahr, Karl 19

Wakhevitch, Georges 173
Weber, Gottfried 227 (n5), 228 (n9)
Weimar 163–4
Wellesz, Egon 98
Wend, Christoph Gottlieb 11
Werfel, Franz 167
Wieland, Christoph Martin (*Dschinnistan*) 8, 25–7, 28, 72, 144
Wild, Franz 160
Wildermann, Hans 174
Wilson, Hamish 174
Wilson, Sir Steuart 170
Winter, Peter von 144, 148–9, 164
Wirnt von Grafenberg 98
women, attitudes toward 40, 203, 217
Wood, Sir Henry 169
Wranitzky, Paul (*Oberon*) 5, 8, 27–9, 42, 69, 71, 88, 143, 164
Wucherer, Georg Philipp 36–7

Yvain 7–10

Zauberflöte, Die
  autograph score 80–6
  change of plan theory 205–7
  characterization 127–9, 194–203
  dialogue 192–4
  direction (*q. v.*) 178–204
  and Freemasonry (*q. v.*) 37–45
  inconsistencies in 212–17
  libretto (*q. v.*) 87–110
  music (*q. v.*) 111–41
  'new' numbers claimed 207–9
  order of numbers and scenes 209–12, 214
  performances 144–52, 160–3, 168–77
  publications of music from 155–7
  reception, early performances 152–60
  recordings 172, 239–41
  scenery 24, 171, 173–4, 184
  sequels and parodies 164–7
  sources (*q. v.*) 4–34
  synopsis 45–66
  writing of 67–75
Zerr, Anna 168, 169
Ziegenhagen, Franz 44
Zinzendorf, Karl, Count 1, 154
Zitterbarth, Bartholomäus 71

ADVANCE PRAISE FOR

you will meet a stranger far from home

"It's a marvelous book. This guy is a major talent.... The stories compliment yet satisfyingly differ from each other, the atmospheres are like different-colour palettes. Jeffers can be cruel, pragmatic, tender, sweet, funny, sexy, and *devastating*. The stories, and their underlying themes and currents, linger. A most collectable collection."
—TANITH LEE,
author of *Disturbed by Her Song* and many more

"These ten stories transport us in smart, dazzling, and sometimes brutal ways into worlds that are both familiar and unfamiliar, near at hand and far over the horizon. Alex Jeffers writes like a man with a thousand years of stories to share. Each is like a prism held up to the sun, refracting hard but rewarding truths unlikely to be found in any other place but these beautiful pages."
—SANDRA MCDONALD,
author of *Diana Comet and Other Improbable Stories*

"Step onto this flying carpet and prepare to be carried away to exotic times and places, where Alex Jeffers has set up camp to tell his tales to both those already familiar with his wonderful wonder stories and to those strangers who happen to be passing by."
—CHRISTOPHER BARZAK,
author of *One for Sorrow* and *The Love We Share Without Knowing*

"What a cornucopia! Each story is a world, and each is more amazing than the one before it. The book is a like a jewel-case filled with these glittering, gorgeous, but very dangerous brooches! The pins are sharp! Barbed at times. And the writing is perfection."
—AGNES BUSHELL,
author of *Days of the Dead*

"...a curious but engrossing blend of cultures, sexualities, and gender identities in worlds where magic is both ethereal and ever-present. ... Jeffers has an elevated writing style that fits snugly with the stories' subtle but persistent titular wonder."

— *Publishers Weekly*

"Whenever I encounter one of Jeffers' stories in an anthology...I usually read it first because I know I will be astounded, not only by the depth of his imagination but by his ability to make those imagined worlds become real. I also know that I will be reading a story layered with atmosphere and meaning—dense and delicious as a flourless chocolate cake."

—Jerry L. Wheeler, *Out in Print Queer Book Reviews*

you will meet a stranger far from home

by Alex Jeffers

Safe as Houses (1995)

Do You Remember Tulum? (2010)

The New People (2011)

The Abode of Bliss (2011)